CBT for Mild to Moderate Depression and Anxiety

DATE DUE

CBT for Mild to Moderate Depression and Anxiety: A Guide to Low-intensity Interventions

Colin Hughes, Stephen Herron and Joanne Younge

Open University Press

Open University Press
McGraw-Hill Education
McGraw-Hill House
Shoppenhangers Road
Maidenhead
Berkshire
England
SL6 2QL

email: enquiries@openup.co.uk
world wide web: www.openup.co.uk

and Two Penn Plaza, New York, NY 10121–2289, USA

First published 2014

A catalogue record of this book is available from the British Library

ISBN–13: 978-0-33-524208-5 (pb)
ISBN–10: 0-33-524208-1 (pb)
eISBN: 978-0-33-524210-8

Library of Congress Cataloging-in-Publication Data
CIP data applied for

Typesetting and e-book compilations by
RefineCatch Limited, Bungay, Suffolk

Fictitious names of companies, products, people, characters and/or data that may be used herein (in case studies or in examples) are not intended to represent any real individual, company, product or event.

Praise for this book

"I have been looking for a book to use as a manual for CBT, and I am glad to say that I have found it! All psychotherapists, whatever their psychological views, will find much to stimulate their thinking in this book. Its depth and scope, the variety of data explored, and the stark nature of the argument will provoke both thought and emotion.

This well-written book provides coverage of a number of important issues and techniques not commonly treated in a didactic manner and specifically not covered in most introductory CBT textbooks. If you are in any way concerned with the practical way to apply CBT for anxiety or depression, you owe it to yourself to read this book."

Dr Mamoun Mobayed, Consultant Psychiatrist, Director of the Program
Department, Doha, Qatar

"Let me put this succinctly - the authors have written a very helpful book. It is essential reading for anyone who is involved in the delivery of low intensity CBT for depression and anxiety.

Depression and anxiety are unfortunately rife within our society and cause significant suffering. Ultimately mental health workers are engaged in addressing and ameliorating that suffering; it is a hard job. This book goes a long way in affording support to those workers through clearly outlining cognitive and behavioural principles and techniques that are proven to help with these types of presentations. Written by highly experienced cognitive behaviour therapists and lecturers for people who are providing low-intensity interventions, the book offers step-by-explanations of evidenced and invaluable CBT approaches and techniques. Although primarily written for people with limited experience and training in CBT I believe all therapists and mental health workers, whatever their level of experience or training, will find much to inform and support them in this book."

Karl Tooher, Centre Director at Northside Counselling Service

"Herron, Hughes and Younge have skillfully woven their passion for CBT and its ability to transform lives with a common sense and useful guide. This book combines principles, theory and practice in a thought provoking and accessible way for any practitioner working with people experiencing a mental health problem. Practitioners of all hues can enhance their core skills in working with sufferers of anxiety and depression.

Lots of health professionals work with the aim of aiding clients in recovery from common mental health problems, however they can often find in real life situations that they have insufficient skills to fully help in this task. This book can provide health care workers of varying professional backgrounds with a really useful road map to do this. The authors clearly integrate their own clinical experiences with the evidence base in an engaging way. Principles, theory and practical aspects of a CBT approach are combined along with helpful suggestions for putting these into practice and integrating these new skills with how people already work.

Everyone from GP's or Student nurses/AHP's to experienced mental health workers will be able to glean useful gems from this book, for example within the chapter on Assessment, the methods described could be fruitful for anyone seeking to establish a collaborative relationship and shared understanding of difficulties."

Catriona Kent, Nurse Consultant, Glasgow Institute of Psychosocial Interventions

To my wife and family. Without your belief and support this book would have remained a 'forever' project', and to my CBT supervisor and lecturers who guided me through my psychotherapy training – 'well done'!

Colin Hughes

To my loving wife, daughter and son, Helen, Meghan and Ben – the best antidepressants in the world! Also to my father, mother, aunt and sister, Eddie, Mary, Margaret and Marie – who taught me 'normal' is nothing to be proud of.

Stephen Herron

In memory of Nanny Younge for her unfailing belief in me. Also to long-suffering Jonny, Robert and Rachel for my endless 'last ever' projects.

Joanne Younge

Contents

Acknowledgements

We would like to thank all at McGraw-Hill Education for helping us to turn this idea into the reality of a book, especially Monika Lee, Priyanka Gibbons and Richard Townrow for their patience and belief that we could (eventually) do it! We thank the publishers and authors for the permissions to use their work within this book, including the previously unpublished work of Fiona Martin and Roy Cheetham. We realize that the training, supervision, support and guidance we have received from many people over a number of decades have made this book possible. We continue to try to learn and value, in particular, the insights of our colleagues on the multi-disciplinary teaching and supervision team at Queen's University. Stephen would like to acknowledge the invaluable contribution that Julia O'Grady, Roy Cheetham, Beverley Bell and Paul Quinn have made to his learning over the years. Colin would particularly like to thank Fiona Martin and Martine Harrower for their guidance. Joanne would like to acknowledge the contribution to her knowledge and inspiration that Dr Michael Duffy, Dr Kate Gillespie and Mr Brendan Armstrong have made throughout her training and beyond. She thanks Karl Tooher for his unwavering friendship and for reviewing and advising on the supervision chapter. All of these people have been trusted companions, colleagues and comrades and have offered endless support during the writing of this book. Last, but definitely not least, we would like to acknowledge the many patients who really taught us everything we know as therapists.

Preface

Do you, as a health care practitioner or trainee health care practitioner, ever experience frustration with your work in helping people? Do you ever feel getting to grips with client problems is difficult and complex? Do you sometimes suffer that 'heart sink' moment when you are overwhelmed with a mountain of client assessment data but struggle to knit it all together? If you answer yes to any of these questions, you are in good company and this book is designed to help you by introducing some interventions that will enhance your therapeutic skills, help you engage more effectively with your clients and help you organize your therapeutic interventions in a much more systematic way.

The inspiration for this book has been the extraordinary advances in the treatment of mental illness since the 1980s which make this moment in time one of the most exciting periods in the mental health field's history. Behavioural and cognitive behavioural treatment techniques, often together referred to as cognitive behavioural therapy (CBT), have had a considerable impact on the delivery of effective treatments for those suffering from common mental health problems. A review of meta-analyses indicates cognitive behavioural interventions offer an effective treatment option for those suffering from anxiety and depression (Butler et al., 2006).

Cognitive behavioural therapy techniques work, and their effectiveness has been clearly demonstrated for decades. Cognitive behavioural therapy appears to have truly come of age and is now a major therapeutic force in modern health care. By 2006 there were 16 methodologically robust meta-analyses of CBT with outcome measures indicating it is efficacious for a large range of conditions. Significant effect sizes were achieved when CBT was compared to other modes of treatment and medication (Butler et al., 2006). In fact, CBT has consistently been shown to be equally as effective as modern gold standard medications for depression and anxiety and in longer-term follow-up studies, CBT seems to have a protective quality that extends beyond the single episode of treatment (Hollon et al., 2005; NICE, 2011).

This level of evidence base is not true for many other psychological approaches or techniques, yet still most health care professionals are not routinely being trained in cognitive behavioural techniques as part of their basic training. If effective evidence-based treatments are to be more widely available for all, then it is our opinion that resources need to be re-allocated to enable the training of existing staff to do what they currently do better, using tried and tested evidence-based techniques. This book represents an attempt to disseminate the basic principles and techniques of CBT to a much wider audience and encourage practitioners to develop, through appropriate supervision and training, a much more proactive psychological approach when dealing with common psychiatric problems.

In the United Kingdom, services follow a stepped-care model that offers clients evidence-based treatments, including CBT at different levels of intensity. The stepped-care model consists of five steps: steps 1 and 2 identify treatments for mild and moderate manifestations of illness while steps 3–5 identify effective treatments for more severe and complex conditions. Each step introduces more intensive interventions. The National Institute for Health and Care Excellence (NICE) recommends that the treatment of panic disorder should be available at step 2 on the UK stepped-care ladder (NICE, 2011). They suggest that CBT is the preferred form of treatment and should be supplemented with appropriate focused self-help information. NICE (2009a) also recommend that the treatment of mild to moderate depression should initially include low-intensity psychosocial interventions such as individual guided self-help, based on the principles of CBT, or group CBT.

In this text we are concerned with the low-intensity application of CBT for the most common mental health disorders, depression and anxiety (Richards and Suckling, 2008). This book therefore sets out to introduce the reader to cognitive and behavioural techniques that can be integrated into your existing skill set. It is not intended to be used as an alternative to formal training in low- or high-intensity CBT. We also strongly recommend the use of good clinical supervision from a trained and accredited CBT practitioner when developing these skills. However, with appropriate training and supervision, we are hopeful that readers in a wide variety of adult mental health services may select and experiment with some of the rudimentary cognitive and behavioural principles and techniques outlined in the following chapters.

The book aims to provide a step-by-step guide and rationale for the use of cognitive behavioural techniques for the most common mental health disorders to aid the understanding of low-intensity practitioners, those undergoing high-intensity training and those mental health practitioners who have an interest in CBT. This text will also be a good introductory 'how to' guide to CBT interventions for GPs and psychiatry trainees. It is recommended that to practise any of the skills within this book, at least basic level CBT training should have been completed and that practice should be under the supervision of a trained CBT therapist. To provide formal CBT, it is strongly recommended that Postgraduate Diploma CBT is completed and there is continued supervision, both of which meet the minimum standards advised by the British Association of Behavioural and Cognitive Psychotherapy (BABCP).

Introduction

The primary aim of this book is to describe how to become more psychologically orientated in your clinical practice, so it does more than merely provide a description or list of therapeutic techniques. We aim not just to describe what to do, but also how to be in practice when treating clients. In this introduction we give a brief overview of the chapters and of CBT and the required competencies, followed by an exploration of the growing evidence base for low-intensity interventions and the evolution of Improving Access to Psychological Therapies (IAPT). Finally we offer our opinion on the need to upskill the mental health workforce for the future.

Overview of chapters

In Chapter 1 we will take the reader through the rudimentary skills of effective engagement and how to get the most out of each therapeutic contact and make every contact with a client purposeful. The aim of this chapter is to dispel the myth that cognitive and behavioural techniques can be applied in a simplistic, mechanistic way without first building a strong, secure and trusting therapeutic alliance. In our experience, even established practitioners pay lip service to the importance of therapeutic relationship skills but are often less able to clearly define what they are. This chapter reviews the core features of a good therapeutic alliance and gives practical tips on elements that need attention.

In Chapter 2, we then take an in-depth step-by-step approach to the process of assessing a client in a more detailed and psychological manner. We attempt to demonstrate how to capture a comprehensive and specific problem list, apply a cognitive behavioural analysis to each problem, establish onset and finally complete a basic mental state assessment. In addition, this chapter will describe the structure of a typical cognitive behavioural treatment session and define the functions of each element of the structure. The structured session allows the client and the practitioner to make the most out of the therapeutic contact, promotes collaboration between the practitioner and client and helps both focus on concrete problems, preventing unhelpful digressions and drift.

Chapter 2 is closely linked to Chapter 3 where we discuss the importance of understanding human motivation and the need to first establish whether a client's current solutions to their problems are working in terms of short- and long-term consequences. The emphasis is on the practitioner and client agreeing on what the client wants to achieve and whether the techniques they use currently are helpful or not. This involves establishing what is important or valuable to the client and how their current problems interfere with those important areas of their life. Chapter 3 will also discuss the task of how we can effectively work with the client in experimenting with other strategies if the practitioner and client can agree current responses to the problem haven't worked. This may include the client initially agreeing to a trial of giving up the current techniques, which so far haven't worked. We discuss the importance of setting goals and targets to aim for by experimenting with new behaviours and alternative ways of thinking.

In Chapters 4 and 5 we look at the nature and maintenance of depression and anxiety, concentrating on mild to moderate depression and panic disorder. We use case examples to examine typical common mental health problems that can have a profound impact on a client's life, and suggest cognitive and behavioural solutions that can be applied to clients in your caseload under appropriate supervision. Although these are typical case scenarios, no actual client data has been used. We concentrate on depression and panic disorder because there is clear evidence that these conditions can very successfully be treated in a low-intensity format.

The overall focus in Chapters 4 and 5 is to introduce the reader to a step-by-step guide to the principles of cognitive behavioural techniques for panic and depression. The intention is that a better understanding of the principles of treatment should help the practitioner to make better use of face-to-face contact and self-help materials.

Chapter 6 deals with sleep and the aim is to give the practitioner essential information on good sleep hygiene and offer specific, targeted techniques for common sleep problems. Chapter 7 outlines the importance of maintaining recovery and wellness and focuses on how to help the client maintain any gains made in treatment and help the client best prepare for any possible future setbacks.

Finally, Chapter 8 concentrates on the importance of supervision when practitioners are delivering any form of psychological intervention. The role and function of supervision are explained and the use of supervision contracts and how a practitioner can best prepare for supervision are discussed. The focus of the chapter is to show what supervision is and what it can be, allowing the practitioner to gain the optimal level of benefit from the process of clinical supervision.

Overview of CBT

The treatment and techniques in this book are firmly rooted in the principles of CBT. Formal CBT is an active, directed, time-limited, structured therapeutic approach that treats a variety of mental health disorders. It is based on the concept that an individual's emotions, physiology and behaviours are determined by the way in which that person interprets the world through their thinking (cognitions) (Beck et al., 1979). Beck's use of the term cognition refers to thinking, beliefs, verbal commentary and images. Our thoughts and beliefs help us make sense of the world and what we are experiencing. Thoughts help us manoeuvre successfully through a lifetime of experiences and situations and help us evaluate who we are and who we are compared to others and help us understand how the world works and what we can expect from life.

This cognitive ability to interpret, understand and make sense of the world allows us to plan and anticipate and offers a powerful problem-solving ability, second to none. However, this powerful ability is a double-edged sword. Planning and predicting the future allow us the ability to imagine all manner of things and it is this imagination that can often lead us into believing things that are inaccurate.

It is actually very common for our thoughts and beliefs to be mistaken or distorted. Think about when you last met someone whom you originally liked and then later discovered they perhaps were not as kind or friendly or as helpful as you first imagined. Or consider the last time your mind told you that something was right, but in fact you had missed something out. These mistakes in reasoning are common but they are much more likely to happen when we are stressed, anxious or depressed. During times of vulnerability, our cognitive apparatus is at its most fragile. Think about how we can overreact when loaded down with flu or a heavy cold. Suddenly our interpretation of what is going on is skewed. When you are ill, your children playing together and laughing and having fun no longer represents a testament of your ability to bring up your children in a peaceful and harmonious way. Instead, when you are ill, the fact that the children are playing can represent their selfishness and self-centredness in making an unholy racket when you most need sleep and rest!

This tendency for humans to misinterpret what is going on can have a profound effect on how we behave and feel and even on how our body responds. This ability to distort and misinterpret events appears to be a significant maintaining factor in both anxiety disorders and depression.

Anxiety and depression are responsible for approximately 97 per cent of the total occurrence of mental health disorders (Singleton et al., 2000). It is estimated that by the year 2020, depression will be one of the largest contributors to the global burden of disease worldwide and will be second only to heart disease (Murray and Lopez, 1996).

There are a wide variety of psychological interventions currently in use to treat these conditions, however, as previously mentioned, CBT has emerged as the most efficacious and therefore the most cost-effective short-term treatment of choice.

As already discussed, cognitive behavioural techniques are recommended for the treatment of depression and all anxiety disorders in the mild to moderate range (Clark et al. 2009). In addition to conventional CBT approaches, clients presenting with persistent depressive symptoms in the mild to moderate range have benefited from emerging cognitive behavioural interventions including individual guided self-help using the principles of CBT and computerized CBT (or CCBT) (NICE, 2009a).

Cognitive behavioural therapy is also recommended for depression in children and young people (NICE, 2005), where it is advised that the child is given guidance including self-help materials. We see this repeated across a variety of conditions and populations; for example, it is recommended that chronic pain sufferers are given support and psycho-education (NICE, 2009a). It is also recommended in the guidelines for antenatal and postnatal mental health (NICE, 2007), and for the management of hypertension in adults in primary care (NICE, 2006).

In spite of the above recommendations, access to psychological therapies is still problematic. This is perhaps due to long waiting lists and because of the cost and time involved in training psychotherapists (Ekers et al., 2006).

McManus et al. (2009) report, in the 2007 Psychiatric Morbidity Survey, that 90 per cent of people who met the diagnostic criteria for common mental health problems were not receiving any psychological treatment and only 2 per cent of patients with common mental health disorders were receiving cognitive or behavioural treatment. It is astounding that, in 2007, the majority of patients with mental health problems were not obtaining any psychological treatment.

We have used the term CBT and highlighted its effectiveness and the fact that it is recommended by the National Institute for Health and Care Excellence (NICE) as the treatment of choice for a wide variety of conditions at a variety of treatment levels. It should be noted that CBT is not the only therapy recommended by NICE, however, it is currently the most efficacious single psychological therapy available. Cognitive behavioural therapy is also a treatment which lends itself to facilitated self-help and has been developed along high- and low-intensity lines in England.

Evidence base for low-intensity cognitive behavioural interventions

The evidence base for employing specific components of CBT, delivered by non-specialists, has yet to be fully explored in the research literature. There is, however, a small but growing data set showing what can be achieved when we disseminate effective treatment components to non-specialist 'coal face' health and mental health practitioners (Clark et al., 2008; Ekers, Lovell and Playle, 2006; Ekers et al., 2011; Whitfield and Williams, 2003). In fact, some clients with more severe depression at baseline show at least as much clinical benefit from low-intensity interventions as less severely depressed clients.

This suggests that clients who may be initially under the care of a non-specialist practitioner could usefully be offered these interventions at a very early stage in their treatment episode, as part of a stepped-care model. The evidence indicates that this is possible if the practitioner receives brief training in cognitive behavioural techniques and continued clinical supervision (Bower et al., 2013).

What this book will and will not cover

Cognitive behavioural therapy (CBT) is used to refer to cognitive therapy, behaviour therapy or a combination of both paradigms. It is not within the remit of this text to debate their particular merits or to scientifically or philosophically debate the underpinnings of cognitive therapy and behaviourism. The purpose of this text is to identify a number of low-intensity CBT approaches and treatment techniques that draw equally from both traditions that we think could be administered by all health care professionals, under appropriate training and supervision, when treating clients with mild to moderate psychological problems. The aim is for clinicians new to working in a psychological way to integrate the techniques into their practice and by doing so to inject a more psychologically focused approach into their work.

The *Oxford Guide to Low Intensity CBT Interventions* by Bennett-Levy et al. (2010) gives an excellent overview of the history and policy which drove IAPT and the various roles of low-intensity practitioners and it is not our aim to replicate this, but we do recommend it as background reading. We will demonstrate particular techniques from both the cognitive and behavioural traditions and it is the application of these techniques and how best to apply them which will be explored.

The basic competencies covered within this book are in part related to the 2007 Department of Health (England) publication *The Competences Required to Deliver Effective Cognitive and Behavioural Therapy for People with Depression and with Anxiety Disorders* (Roth and Pilling, 2007), which explicitly details the knowledge and skills competency required for those delivering CBT at both low and high intensity:

- *Practitioner knowledge* Three areas of basic knowledge: the basic principles of cognitive behavioural interventions, common cognitive biases relevant to anxiety and depression, and the role of safety behaviours in maintaining mental health difficulties.
- *Practitioner's role in building a therapeutic alliance* Successfully engaging the client and building a positive therapeutic alliance and improving the likelihood of maintained engagement in treatment and ultimately better outcomes.
- The ability to understand and complete a cognitive behavioural assessment. This is crucial if the practitioner and client are to begin to understand the difficulties presented in treatment, from a thinking and behavioural perspective. This also requires the practitioner to complete a cognitive and behavioural analysis of current difficulties, focusing on patterns of thinking and current ways of responding.
- *Understanding of the rationale and basic premise for CBT* Orienting practitioners to important features of the generic CBT model and its basic treatment components.
- *Structuring sessions* The ability to structure sessions through dividing each clinical interaction into a set of overlapping, but distinct, sections that allow both the client and practitioner to extract as much as possible out of each clinical contact. A fundamental characteristic of this structuring is that practitioners need to ensure that they work in a way that ensures collaboration and a true sharing of responsibility for the session and the therapeutic work. The structure should facilitate the agreeing and reviewing of homework tasks and facilitate time for giving and receiving feedback.
- *Setting agreed goals and using measures and self-report records to monitor progress* This is essential to help to focus and anchor treatment and ensure treatment has a specific and measurable destination with a specific time scale agreed.
- *Developing hypotheses about a maintenance cycle* It is helpful to conceptualize how the client's thoughts, physical symptoms, behaviours and

emotions interact to maintain their problems, and to share this with the client. This is not a matter of telling the client about the maintenance cycle, but of sharing an initial hypothesis with them and using their feedback to arrive at a jointly constructed understanding of their current 'here and now' problems and what is maintaining them. This can be used to guide treatment, assess whether current tactics work for the client, plan alternative tactics and provide a framework that helps the client to begin resolving their difficulties.

- *Problem identification and problem solving* This is important for helping clients to identify what precisely maintains their difficulties and then, in collaboration with the client, develop, appraise and implement solutions to specific difficulties. This includes hypothesizing and then testing current strategies in the spirit of collaborative experimentation.

If you would like to explore further the different paradigms that make up the CBT family of therapies, we suggest Westbrook, Kennerley and Kirk (2007) and Baum (2004).

Improving Access to Psychological Therapies (IAPT) and the growth in intensity treatments

It has been acknowledged that the demand for treatment from the population has placed a significant burden upon existing mental health services. Until very recently, only 24 per cent of those who needed it would actually receive any treatment for mental health problems and this was mostly in the form of pharmacotherapy (Richards and Suckling, 2008). Layard et al. (2006) highlighted the impact mental illness has on the economy as a whole and go on to show that while the NICE guidelines have indicated that CBT should be offered to clients with a wide range of common mental health problems, there remains little evidence that this is offered in the vast majority of cases who first present for treatment in local community mental health teams.

One of clients' biggest complaints across the United Kingdom National Health Service is the lack of access to psychological therapies. In 2005, of those suffering from depression, only half received treatment, 8 per cent had seen a psychiatrist and 3 per cent had seen a psychological therapist. Layard (2005) outlined several UK national objectives: clients should have a choice of psychological therapy as part of routine clinical practice; there should be waiting time targets for those awaiting psychological therapy; those who access their GP for treatment in the first instance, but who do not improve, should be referred to psychological therapy services; clients should have access to high-quality self-help facilitators; stigma must be reduced by all possible means and clients should be helped back to work (Layard, 2005: 4).

In recognition of this, in October 2007 on World Mental Health Day, the UK government launched a large-scale initiative for improving access to psychological therapies (IAPT) for depression and anxiety disorders in England (Ekers, et al., 2006). The IAPT programme has one specific goal, which is to help primary care trusts implement NICE guidelines for people suffering from depression and anxiety disorders (DoH, 2008). It is acknowledged that there is a role for non-specialist mental health trained practitioners to work as low-intensity workers delivering evidence-based care from the first point of contact.

Following on from Layard's report (Layard et al., 2006), the Department of Health funded two demonstration or pilot sites in Yorkshire (Doncaster) and inner London (Newham). Both these sites commenced work in the summer of 2006 and focused on depression and anxiety disorders. In order to assess outcomes, clients were required to complete the PHQ–9 (Kroenke et al., 2001), the GAD–7 (Spitzer et al., 2006), the Core-OM (Barkham et al., 2001) and an employment questionnaire developed by the Department of Health (DoH, 2008). At each subsequent treatment session, the client was required to complete both the PHQ–9 and the GAD–7; the other two measures were completed at assessment, every sixth session and on completion of treatment.

Overall the outcomes of these pilot sites appear positive, with 55–56 per cent of clients who were referred, assessed and attended being classified as recovered and a further 5 per cent having improved their employment status (Clark et al., 2009). These treatment gains also appear to have been maintained over a ten-month follow-up. For more detailed information on these pilot programmes, please see Clark et al. (2009) and, for the full report, Clark et al. (2008) (accessible at www.iapt.nhs.uk).

It appears that providing clients with easy-to-access low-intensity treatment is effective and while it is acknowledged that it may not be beneficial for all, its use in a structured stepped-care model is not only recommended, but appears to be economically and clinically effective.

These most recent exciting developments are the latest in a long line of sound and sometimes groundbreaking research. Of course, being the most researched psychotherapy does not indicate anything if that research is not robust and rigorous. However, only time will tell if the clear benefits of standard CBT treatment can be equalled by lower-intensity cognitive behavioural interventions. So far, however, the results from IAPT are promising, especially as the results at the Doncaster site were mainly of clients who received low-intensity interventions (Clark et al., 2008).

Upskilling the current mental health workforce

The achievements of the IAPT initiative in England are astounding and have been realized by the creation of a brand new workforce of graduate mental health workers called psychological wellbeing practitioners (PWP). This IAPT interpretation of low-intensity training is in its infancy and is still evolving. It quite naturally has experienced a number of teething troubles with Shepherd and Rosairo (2008) suggesting that there is a mismatch between the training and expectations of low-intensity practitioners or primary care mental health workers. The problem is that the role includes sign-posting, guiding clients in the use of self-help materials including computerized CBT, and also a face-to-face 'limited clinician' role

(Strain et al., 2006). It is this face-to-face direct treatment role which can predominate due to local pressures on services.

These roles require very diverse skills and training someone to be proficient in sign-posting clients to appropriate services requires a very different skill set to training someone to oversee good quality facilitated self-help treatments, which incorporates (depending on the needs of the client) a variable degree of actual face-to-face treatment sessions. If the dominant low-intensity treatment paradigm is CBT, then the fundamental basic competencies required to deliver treatment in that form are required.

In fact it could be argued that because the low-intensity practitioner is working in a high volume, more intensive environment, a thorough grounding in the principles of the treatment they are administering is even more essential. Practitioners need to understand the core principles and rationale for the treatment they are promoting even if, for the majority of practitioners, they deliver treatment at a distance.

Improving Access to Psychological Therapies is an English model of low-intensity treatment delivery, based on the premise of training a brand new workforce and this is admirable. However, across the rest of the United Kingdom the concept of low-intensity treatments is not so well operationalized.

To date, the use of self-help strategies has often involved a fully trained CBT therapist, using their skills in a different way. This, however, is not an effective use of resources (Ekers et al., 2007). A much more effective and efficient method of delivering good quality mental health care is to utilize the staff already delivering mental health treatments at primary care level. For example nurses, social workers, doctors and occupational therapists are the largest professional groups currently charged with the 'coal-face' delivery of mental health treatment in health services across the world. The effectiveness and efficiency of this resource could only be enhanced by augmenting generic mental health knowledge and skills with modern effective techniques based on CBT principles (Lovell et al., 2003).

In the absence of, or in addition to, a new tier of mental health worker we suggest there also needs to be a commitment to radically overhaul existing traditional mental health care training. Creating a brand new workforce has obviously been accepted as one solution in England, yet the vast majority of health care professionals involved in mental health are not routinely offered high-quality psychological therapy training and supervision. Mental health nursing, medical, social work and occupational therapy training have, in our experience, been left relatively unchanged despite the growing evidence that specific structured psychological interventions work.

The only way to truly address the vast untapped need for psychological therapy is to train our existing workforce in evidence-based, NICE-approved, treatments. Core training in psychology, nursing, medicine, social work and occupational therapy should contain robust low-intensity training in specific evidence-based treatments. These trainees should have a thorough grounding in specific therapeutic techniques as part of their core professional training, or, on completion of training, be offered high-quality postgraduate certificate level training in these effective treatments.

Grimshaw and Russell (1993) demonstrated that if practitioners are equipped with the necessary knowledge and skills to enable them to adhere to health guidelines, this can directly improve health care outcomes. Grimshaw et al. (2002) note that one of the most frustrating findings in health service delivery is the gap between the research evidence and clinical practice. They suggest that the lack of knowledge and skills training constitutes a real obstacle to the successful implementation of guidelines.

Alas, a still too common complaint of newly trained and experienced mental health care staff is that they emerge from core professional training with very few actual treatment skills. Too often, in the authors' opinion, clients arrive for high-intensity therapy following a long treatment spell with community treatment teams with little or no meaningful therapeutic work completed. Monitoring mental state and some relaxation techniques may have been trialled but there has frequently been no attempt to actually treat the client's underlying condition. Our experiences are not unique; research with a community mental health team in a South London borough showed that the National Institute for Health and Care Excellence guidelines for depression were not being implemented. Staff reported that the services did not have sufficient resources to provide the recommended treatments for all people with depression. The majority of staff also reported low levels of confidence in using the guidelines and very few had received any formal training on implementing the guidelines. Many staff stated they would like more support and training in using the guidelines (Rhodes et al., 2010).

This book was forged out of a belief that tried and tested low-intensity skills should be incorporated into core professional training or practice enhanced through the use of high-quality postgraduate training and supervision. It is our belief that to be able to effectively conduct time-limited face-to-face treatment and guide clients through self-help resources and computerized CBT packages, then practitioners, whether they are PWPs or experienced mental health professionals, need to have a good understanding of the underlying CBT principles of treatment of those disorders, particularly disorders which commonly present and are usually treated in primary care, such as mild to moderate depression and anxiety disorders, for example, panic disorder. This is essential if we are to dramatically improve the current treatment, which, as already mentioned, often consists (in our experience) of supportive counselling, monitoring mental state and relaxation training within community mental health teams. Our wish is that this book will go some way in starting to bridge the gap by providing a 'how to' and 'why' rationale that may spark the reader's interest in further training.

If the gains achieved in IAPT are to be replicated across the rest of the UK and further afield, then upskilling the existing workforce offers a viable and realistic solution. We consider that disseminating cognitive behavioural intervention approaches across the entire mental health workforce would help many more clients reclaim their lives. Access to good quality psychological practice should be the norm for all clients accessing mental health care and we suggest training in selected cognitive behavioural techniques offers an excellent vehicle to deliver this.

Many of the elements that make up formal cognitive behavioural psychotherapy may be inherently helpful in all routine clinical practice. One example of

CBT practice that should be taught to all health care professionals is the establishment of an agreed agenda at the beginning of any therapeutic consultation. This allows the clinician and client to reflect, plan and prioritize what is going to be discussed and establish what time is available to discuss these items in an explicitly negotiated way. This then creates a clear, unambiguous, collaborative and concise context, in which the client and professional consultation occurs. This is just one example of how an element from CBT (agenda setting) may be incorporated into and can enhance routine health care consultations. In our experience, the dissemination of skills practised routinely in CBT to other areas of mental health treatment greatly enhances the effectiveness of that consultation and treatment.

It is important to reiterate that we are not suggesting that the skills outlined in this book offer anything more than a set of tools to aid routine clinical practice. This is not a formal therapy manual, but it is an opportunity to expand the reader's treatment repertoire and explore new ways in which routine care can be delivered. Remember that to practise any of the skills within this book it is recommended that at least basic level CBT training should have been completed and that practice should be under the supervision of a trained CBT therapist.

1 Interpersonal communication

Introduction

This chapter will introduce you to the concept of effective therapeutic communication and the impact of the client/practitioner therapeutic alliance on treatment. This involves being aware of both practitioner and client characteristics that might hinder or enhance the client/practitioner partnership. In addition, the chapter will reinforce the importance of maintaining that therapeutic alliance throughout the treatment process.

Establishing the therapeutic alliance

It is a quintessential human desire to be seen by others in a favourable light. Therefore, describing our difficulties and explaining to another person that we may not be coping so well is incredibly difficult. Telling someone that we feel helpless or that we are terrified doesn't come easy to any of us. Even mild to moderate anxiety or depression can create a sense of inadequacy and shame that makes disclosing to others how we are really feeling difficult. In a species that depends so much on each other, it seems only reasonable that the only thing worse than you 'knowing' that you are vulnerable or not coping so well, is that 'others' discover it.

Successful engagement in psychological treatment is therefore not possible unless the client feels able to disclose how they really think, feel and react to the practitioner. The practitioner must therefore be able to facilitate the establishment of a sound, therapeutic working alliance. An environment where the client feels comfortable enough to explore their problems, without fear of being negatively judged is essential. Empathy, warmth and genuineness are considered essential to create effective conditions, under which safe, secure engagement can occur (Patterson, 1984).

Ackerman and Hilsenroth (2003) present a comprehensive examination of practitioners' personal attributes that positively influence the therapeutic alliance; these include flexibility, honesty, respect, trustworthiness, confidence, warmth, interest, and openness. Further to this, other aspects which improved the therapeutic alliance include noting past treatment success and exploring and accurately interpreting the client's story (Ackerman and Hilsenroth, 2003).

The cornerstone of good communication is remaining client-centred throughout. This means remembering the following:

- A client should be considered as having a unique understanding of their own illness and their experiences of that illness.

- The client's unique understanding of their own illness should be used to guide and inform assessment and treatment.
- Those suffering from any health difficulties are people like you, with desires and aspirations to have their opinions heard and to feel that they belong and that they have intrinsic value.
- Those suffering from any health difficulties have a right to exercise self-efficacy and self-determination.

(Safran et al., 2006)

This is achieved by first making it very explicit that you intend to negotiate what the contacts between you and the client are intended to achieve. From the outset, the aim is to motivate the client to participate fully in the process of treatment. This involves giving the client choice and allowing them equal opportunity to decide or negotiate what treatment priorities are agreed. The overarching aim is to generate hope, so that the client truly believes that they can be helped through a partnership with you.

Where to start

The process begins with your first meeting with the client. Greet them with a warm smile, introduce who you are, ask how they wish to be referred to and offer them an appropriate, comfortable and private place to talk (see Figure 1.1).

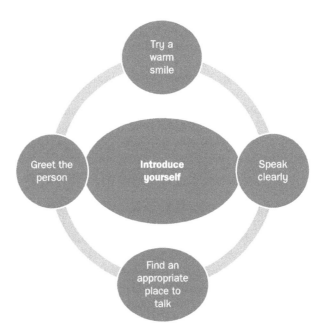

Figure 1.1   Introduce yourself

(Reproduced by the kind permission of Fiona Martin.)

Establish from the outset who you are, your job title, your level of expertise, what your role is and what you plan to do each session (Figure 1.2). It is important that the client is fully aware of who they are seeing, what your official job title is and what treatment will entail. It is particularly important to highlight if you are a fully qualified practitioner or a trainee under supervised practice. If the client is seeing a trainee, then the details of supervision should be explained. Consent from the client to continue treatment with a trainee should be sought. Also, the client should always be given the opportunity to express any reservations about treatment. If your service permits a choice of male or female practitioners, then this choice must be offered to the client.

It is important, at this early stage, to explain the bounds of confidentiality to the client, i.e. that any discussion is confidential, but if the practitioner has concerns about risk to the client or others, particularly children, or if required to by law, then the practitioner may need to disclose relevant information. Also, pertinent information will be shared with others involved in the client's care, including the practitioner's supervisor, in order to ensure the client is getting the right care. In most circumstances, with the exception of the most urgent, the practitioner would discuss relevant disclosures with the client in advance. Understanding the parameters of confidentiality from the outset permits the client to make an informed decision about proceeding with treatment.

Figure 1.2   Establish who you are

(Reproduced by the kind permission of Fiona Martin.)

In the early stages of engagement, it is the attitude you convey that is often the crucial deciding factor that determines whether the client chooses to work with you (Figure 1.3).

It is important the practitioner remains interested and stays focused throughout the interview. Acknowledge what is being said by the client and note how they communicate. Be aware of your own reactions and curtail any responses that could be viewed as being judgemental. Be positive and convey a desire to want to know what the client's problems are and display an interest in wanting to understand and help with finding a solution.

This is best achieved by being aware of both your verbal and non-verbal communication (see Figure 1.4).

Maintain eye contact, but don't stare. Sit upright and attend to the client and be aware of your facial expression at all times. In treatment, practitioners can come across distressing and disturbing material and it is important the client doesn't leave the session believing they have distressed or disturbed the practitioner.

There is a lot written about empathy and its importance to the therapeutic alliance. Empathy is essentially a communication process, which aims to facilitate the client being heard. The client expresses ideas and concerns and the practitioner's task is to ensure they accurately hear what is being said. This requires the practitioner to attend to the way information is stated, not just the content of what is

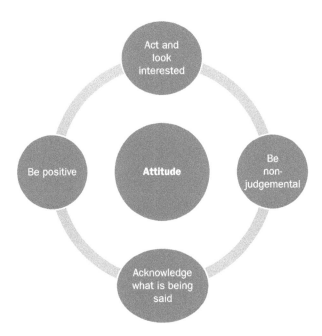

Figure 1.3 Attitude

(Reproduced by the kind permission of Fiona Martin.)

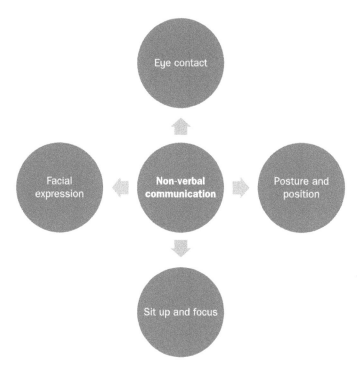

Figure 1.4   Non-verbal communication

(Reproduced by the kind permission of Fiona Martin.)

being said. Empathy can be seen as a two-way process that requires a number of elements (see Figure 1.5).

Active attention or listening

Listening is the first important skill in therapeutic communication. Active listening is the act of receiving, perceiving and processing both verbal and non-verbal communication. It is cited by almost everyone involved in the field of health care (and those in other walks of life) as the most important skill, yet is practised very little in training. Apart from being the best method available to gather a lot of information in a very short period of time, it also requires that we set aside our prejudices and assumptions and try to really 'get' what the client is conveying. The aim is to truly get to grips with the client's story from their point of view.

Reflection of content and affect

Active listening is more than just listening. To fully grasp what the client is saying, there is a requirement for the practitioner to convey their understanding back to

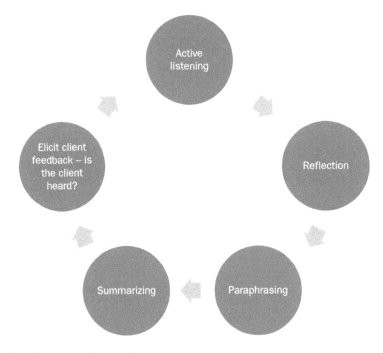

Figure 1.5   Elements of empathy

(Reproduced by the kind permission of Fiona Martin.)

the client. We need to check with the client to confirm we accurately perceive their story, from their point of view. Reflection is more than simply restating verbatim what the client says in a repetitive way. Reflections should instead highlight what the practitioner views as the essential message conveyed by the client. This will include not just the words used by the client, but also the emotion associated with those words. This ensures the practitioner has both a cognitive and affective sense of the client's story.

Paraphrasing and clarification

Once the client's message and the mood associated with that message are understood by both the practitioner and client, the practitioner can then use paraphrasing to test if they truly understand the facts and ideas conveyed by the client (the more detailed cognitive component of the client's story). Paraphrasing is often linked with clarification. It is used by the practitioner to try to get to the detailed, important aspects of the client's story. For example, *'You seem to be saying that you think that your family is feeling fed up with you being depressed.'*

The client might then agree with the practitioner's understanding, but, if the client does not agree, or if it is not altogether clear they agree, the practitioner can seek further clarification by paraphrasing, *'Can you tell me a bit more about that? Can you give me more details on what you think the effect your depression/ anxiety has on your family?'* This clarification process can actually begin to help the client to come to understand themselves better. By asking the client to explain something in more detail, or in a different way, they are encouraged to explore their own thoughts on the situation in more detail. This should also convey to the client that you too are trying to understand their situation.

Summarizing

Many clients who are suffering from distress may respond by talking quickly and trying to provide a lot more detail than a practitioner can comprehend all at once, or they may be depressed and conversation may be disjointed. The practitioner needs to sensitively pause the session periodically, to try to 'chunk together' and feed back to the client those points that seem most important. Client feedback is then necessary to ensure the practitioner is accurately picking points that are truly important to the client. This is similar to paraphrasing and helps to ensure that the practitioner and client understand each other correctly.

A summary is when the practitioner paraphrases and reflects back to the client what they have heard. If the practitioner notes a possible link between thoughts and feelings expressed by the client, this would be an important point to summarize. Summarizing also aids empathy as it helps the client know you have been listening to what they have said and are trying to understand. In addition, a final summary at the end of the session, which includes all of the important points of the discussion, is the final opportunity for the practitioner and client to check they understand each other.

Eliciting client feedback

The process of summarizing is clearly a two-way communication process. It is therefore important that feedback remains a two-way process throughout. This helps ensure that both the practitioner and client understand what each other means, helping to prevent misunderstanding. This can be achieved by gently and sensitively asking, or better inviting, the client to periodically reflect back to the practitioner what they understand. In addition, as treatment progresses, eliciting client feedback should become so routine that the client is encouraged to give the final summary as treatment progresses.

Collaboration throughout treatment

Collaboration is necessary in order for truly effective therapy to take place (Bordin, 1979). Both the client and practitioner work together to agree goals and tasks, specifically designed to help the client to move towards recovery. The client should not be viewed as a passive recipient of care; instead collaboration and co-operation between practitioner and client need to be at the heart of treatment, if success in goal attainment and recovery is to be realized. The practitioner can achieve this by always remembering to share information, encouraging the client to prioritize what tasks are best attended to in treatment and asking the client to contribute to writing on forms during exercises or when completing self-help literature. The practitioner must remember that the client is the 'expert' in terms of their own difficulties. Treatment is a partnership and, as in any partnership, success is only achieved if both parties work together.

The practitioner must also be aware, however, that skill in the application of cognitive behavioural interventions, as well as a good working alliance, has been deemed to be indicative of positive treatment outcome (Trepka et al., 2004). Perhaps what can be drawn from this is that competence in the use of cognitive behavioural interventions is necessary, however, not enough, as the establishment and maintenance of a good quality therapeutic relationship may well provide the optimal conditions for positive treatment outcome (Leahy, 2008).

How do we positively influence the therapeutic alliance/relationship?

Rogers (1951) identified four components necessary to ensure that the practitioner–client alliance would remain therapeutic. They are warmth, empathy, genuineness and non-judgemental respect for others. The four components could be deemed as the fundamental foundation on which a practitioner practises in a client-centred way. In fact, often when clients are asked to evaluate best practice, they use descriptions such as 'pleasant, caring, practical and honest' to indicate a sound and productive therapeutic alliance with a health care practitioner (Lovell et al., 2008). Hence, from a client's perspective a good practitioner is valued in terms of attitudes and feelings (Mead and Bower, 2000; Gask et al., 2003; Lovell et al., 2008).

Why it is important to remember that therapeutic alliance and technical ability are both important in low-intensity working

As low-intensity working depends upon the use of manualized facilitated self-help materials, the potential problem is that the emphasis may be placed on the technique. The focus may be on the rigid adherence to the completion of a manualized treatment programme, with less emphasis given to the important aspects of the therapeutic alliance.

As an aid to the development of the therapeutic alliance, Egan (2010) provides a useful guide to the practical creation of a therapeutic environment. This is embodied in the acronym SOLER (Egan, 2010):

- Sit squarely (although some prefer up to a 45° angle)
- Open posture
- Lean towards the client
- Eye contact (is maintained)
- Relax (as this improves the quality and comfort of the session)

The impact of the practitioner's beliefs and values on communication

This section will explore in more detail the need for the practitioner to be self-aware of their own beliefs and values. It is important to be aware that your own beliefs and values can have an adverse effect on the communication process and the therapeutic alliance.

In treatment, we can see the influence of the practitioner's beliefs in several ways, for example, the practitioner may hold a belief which demands a very high standard of themselves and others and they therefore may feel they have to 'fix' all of their client's problems. This may create a situation where the practitioner drives the treatment process and abandons a more collaborative approach to treatment. The problem with this is that the practitioner may set goals which they deem are important for the client, rather than collaboratively setting goals with the client. Note in this instance, there is no true collaboration.

In order to successfully deal with this process, it is important, first, that the practitioner is aware treatment is not progressing. If the practitioner perceives their beliefs and values are interfering with the treatment process, this should be discussed with the practitioner's supervisor and a way forward devised. In addition, the practitioner should engage in self-reflection. It must be noted that reflective practice and supervision are not optional; this is a necessary requirement in the provision of quality treatment. This will be looked at in Chapter 8 on supervision.

The importance of questioning

There are a variety of questions which can be asked to assist the practitioner and client to get the most out of each session. Here we look at the importance of questioning in general.

In treatment, it can be quite easy to assume the role of the 'expert', especially if there appears to be an obvious solution to a problem that seems to evade the client. The focus should always be on asking questions designed to bring the client's attention to information which they have access to, but may not be attending to due to their current level of distress. The aim, therefore, is to use questioning to create an environment where the client can examine their current situation, thoughts, behaviours, bodily sensations and emotions. The best way to think about this is to consider questioning in a gentle and compassionate way, using both open and closed questioning techniques.

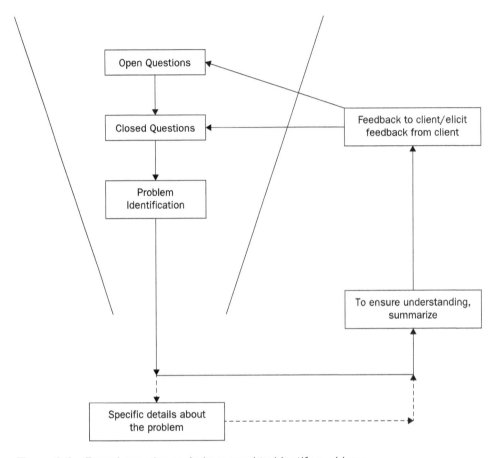

Figure 1.6   Funnel question technique used to identify problems

This can be conceptualized through the use of the 'funnel assessment technique'. This is achieved by the client's problem areas being broken down into phases that resemble or form a funnel, starting by eliciting broad, general descriptions of the client's difficulties by using open questions, with a subsequent narrowing of focus until the detail of the problem is established, using closed questions (Cone and Hawkins, 1977). Questioning therefore takes place in the context of three phases which are as follows (see Figure 1.6):

1   eliciting general problem areas;
2   defining, clarifying and general quantification of a single problem episode;
3   pinpointing precise specific triggers and subsequent thoughts, emotions, bodily sensations, behaviours and consequences.

While there are a variety of different types of questions, our focus is on the use of open and closed questions. Open questions are designed to allow the client to divulge broad problem areas. This can be seen in questions such as the following:

Practitioner: *Could I ask, what do you think your main problem or problems are at the moment?*

Client: *I find I have difficulty doing anything, I stay in bed a lot, have little interest or energy (this may be a client with low mood).*

Or

Client: *I worry a lot and I cannot leave the house and when I think about leaving the house I get very panicky (this may be a client with an anxiety problem).*

Closed questions are used to elicit more specific information and traditionally have only very limited responses.

For example:

Practitioner: *Can you tell me a bit more about that, when was the last time you experienced a panic attack?*

Practitioner: *In the last week how often have you experienced a panic attack?*

Practitioner: *What specific bodily sensations did you notice when you had your last panic attack?*

As can be seen from the funnel model (Figure 1.6), it is important to summarize and check understanding throughout. The use of open and closed questioning will allow you to gain access to the client's problem situations, thoughts, behaviours, bodily sensations and emotions. The appropriate use of this funnel model can help enhance the therapeutic relationship; the practitioner has the opportunity to collaboratively show an understanding of the client's problems. The practitioner should try not to use too many closed questions as this may lead to an interrogative style, which may be viewed as overly intrusive by the client. In addition, beware of leading questions specifically designed to direct the client to state a specific answer. For example, 'When you panic, do you think you will die?' is a leading, closed question, which will only get a 'yes' or 'no' answer.

Remember, do not move too quickly, do not directly challenge the client and do not seek a concrete answer too early. Do not give the answer to the client and do not assume an 'expert' stance.

Conclusion

Communication skills are of supreme importance, without which we cannot begin to construct the working therapeutic alliance upon which successful treatment is based. However, as already discussed, the practitioner should remember that these skills are simply not enough; in addition, we require the technical skills in order to provide successful treatment. Self-awareness and good quality, frequent supervision, as well as constant reflective practice are also essential.

Summary

- Introduce yourself and establish who you are.
- Pay attention to verbal and non-verbal communication.
- Active listening, reflection, paraphrasing and summary are key skills.
- Treatment is seen as a partnership between the practitioner and client.
- Successful treatment depends upon the client feeling safe.
- Empathy, warmth and genuineness are important factors in the therapeutic alliance.
- Clients view honesty, respect and trustworthiness as important practitioner attributes.
- Promoting self-efficacy and self-determination is the cornerstone of treatment.

Recommended reading

Hawton, K., Salkovskis, P.M., Kirk, J. and Clark, D.M. (1989) *Cognitive Behaviour Therapy for Psychiatric Problems: A Practical Guide.* Oxford: Oxford University Press.

Kahn, R.L. and Connell, C.F. (1967) *The Dynamics of Interviewing.* New York: Wiley and Sons.

Leahy, R.L. (2008) The therapeutic relationship in cognitive behavioural therapy. *Behavioural and Cognitive Psychotherapy,* 36(6): 769–77.

Richards, D. and Whyte, M. (2009) *Reach Out: National Programme Educator Materials to Support the Delivery of Training for Psychological Wellbeing Practitioners Delivering Low Intensity Interventions,* 2nd edn. Rethink Mental Illness. Available at: www.cedar.exeter.ac.uk/iapt/iaptworkbooksandresources (accessed 23 May 2014).

Rogers, C.R. (1951) *Client-centered Therapy.* Boston, MA: Houghton Mifflin.

Safran, J.D., Muran, J.C. and Rothman, M. (2006) The therapeutic alliance: cultivating and negotiating the therapeutic relationship. In W. O'Donohue, N.A. Cummings and J.L. Cummings (eds) *Strategies for Becoming a Master Psychotherapist.* New York: Elsevier.

Simmons, J. and Griffiths, R. (2009) *CBT for Beginners.* London: Sage.

Westbrook, D., Kennerley, H. and Kirk, J. (2011) *An Introduction to Cognitive Behaviour Therapy: Skills and Applications,* 2nd edn. London: Sage.

2 Cognitive behavioural assessment and session structure

Introduction

The first interview with the client is important and should be used to obtain specific information on their main problem areas. This includes precise details of when those problems arise (triggers) and the client's physical reactions, emotional reactions, cognitive reactions and the way the client currently responds (behaviours).

In this chapter, we will describe the format of a cognitive behavioural assessment and take you through the step-by-step process for the identification of key problem areas using a cognitive behavioural analysis. In addition, how this information is used to obtain a comprehensive problem list will be highlighted, as well as any maintaining factors for the client's problem/s. A cognitive behavioural assessment not only complements, but also greatly enhances, the data gathered by routine general assessment procedures. In addition, we will examine how the practitioner can use their time with the client more productively by following a cognitive behavioural session structure.

We suggest that if you are already a practising clinician, you follow your current history-taking procedures, including risk assessment, as client history is vitally important. Basic mental state evaluation and risk assessment and their role in deciding if low-intensity treatment is suitable for the client are also discussed. However, when it comes to exploring the client's current problems, we suggest you follow the steps in this chapter and then evaluate how relevant and detailed the information is compared to your current method of assessing the client's 'here and now' difficulties.

The aims of a cognitive behavioural assessment

The overall aims of a cognitive behavioural assessment include:

- eliciting detailed information about the client's main problem area/areas;
- analysing these problems in terms of their triggering events or experiences, cognitions associated with those triggers and the client's behavioural responses to those triggers;
- analysing the impact of behaviour and cognition on the individual's bodily sensations and mood;
- identifying key maintaining factors;
- arriving at a shared understanding of the client's main problem areas;

- identifying shared goals that address key maintaining factors;
- allowing the client to make an informed decision regarding treatment.

The overall aim is to assess the problem with respect to:

- *Who* Who is involved in the problem situation? Who makes it better or worse?
- *What* What precisely happens in the problem situation? What helps? What does not?
- *Where* Where does the problem mainly occur? Where does it not occur? *Why* What is the client's explanation for this occurring?
- *When* When is the problem most likely or least likely to occur?

In addition to the five W's above, we need to also consider the following:

- frequency: how often the problem occurs;
- intensity: the degree of distress it produces;
- duration: how long the problem lasts each time it occurs;
- onset: both in terms of what happens just before the problem occurs and when it all begin.

Conditions necessary for an effective assessment interview

The assessment interview is too often viewed by practitioners as simply a data-gathering or fact-finding mission. Gathering accurate data is certainly important. However, the assessment also offers an opportunity to find out what the client is hoping to achieve in a number of areas of their life, how they are going about life currently and to explore collaboratively with the client whether the methods they currently employ are working for them, both in the long and short term. It also allows the practitioner to evaluate how the client previously functioned, before their problems began. If the practitioner and the client agree there are specific problems or areas of their life where the client's reactions don't seem to be working as effectively as they would like, then they can begin to discuss the possibility of change.

This can eventually be accomplished by asking the client to experiment with new ways of reacting or behaving, rather than continuing to behave and react in ways that the client and practitioner agree don't seem to work. The client doesn't necessarily need to engage with the idea of change immediately during the first interview; however, the assessment should introduce the notion that change is possible.

The assessment may be the first time the client has been afforded the opportunity to explore their current way of functioning, investigate if what they are doing currently works for them and identify if change is needed. As discussed in Chapter 1, your client will probably feel more able to engage collaboratively in the assessment process and present their difficulties openly to a warm, empathic and non-judgemental practitioner. You need to communicate effectively and instil hope that things can change. An assessment is never an interrogation, but is instead a planned, structured and systematic attempt to better understand the client's current life difficulties and problems. This obviously needs to be done in a safe and secure environment to enable the client to openly and honestly evaluate if current ways of dealing with their problems are working or not.

Explaining what you are doing each step of the way

Keep in mind that your client should have a clear idea of the function and format of the assessment session as this should help reduce anxiety, introduce them to the open and collaborative nature of this way of working and socialize them to working in a very structured way, in order to make the best use of the available time. Once introductions are complete, the structure of the assessment interview should be explained.

Throughout this chapter, we will give examples of how to introduce each section of the assessment process. These are merely suggestions to help guide the novice practitioner.

Introducing and explaining the assessment session

The outline of what the practitioner hopes to achieve in the first session is explained and then permission to continue is sought.

> *Thank you for coming today, I have one hour scheduled for our interview. Is this OK with you? In order to make the best use of our time together, I would now like to explain an outline of what we will be doing in today's session. First, I'd like to look at, and try to understand, the current problems you have been experiencing – this will allow us to generate a list of the key difficulties that brought you here today. Then I hope we can draw down and analyse those problems in detail. This will hopefully help us both understand what is going on during these difficult periods. If we have time today I would also like to briefly look at how long these problems have been with you and finally I would like to check your mood and the effect of your mood on other parts of your life. Please don't worry if we can't get all the information we need today. We can finish the assessment next session, if necessary, and then I will feed back to you what I find, to make sure I've understood you properly. Before we go on, do you have any questions or concerns?*

With experience and practice, the practitioner will be able to complete most of the initial assessment in one or two sessions, however, in order to get detailed, accurate information, it is important not to rush. In addition, your assessment of the client will change over time as you learn more and as the client becomes more comfortable with you. Remember, do not make the mistake of seeing the assessment as simply a data-gathering exercise that should be dispensed with as quickly as possible.

The pacing of the session and the attitude of the practitioner should facilitate the client's comfortable disclosure of their major problem areas. Only by completing a thorough assessment can a practitioner and client identify the key components of the problem areas and go on to agree effective interventions.

A four-step approach to assessment

Step 1 – *Obtain a detailed account of current problems and generate a problem list*

The practitioner needs to first establish a comprehensive list of current problems. These presenting problems need to be defined in very specific, concrete, measurable, behavioural terms. We could start by asking:

> *'If you're comfortable about beginning the assessment, could we start by you telling me what current difficulties led to you being here today?'*

Alternatively, the practitioner can start by asking:

> *'Could we take some time to list those things that you think you should be doing and can't or those things that you once were able to do but now can't?'*

The secret here is to remain focused on current difficulties and not get drawn too early into a history-taking session. If this happens, gently inform the client that this information is important and you will address it, but for the purposes of today's session you would like to establish current difficulties. Explain that it is important for you to try to understand what the current problems are; this allows the practitioner and client to consider some immediate help, thereby instilling hope. The difficulty with obtaining a long, convoluted history of the client's problems immediately is that it may prevent you establishing what is going on in the 'here and now'. It is, after all, in the 'here and now' that we solve problems.

Obtaining a comprehensive history may be very useful in terms of explaining what caused the current problem but can often offer little help in terms of speedily correcting the problem. Your dentist, when dealing with a toothache that is painful and inflicting huge difficulties in the 'here and now', will not, in the first instance, ask for a detailed account of your sweet-eating history. This is not to suggest client history is unimportant. Of course, it can eventually allow us to understand how long-standing patterns of thinking and behaving have contributed to current difficulties. The first aim of assessment, however, is to understand what is happening currently in order to offer the client a realistic solution in a timely manner.

Again, always remember that questioning the client on current difficulties should be done sensitively and compassionately. Clients are often only too aware of the emotional component of their difficulties and will therefore identify their emotional reactions in the first instance. For example, the client suffering from panic disorder may describe their problem as being 'frightened or worried' or a client suffering from depression may initially describe their primary problem as 'being weary' or that they simply 'can't be bothered'. Even after many years of practising CBT, the authors still tend to describe their day with reference to how they feel (e.g. 'the day was lousy'), rather than describe what precisely happened to make the day 'feel' lousy, or what thoughts they experienced.

Eliciting vague, general statements about how someone feels emotionally is important, but is only the first step. It is important that you acknowledge what the client feels. Feelings tell us subjectively how the person experiences their current situation and can offer invaluable information on how feelings affect the person's thinking, behaviour and body. Feelings alone, however, tell us practically nothing about the detail of the client's problem. As they are often a consequence of how we think and how we behave, they can offer a chance to explore underlying thoughts and behaviours. The difficulty most practitioners face is that individuals assign individual meanings to the words they use to describe how they feel. The phrase 'I just feel lousy' can convey that the individual is simply experiencing a transitory, very mild sense of stress, or it can convey a fairly permanent state of severe distress.

Eliciting these general statements is therefore not enough. We then need to clarify what the person means when they say they feel a certain way. This often means using clarification questions to probe for a better understanding of the problem.

Simple clarification questions include:

'When you say you are having panic attacks, tell me what you mean.'
'If you suffered this reaction now, can you describe to me what actually would be happening?'
'What would I see and where would you feel it most in your body?'
'I would like to understand what exactly happens when you feel that – can you describe a recent example?'
'Tell me not just what you felt emotionally but where you felt it in your body – what physical sensations were you aware of?'

Clarification questions allow a more elaborate discussion about what the person actually experiences when they report a particular emotional state. This prevents assumptions being made by the practitioner and keeps the focus squarely on the client's experience. Clarification questions should be used for any term the client refers to that the practitioner is unclear of or where the meaning may be ambiguous.

First, focus on eliciting specific behaviourally defined problems. This gives the practitioner a good concrete sense of things that the client is perhaps doing too much of and/or the things that the client does too little of. Instead of

'I just feel awful all day and cannot be bothered.'

define what 'awful' means and get a recent example.

> Practitioner: *Could you tell me a bit more about what feeling awful actually means to you by giving me an example of when you last felt like this? What did it look like the last time you experienced this feeling 'awful'?*
> Client: *Yesterday was the last time it happened. I felt tired all day, had a constant headache and thought about doing things all day (like the washing up and ironing) but didn't actually get round to doing them.*

Another example might be when a client says, *'I feel panicky when I'm out.'* Ask the client to elaborate on this:

> *'Can I ask you to give me some more detail of the last time you actually felt panicky? What did that look like and what did you think was happening?'*

This is then converted into:

> *'Today, and, in fact, every time I try to leave my front door alone, I feel frightened. My breathing goes all wrong and I end up gasping for breath. I almost stop breathing, I think I'm going to collapse and die all alone. Therefore I cannot collect the kids from school, cannot go out to shops alone and cannot visit friends alone.'*

By obtaining this additional information, we now have a much more detailed account of this particular problem situation. We have established a typical event/ situation, the behaviour associated with this situation, the negative frightening thoughts, the emotion these thoughts generate and the actual physical reaction to this situation. In other words, we get a tiny but very important insight into this client's perception.

> Situation/s: thinking about going out alone to pick up kids, shop, and visit friends.
> Behaviour: avoid going out alone
> Mood/Emotion: fear
> Thoughts: 'I will collapse and die alone'
> Body/Physiology: gasping for breath

The next task is to reflect this back to the client to ensure you understand fully their interpretation of what is happening and then ask if there are any other problems or problem situations.

Eliciting avoidant or protective behaviours

A common problem encountered when trying to elicit a precise problem list is that the client only offers up their distant past emotional reactions. This can occur when a person has developed a range of strategies that have successfully shielded them from current distress. For example, if an individual experienced panic symptoms in the past, when away from home, they may have learned that it is better not to be away from home and have adapted their behaviour accordingly, i.e. stopped going out. They therefore may report that they only felt distressed in the past.

When faced with this, the practitioner could consider moving on to any areas of the person's life that are currently avoided: *'Is there anything at the minute that you have stopped doing or that you avoid because you find it difficult?'* Once you have elicited avoided activities, the next question involves asking the client to think about or imagine doing this activity now, and then eliciting what they think they might feel. This may even provoke the thoughts and emotions in session, which can then be used to complete the problem list. As you already have the avoidant behaviour, use it to elicit the thinking and emotions that led the client to employ avoidance.

For example, if a client reports that she no longer suffers any emotional reaction because she has learned to avoid going out of her house, ask, *'If you were to think about leaving the house alone today, what do you imagine that would feel like?'* Then: *'What would be the worst thing you imagine would happen?'*

As each problem area is elicited, the practitioner needs to reflectively feed back to the client the problems described, in order to clarify that they understand precisely what is being said. The aim is not to interpret or assume anything, but deal with and record the facts, as conveyed by the client. At the same time, encourage the client to elaborate on and expand their description of their experiences so you understand them more fully. Once you have established a problem area (and are sure you clearly understand what the client is saying), then ask if there are any other problems; the process of clarifying what the client is saying then begins again. Once you have clearly identified a number of problem statements, recap by summarizing, check that you've understood the client and move on to step 2. Problems are defined by the client, not the practitioner. The practitioner should also establish how the client functioned before their problems arose. This comparison between then and now can be used later by the practitioner and client to reflect on the differences between how they are currently reacting while ill and how they once reacted while well.

Step 2 – *Prioritize problems and ask the client to select the most important problem for further detailed cognitive behavioural analysis*

To help make sense of the client's problems, we now need to start mapping out what exactly happens to them, their reaction or interpretation of what is happening, their emotional responses and how they cope or behaviourally respond. This is completed before a decision is made by the client and practitioner on whether the client's current thinking and behavioural responses are helpful. A generic cognitive behavioural maintenance model can be used to achieve this (see Figure 2.1 on p. 32). The generic maintenance model focuses directly on the inter-relationship between the client's current problem situation or experiences and their resultant cognitions, emotional reactions, bodily responses and subsequent behaviours. As mentioned before, it is the interpretation of these experiences that often generates the client's resultant problems and it is often the client's behav-ioural responses that maintain them. It is important to recognize that the generic cognitive behavioural model does not prioritize one domain above another. Therefore a change in behaviour can effect a change in cognition or an increase in bodily symptoms can effect a change in thinking, behaviour and/or mood. Let's look at the model in more detail.

- **Environment or trigger situation** This is also referred to as the ante-cedent or precipitant and is anything (an event, a situation, a thought, a memory, a physical sensation, a mood or behaviour) that precedes a current shift in mood, thinking and/or behaviour. It captures the precise moment the client suffers a change or shift in mood.
- **Internal and external triggers** Triggers broadly come in two forms. External triggers are real-life situations or events that we come across or find ourselves in. They are by definition external events, for example, actually being in a shopping centre or town centre or actually walking into a crowded party. Internal triggers are internal experiences, not often obvious to others. They include thoughts/memories that just pop into our heads, sudden emotional reactions and physiological changes to our bodies. They are private internal experiences.
- **Cognitions or automatic negative thoughts/intrusive thoughts or images** These are negative automatic thoughts, images or memories that may appear to be related to, or provoked by, the trigger. They can be unwanted, negative, catastrophic or derogatory and are affect- or emotion-laden. They are not wilfully generated by the client but seem to just arrive and seem credible to some degree to the client.
- **Bodily sensations** These are real physical sensations that are initially experienced privately (e.g. shaking, trembling, sweating, butterflies in the stomach) that may also be apparent to others (e.g. shaking, trembling and sweating). They are often very apparent to the client and can feel over-whelming and cause a great deal of added concern and worry.
- **Emotion (mood/feelings)** These are the subjective feelings experienced and reported by the client. The practitioner aims to map the client's

separate problem situations onto the model. The practitioner needs to understand the impact of the client's recent experiences, in terms of how they interpreted that experience, the impact of that interpretation on mood and physical sensations and the behaviours they employed in response to their negative automatic thoughts and feelings.

- **Behaviour (particularly protective/safety behaviours)** These include any behaviour employed, knowingly or unknowingly, that the client uses to quell emotional distress temporarily, or to prevent the negative automatic thought occurring.

As mentioned, the generic cognitive behavioural maintenance model is a very useful tool that helps achieve a better understanding of the problem for the client and the practitioner and hopefully helps both to jointly construct a treatment strategy. Each problem is analysed using the model (Figure 2.1).

The practitioner and client now have a map on which to plot and explore in more detail the sequence of events which occur when a client experiences a typical problematic situation.

To select or prioritize which problem situations are analysed, first, the practitioner simply asks the client to pick out a problem from their problem list (often starting with the most distressing or the most recent). The practitioner and client then explore, in more detail, the precise nature of the triggering event; what was going through the client's mind at the time and how much they believed those thoughts; what impact those thoughts had on their mood and body; and what they specifically did in response to any negative shift in emotion. Finally, the practitioner needs to discuss with the client the workability of the strategies they currently employ. This includes whether the strategy works all of the time, some of the time or no longer works at all. The practitioner also needs to bring the client's attention to the short-term consequences of current responses versus the longer-term consequences.

The process involves asking questions that enable the client to think about and explore their current strategies, when confronted with adversity, and whether they work or not. The aim is to gently point out all of the consequences of current behaviour and to avoid bluntly identifying potential flaws in current responses. Your aim has to be to promote an environment where the client themselves can begin to challenge the validity of their current thoughts, beliefs and actions. The practitioner never directly challenges a client's beliefs or actions. The consequences of doing this may lead the client to believe they are being attacked and criticized or that their experiences are invalidated by a challenging practitioner.

Questions to help triggering situations

Now that you've selected this particular problem from our problem list, can we look at the start of the last distressing episode?
Could we take the last episode you experienced?
Can you close your eyes and imagine being back there?

> *Now can you tell me precisely what was going on?*
> *Where were you?*
> *Who were you with (if anyone)?*
> *What were you doing just prior to feeling this way?*
> *What were you focussing on or concentrating on?*

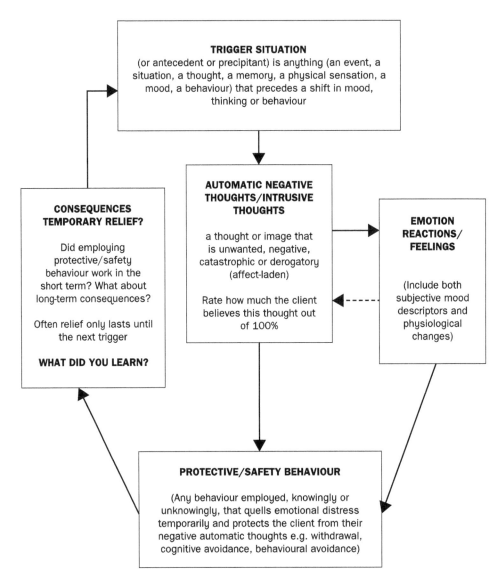

Figure 2.1 Generic cognitive behavioural maintenance model

The aim is to try to establish precisely what the circumstances were just prior to the client experiencing a negative shift in emotion. The trigger could be an external event, such as being in a particular place, at an event with a particular person or noticing a specific object. Alternatively, the trigger could be an internal event, such as noticing a particular bodily sensation, thinking about a specific thing, having a particular memory pop into their head or simply experiencing a sudden shift in mood. You need to check for all of these types of triggers. Remember, also, that more recent specific examples of problematic situations are easier to recall in detail than more distant examples. The importance of asking the client to cite a *recent* and *specific* incident when they noticed their mood shift cannot be emphasized enough.

Questions to elicit negative thoughts or intrusive thoughts

The following questions may be helpful in eliciting negative automatic thinking:

What was going through your mind at the time?
Can you remember what you were thinking at the time?
What did you make of this particular trigger situation?
How did you read what was going on?
What did you think was going to happen?
What was the worst thing that might happen?
How much did you believe this thought at the time?
How credible did that thought seem at the time out of 100 per cent, with 10 per cent equalling not so believable and 90 per cent equalling very believable?
How real for you was the thought at that time?

Thoughts flash through our minds in an instant and we don't often attend to our thoughts, but instead respond to the negative emotion associated with the thought. Therefore, this process of eliciting pertinent negative automatic thoughts is difficult initially. It may be necessary to ask the client if they would be comfortable closing their eyes for a few seconds and trying to revisit the situation in question, in order to remember what was going through their head at the time.

In addition, clients may be very hesitant about revealing what they were thinking, as they may think their thoughts are foolish or strange. Creating the right atmosphere, in which a client feels able to divulge personal thoughts, requires good therapeutic relationship skills, as noted in Chapter 1. Remember, clients are usually very aware of the emotional component of their difficulties and will often identify their emotional reactions in the first instance.

If the client continues to experience difficulty either in revealing their thoughts or accessing them, then move on to exploring the emotions associated with the triggering situation and all noticeable bodily sensations. You can see that we are not just capturing the negative automatic thought but also how credible that thought was to the client in the problematic situation. This is important as it is not just having a negative automatic thought that disturbs people; it is how believable that thought is at the time to us that determines how we feel and the intensity of that feeling.

Questions to help the client elicit feelings and associated physical sensations

What word or words would best describe how you felt at the time of this specific problematic situation?
What word or words would best describe your mood at the time?
Can you tell me more about this?
What does that word mean to you?
Did you notice any changes in your body?
Where did you notice this most in your body?
Is there anything else you noticed about your body at that particular time?

As mentioned before, when exploring feelings/mood, it is always important to ask clarification questions in order that you can understand fully what the client means when they say they felt 'awful', 'depressed', 'frightened', 'panicky', and 'dreadful', etc. Simple clarifications questions include:

'When you say you are having . . . (e.g. panic attacks) tell me what you mean.'
'If you suffered this now, describe what would actually happen.'
'I would like to understand what exactly happens when you feel that.'

Asking the client to recall the situation in their imagination may help them remember how they actually felt at the time and help establish any notable bodily sensations at the time. In fact, revisiting the situation in the imagination may actually provoke a return of those actual sensations in session and this allows a much clearer understanding of what actually happened during the problematic situation.

Questioning throughout treatment should not be seen by the client as an interrogation, so allow time for the client to respond to your questions, and listen, reflect and summarize their responses until there is a mutual understanding of what the client is actually describing. Use the techniques described in Chapter 1 to assist with this.

The connection between emotions and cognitions

Two important aspects of exploring in detail the emotions expressed by the client are:

- First, the client, in giving an account of their feelings, may also volunteer the underlying cognitions or thoughts behind those feelings. For example, in response to a clarification question from the practitioner about how the client felt during a difficult situation, they may very well express their perception about what they believed was happening. The client may disclose 'God, I just felt so terrible. I felt I was going to collapse or die.' In attempting to explain the emotional content of the event, the client has expressed a very potent thought ('I'm going to die'). The practitioner needs to be alert for such important disclosures throughout the entire assessment and treatment process. People often express thoughts as feelings and use the words 'thought' and 'feel' interchangeably.

- Second, the practitioner needs to pay attention to the impact of particularly catastrophic thinking on emotion and the reverse impact of the subsequent emotional and physical changes on thinking. For example, the person who notices his heart rate increase (the trigger) may interpret this as a sign of an imminent heart attack (cognition). This frightening thought, 'I am having a heart attack!' (if credible to the client) will obviously increase anxiety and therefore the rise in anxiety may confirm the original catastrophic thought. The interplay between thinking something is frightening and the activation of the fear response establishes a potent vicious cycle, which may help maintain the belief and may produce a panic attack in session. If this happens, it gives the practitioner an excellent opportunity to investigate the anxiety in detail. Again this must be done sensitively, by first empathizing and then asking the client to describe in detail what they are experiencing.

Questions that elicit information regarding protective or safety behaviours

When you experience these feelings, what did you do?
When in this difficult situation, is there anything you did that helped?
Is there anything you do or is there anything anyone else does that makes the problem better?
Can you take me through precisely what happened, once you experienced this feeling?

The aim here is to elicit the client's current coping strategies or their preferred way of dealing with the problem, at this moment in time. It is important to investigate this fully, as very often people employ techniques for so long that the protective or safety behaviour now seems so natural that they no longer view it as a response to anxiety. For example, a client who experiences panic symptoms, with a racing heart, breathlessness, sweating, dry mouth, palpitations and a mistaken belief that these symptoms mean they are going to stop breathing and die, may use some or all of the following protective behaviours:

1   Always carry water to cool them down and make their symptoms subside.
2   Make sure their mobile phone is always fully charged before they leave home in case they need an ambulance.
3   Have the caller number always ready on their phone with key people who might help them in case of the perceived catastrophe.

4 Always carry a brown paper bag because they saw this used on the TV programme *Casualty* when someone was having breathing difficulties.
5 Always carry a diazepam tranquillizer in their bag because it worked once when they felt panicky.
6 Never go out alone in case they pass out quickly and can't get to their phone.
7 If going out in the car, ensure there are back-up supplies of water in the car in case they break down and need to wait for assistance.
8 Test their pulse to check whether it is 'racing' or not, as this may be a sign of impending heart failure.

Taking the time, during the assessment phase of treatment, to fully assess the extent and range of protective or safety behaviours is worth the effort, so that later treatment is not unnecessarily hampered by the client continuing to inadvertently employ very subtle behaviours that maintain the problem.

As we will see in the next three chapters, the key point is that, although protective or safety behaviours are completely understandable and even appear logical, they actually prevent the client testing out their catastrophic beliefs and therefore prevent the client from learning new, more adaptive strategies. They therefore, act as a potent maintaining factor in terms of the illness. Protective or safety behaviours often work very well in the short term. For example, the client mentioned above has experienced that cooling their body down by using copious amounts of water does seem (time and time again) to prevent them from suffering 'cardiac arrest'. Therefore, it may appear to the client that it is a strategy that works.

Given that your client is a fully functioning problem-solving human, the discovery that protective or safety behaviour helps in the short term prevents them from solving their current difficulties. To overcome this, we need to elicit and appreciate the client's perception or model of what is going on. Very often, we all stumble across or design solutions that work very well in the short term and then revert to these solutions time and time again because they seem to work. Many of us are blind, or decide not to pay attention, to the long-term consequences of our behaviour. We instead opt to continue doing things that are unhelpful, but bring relief or even pleasure in the short term.

Take a look at these examples:

Smoking
Drinking alcohol
Eating a deliciously fat-laden diet
Taking drugs
Gambling
Putting off opening bills
Putting off paying bills
Avoiding confronting someone

These behaviours can be used to put off or delay discomfort and distress in the short term. The problem is that they often work incredibly well in the short term but can stall us from recognizing other longer-term, more healthy solutions. They therefore become potent maintaining factors that prevent us from learning or designing more appropriate long-term solutions.

For example, if someone has panic disorder with agoraphobia and discovers that by quickly returning home when they have an increase in distressing anxiety their anxiety reduces, then this behaviour (returning to the safety of home) may be reinforced (actually negatively reinforced). This then becomes the preferred method of dealing with anxiety. Cognitively, the person may also develop what might appear to be a reasonably rational belief that going outside alone is not for them. The more the person uses returning home as a strategy, the more they continue to confirm that going out is dangerous for them and the less likely they are to risk testing out this assumption and free themselves from being trapped inside their house. This behaviour is likely to be maintained or actually increase in frequency if it is reliably followed by a reduction in distress. This is referred to as negative reinforcement and is by far the most potent form of learning (Baker et al., 2004).

Step 3 – *Evaluating the advantages and disadvantages of current methods employed to deal with the problematic situation and the distress it causes*

Once you have elicited protective or safety behaviours, some time needs to be dedicated to establishing how they work for your client. Explore with the client what happens after they employ the protective or safety behaviour. Acknowledge the benefits and understand that these behaviours may have worked to some extent. Note that the client's current pattern of behaviour is evidence that your client has been working hard at employing techniques to help themselves and to prevent the problem getting worse. Once you have elicited all protective behaviours, point out that you recognize that they have worked extremely hard at finding their own solutions.

Once all the advantages of current behaviour have been elicited, the practitioner can then ask about how long the benefits last and whether there are any adverse side effects to using their current strategies. The aim here is to test the overall workability of current strategies being employed and begin the search for more permanent solutions to the client's current problems. This can be done as you move through each problem situation from your problem list or it can be done as part of the next treatment session. If you address the workability of the client's current protective or safety behaviours at the next session, we would suggest you list all the protective/safety behaviours elicited from your assessment session and then, taking one at a time, explore each in terms of its benefits and explore potential problems with their preferred current behaviour. With depression, the client may use protective behaviours that are designed to prevent the occurrence of perceived catastrophic predictions that their situation will get even worse, or that others will see how weak, incompetent or unlovable they are. Depression-fed protective behaviours often take the form of social withdrawal and a reduction in activity (Beck et al., 1979).

Some questions that may help establish the long-term consequences of protective or safety behaviours

---

Does doing this help you find out if your current beliefs are correct or not?
How long does the effect last?
Has it ever offered a long period of relief?
When employing these strategies, is there anything you sacrifice in terms of things you would like to do but can't because of these strategies?
How long have you used this particular strategy?
What does this tell us about its ability to help you in the long term?
Does this behaviour help or prevent you testing out the reality of your negative thoughts?
Name me the three most valuable and important things in your life. Does using these current strategies affect the things that you value or get in the way of attending to important areas of your life?
Does it hinder or help your relationships, your social life or your working life, etc.?

As mentioned above, we are trying to acknowledge and understand the use of protective and safety behaviours, but also introduce the idea that they prevent the client from really testing their negative beliefs.

Once all or most of the problems on your initial problem list have been explored using the cognitive behavioural analysis described above (and you are both clear you fully understand the triggers, cognitions, bodily sensations, emotions and behaviours involved in each problematic situation), the next stage is to ascertain the onset of these problems.

Step 4 – Onset

The practitioner now needs to investigate the onset of these problems. This is done by asking the client to consider the first time they noticed these difficulties. The practitioner explores whether the client's problems represent a relatively recent change in functioning or if they represent a more enduring pattern of functioning that has been resistant to change. The use of brief low-intensity cognitive behavioural interventions (as opposed to a formal course of CBT) is going to be of benefit mainly to clients who have problems that have developed relatively recently. The practitioner is advised to speak to an experienced and accredited supervisor regarding 'stepping up' more severely ill clients to appropriate formal therapy.

Questions to elicit information on onset and fluctuations

Can you remember when these problems first occurred?
Could we examine your earliest memory of these difficulties occurring?
Think carefully – was there anything significant at the time of onset?
What is your impression of what happened to bring on these difficulties?
Has there been anything in the past that has improved or considerably helped with this problem?
Has there been anything in the past that has made the problem considerably worse?

It is then useful to carry out a cognitive behavioural analysis of the earliest remembered episode.

The above questions not only help establish onset but also explore the client's impressions of any positive or negative fluctuations in the condition. This may help the practitioner and client identify cognitive, behavioural, social, recreational, spiritual and occupational variables which may have been useful in the past but which are now maintaining the problem.

We also advise offering the client the Client History Form as part of their early homework assignment (Appendix 1). This allows the client to think about, record and review their history relevant to their illness.

Mental State Evaluation

An important aspect of history taking is the Mental State Evaluation; this can be seen at the end of the Client History Form (Appendix 1). The format may be used to elicit current mood and its impact on risk, appetite, sleep, memory, concentration and motivation. In addition, this should be noted by the practitioner during the assessment:

Appearance and behaviour

Does the client appear to be caring for themselves? Is there any weight loss apparent e.g. loose clothes? Do they appear anxious or agitated? What are eye contact and expressions like?

Speech

Are there any speech changes, e.g. slow, fast or monotone?

Thought content

Are there any cognitive features of depression? Are there any expressions of worthlessness, hopelessness or thoughts of being a burden on others? Are there

---

any cognitive features of anxiety? Does the client talk about fearing the worst will happen, e.g. having a heart attack during panic symptoms?

Mood

Is there objective evidence of depression or anxiety? How do they describe their mood? Interest? Appetite? Sleep? Enjoyment?

Energy? Is life worth living? (If the client expresses thoughts of life not being worth living, see the risk assessment section for further detail (pp. 43–6). It is recommended that this is discussed with your supervisor/client's GP. It may not be appropriate to proceed with low-intensity interventions.)

Perceptual abnormality

Do they describe any odd experiences, e.g. hearing or seeing things others have not reported hearing or seeing (hallucinations)? (This requires further assessment and discussion with your supervisor and/or client's GP before considering proceeding with low-intensity CBT interventions.)

Insight

What do they think is wrong, if anything? What do they think may help?

Memory, concentration and motivation are also assessed in order to establish if the client is ready to commit to what can be quite intensive (for them) cognitive behavioural interventions.

Client's expectations of therapy

Questions to elicit expectations

Given what we have covered today, what would you like to achieve by undertaking treatment?
If treatment works, what do you think would change in terms of your current behaviour?

This permits you to tap into the client's overall goals for treatment and also allows you to convert these goals into concrete short-term, medium-term and long-term treatment targets. This is covered in more detail in Chapter 3.

Setting treatment targets

Once all of this data is gathered, the practitioner draws up the problems identified onto a fresh cognitive behaviour analysis sheet (one for each problem analysed) and then, in a subsequent appointment, slowly reviews the sheet with the client. During this stage of assessment, the practitioner and client begin making the possible connections between triggers elicited, negative automatic thoughts, emotional and physiological reactions and the use of any identified protective or safety behaviours. It is important to establish that the client understands and agrees with the links. If not, the practitioner and the client need to revisit the analysis and come to a shared agreement before moving on.

If there is a shared understanding, then the practitioner can bring the client's attention to the notion that they seem somewhat trapped in the cycles they both have analysed. The practitioner can then ask the client to describe how they have so far tried to break the cycle. It should become clear to the client that they have attempted to break the cycle in a number of ways. The generic cognitive behavioural maintenance model (Figure 2.2) can be used with the client to help accomplish this; a blank worksheet is provided in Appendix 1.

The problem with avoiding triggers

The client may have tried to avoid the triggers that they consider to provoke the distressing cycle of negative or catastrophic thoughts, and their associated negative distressing emotions. This can mean avoiding external triggers either by simply not going out or by ceasing to engage with life. This shuts down the individual's life and limits their capacity to do what is really important to them. Second, the client may attempt to avoid or stop unwanted internal triggers. The problem with this is that if you try to suppress a negative thought or memory, paradoxically you increase that thought's frequency. Try not to think of a big, fat, white rabbit. What pops into your mind? Try not to think of the numbers 1 2 3, well, have you successfully expelled them completely from your mind? Thought suppression

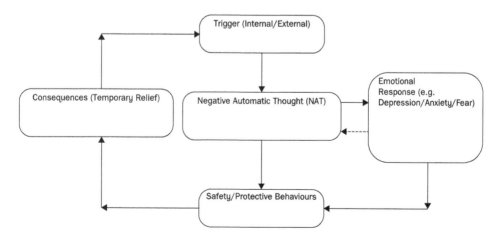

Figure 2.2   Generic cognitive behavioural maintenance model blank version

is not possible. Another strategy is to become overly vigilant for physiological sensations (in an attempt to be at least prepared for the possible onset of a physiological catastrophe). This can lead to constant body scanning and only serves to focus the client's attention towards even normally occurring physical changes that may be misinterpreted as a sign of impending physical doom. Thought suppression and scanning are also examples of protective behaviours that then backfire and keep the client's focus of attention on their problem.

To show this in action, note what happens if you overly scrutinize an otherwise perfectly healthy physical mechanism. Notice your throat and pay particular attention to your next swallow. What do you notice? Try swallowing again to test your ability to swallow – what do you get? Is it difficult? Do you notice your tongue, the muscle in your throat contracting and relaxing? Is it a tiny bit weird? Is it tight? Is it lumpy? Do you feel your throat is constricted? Now, hopefully you have been happily swallowing all day up to this point, but you will have noticed what happens to your experience of swallowing when you overly focus attention on this most automatic and routine physical activity. If a client begins to body scan in search of signs of potential illness, this often offers the client a whole new set of experiences to worry about.

Safety or protective behaviours block learning and reality testing

The client will begin to see that they also use protective behaviours and safety behaviours to avoid distress. In doing so, the practitioner needs to ask the client to consider, while this continues, how you and the client can really test the accuracy of their catastrophic thoughts. If the client doesn't go out and instead stays at home because of the thought that they are going to collapse and die, how can the client ever test out whether this thought is true or not? Therefore, the protective and safety behaviours are not merely a benign side effect of negative thinking; they are, in fact, a potent maintaining behaviour and help to keep the problem from ever resolving. The more safety behaviours are employed, the more they need to be employed and the more the client relies on them, the stronger the response. They are, in fact, highly addictive behaviours. The aim, therefore, is to begin to dismantle these responses and to reality test the client's thoughts.

It is, therefore, vitally important to open the debate with the client as to whether their current reactions are working for them or not (the 'workability criteria'). Only when a client comes to the conclusion that current strategies don't work might the client be willing to agree to work with the practitioner on alternative anti-avoidance strategies. The hope is that if the client and the practitioner truly agree current strategies may in fact not be helpful, the client may then agree to experiment with different approaches, rather than to persevere with the unproductive strategies.

As you can see, the process of completing a cognitive behavioural assessment is structured and thorough. It should provide you with a detailed analysis of the problem the client wants addressed and help you and the client to explore what maintains the problem. The following section covers the importance of risk assessment, which will also inform your decision about whether low-intensity treatment is suitable for the client.

Risk assessment

When completing an assessment of any client, one of the areas of paramount importance is the issue of risk. Clients should be told about the bounds of confidentiality at the outset of assessment, so that if there are any concerns about risk to self or others, these can be dealt with appropriately, without causing a rupture in the therapeutic relationship. Risk assessment must be carried out at each appointment and should be seen as an ongoing process. Obviously, if risk issues are raised, they will be the main priority for the session. As a health professional, there is an expectation that risk assessment is a core competency: one we should all be familiar with, including local policies regarding risk and child protection and risk assessment tools used within services. When engaged in an assessment, the practitioner should be aware of 'at risk' groups and any specific indicators of increased risk such as:

- age and gender – there is a peak in completed suicide between the ages of 15 and 35 years and over 65 years, especially in males (Gask et al., 2008);
- history of deliberate self-harm or suicide attempts, particularly more violent methods, e.g. shooting, hanging;
- history of misuse of drugs or alcohol;
- family history of completed suicide;
- history of serious physical illness/disability;
- low income;
- divorce or recent relationship loss;
- unemployment;
- prisoner or forensic history;
- expression of hopelessness (Beck et al., 1985).

Obviously some of these factors are relatively stable, for example, age and gender represent a statistical increase in risk, whereas others may change, for instance, hopelessness. In psychological autopsies of completed suicides, the incidence of evidence of mental disorder is high; however, there are major methodological limitations to this type of retrospective analysis (Appleby et al., 1999a). Nevertheless, one in four people who complete suicide were found to be in contact with mental health services in the year before their death (Appleby et al., 1999b). Interestingly, a recent study has shown that the risk of suicide is greater following a general hospital admission, suggesting that risk assessment and opportunities for suicide prevention are not just the business of mental health services (Dougall et al., 2014). With this in mind, remember to use the PHQ–9 (Kroenke et al., 2001), which includes questions regarding hopelessness and suicidal ideation, at each appointment and use these results to inform your risk assessment.

Occasionally, we can be shy about asking questions about suicidal ideas. This can be for many reasons, for example, inexperience or simply not wishing to confront the issue. Inexperienced clinicians can sometimes think that asking the question can increase the risk. This is not the case and asking the question quite often can allow the person to discuss the problems they are facing and may overall reduce risk (Gask et al., 2008). Dealing with suicidal ideas can be upsetting for both the client and the practitioner. If you have concerns about a client expressing suicidal ideas, it is advisable to consult a senior colleague/supervisor for advice and support.

Having a good, trusting therapeutic relationship is obviously an important prerequisite for risk assessment, which needs to be done sensitively and empathically. It is likely that the client may feel ashamed about having thoughts of harming themselves and may not have told anyone else about this. It is important to assess the degree to which the client has considered this and if there are any protective factors, which may reduce the risk of completed suicide.

> Practitioner: *Do you feel as if life is worth going on at the moment?*
> Client: *Well, no, not really . . . sometimes.*
>
> [The practitioner empathizes and probes further about suicidal ideation.]
>
> Practitioner: *So things are really difficult for you at the moment and at times you feel as if life is not worth living. Have you ever thought of doing yourself any harm?*
> Client: *Well, I did think of taking sleeping tablets, just to get away from things for a while.*
>
> [Then the practitioner probes about suicide plans.]
>
> Practitioner: *Have you made any plans to take extra tablets or harm yourself in any other way?*
> Client: *No, I wouldn't do it to my husband and the kids – that would kill them. I just wanted to sleep.*
>
> [The practitioner summarizes and enquires about other protective factors.]
>
> Practitioner: *So you have had thoughts of taking sleeping tablets but thoughts of your family stopped you. Is there anything else you think stopped you?*
> Client: *Well, I don't think it's right, you know, taking your own life. I used to be quite religious. I was brought up to believe it is wrong.*
>
> [The practitioner summarizes and asks about access to means to harm.]
>
> Practitioner: *OK, so thoughts of your family and your religious beliefs have stopped you acting on these thoughts. Have you access to sleeping tablets or any other way of harming yourself?*
> Client: *Yes, but I only have a few tablets left. The GP just gave me 2 weeks' supply.*

[The practitioner asks about final acts.]

> Practitioner: *Did you tell your husband or anyone else goodbye or write any notes?*
> Client: *No.*

[The practitioner asks about protective confiding relationships.]

> Practitioner: *If you have thoughts like this again, is there anyone you could confide in? It can be really difficult holding on to thoughts like these, sometimes it helps to talk about it.*
> Client: *Well, my GP is good. I used to be able to tell my husband everything.*
> Practitioner: *Do you think it would be helpful for your husband to know how you are feeling?*
> Client: *Yes, I will talk to him. I know he is worried about me.*

[The practitioner seeks permission to discuss this with her family.]

> Practitioner: *Would you like me to discuss this with your husband?*
> Client: *Yes, he is waiting for me in the waiting room. I think that would be good.*

[Harm minimization strategies and information sharing are discussed.]

> Practitioner: *As you know, I will be sending a report to your GP and I will discuss your case with my supervisor as you may need more intensive support. I think it is important for your care that I share this information with them. Your GP may decide to give you smaller prescriptions of medication or ask your husband to look after your medication until these thoughts subside.*
> Client: *OK.*

[A final summary includes an agreed action plan in the event of further thoughts of life not being worth living and may instil hope that they can be helped.]

> Practitioner: *OK, so we have agreed to talk to your husband, your GP and my supervisor and if you have these thoughts again, you will try to speak to your husband or GP. Here is a 24-hour helpline number that you can also contact at any time.*

Development of a management plan, which involves others caring for the client and family members, is very important. The most common findings to come out of suicide inquiries are that there was poor communication between professionals and with family members. The plan will be dependent on the history and current findings. There is much debate about the reliance on risk assessment tools. These tools can themselves sometimes engender a sense of detachment. If the clinician engages in a form-filling, tick-box exercise it can become more about the assessment tool and less about the client. This may create an illusion for the clinician that an effective risk assessment is being conducted, while the process may actually prevent full and frank disclosure (Martin and Hamilton, 2006). Therefore risk assessment tool use can create an erroneous and dangerous sense of security for the clinician (Simon, 2009).

The assessment of risk is every practitioner's responsibility and should be considered a core competency. There will always be a balance of risks which will have to be negotiated, taking into account the client's presentation, autonomy and the multi-disciplinary team's and the family's views. We should all be actively engaged in the process and while we should ensure we adhere to whatever local policies are in place and are aware of those at more statistical risk, we should not lose sight of the client in front of us and should see beyond the assessment tools.

Session structure

This section suggests how each subsequent therapeutic session should be structured.

Following the assessment interview, each subsequent session can use the following format. This ensures the process of treatment is clearly understood by both the practitioner and the client and that each session is used as effectively and efficiently as possible. A constant session structure throughout the course of treatment helps the client and practitioner to focus attention on problem-solving the client's difficulties and thereby prevents unnecessary digression. In addition, it encourages client collaboration, as each session affords the client the opportunity to contribute to the session agenda.

Adhering to a standard structure is associated with successful treatment outcome (Feeley et al., 1999). The authors believe that using elements of CBT session structure, such as noted below, forms a robust format for any therapeutic intervention. The rationale for employing structure is that every session counts and for brief interventions to be effective we must, as practitioners, optimize session time. Almost all sessions, except the first intake session (start of treatment), follow several discrete steps (see Table 2.1).

Table 2.1   Session structure

Mood check
Review of previous session
Homework review
Set agenda
Set homework
Final summary
Check for any problems/issues from the current session, check for learning

All of the suggested session structure items are carried out in the spirit of collaboration, in an attempt to establish a shared understanding and ultimately a resolution of the client's problems. The structure is often written about but the functions are rarely defined; we shall now break this down and explain each section.

Mood check

A brief mood check is completed at the beginning of each session. The functions of a mood check are:

- to establish the client's current mood;
- to measure the client's mood from the last session;
- to note any change and attempt to establish why this may be the case;
- to identify any potential risk of harm to self or others;
- to highlight any possible issues to be included in the current session agenda.

Regardless of the change in mood – up or down – the practitioner and client need to establish why this may have occurred. The mood check may include the use of subjective units of distress scale or SUDS (Wolpe, 1982), session-by-session objective measures such as the PHQ–9 (Kroenke et al., 2001) and the GAD–7 (Spitzer et al., 2006), as well as any condition-specific measures (such as specific depression or anxiety scales). The subjective units of distress scale, as originally described by Wolpe (1982), is a scale for assessing the level of subjective discomfort the client may be experiencing. This traditionally runs from 0 to 8, with 0 being described as no distress and 8 being the maximum level of distress (Wolpe, 1982). Quite often a scale measuring intensity of emotion from 0–10 or 0–100 is used. The important thing is that the number increases with the increasing intensity of emotion. If there was a particular event associated with a high level of emotion, this may be a suitable topic for that particular session agenda.

The overall aim is to measure the client's progress as treatment moves forward or, indeed, to quickly and effectively establish deterioration, which allows the practitioner and client to ask why, and then take corrective action. Traditionally, practitioners have been poor at measuring the effectiveness of the interventions employed. This can often lead to poor treatment outcome and client drop-out. The client should be encouraged to actively engage in measuring their own progress throughout treatment, as this has proven to be a powerful therapeutic tool in its own right (Lambert and Hawkins, 2004).

Review of previous session

The functions of the review are:

- to establish if the client can recall last session's content;
- to establish what learning has taken place between this and the previous sessions;
- to identify if there are any problems from the previous session content;
- to establish if there are problems with the therapeutic alliance.

If there are any problems in any of these areas, then the practitioner and client need to consider putting them on the current session's agenda. When dealing with the review some of the typical questions which can be considered are:

'Can you recap the headlines or main points from our last session together?'
'Let's start by reviewing the last session. I would like to hear how you thought the last session went.'
'Was there anything that upset you or requires clarification?'
'Was there anything you found useful?'
'How do you think the last session addressed the goals and targets we have set?'
'Can you tell me if/how the last session moved us forward towards your goals?'
'If you are unsure what we covered, could I suggest it would be important to review the material again in this session's agenda?'

Homework review

Homework is an essential part of employing CBT interventions. It can be considered to be 'self-therapy' tasks, where the client continues to work on their problems in between meeting with the practitioner.

The functions of the homework review are:

- to ensure the client understood the purpose of the homework/self-therapy task;
- to ensure it was completed without difficulty;
- to establish what learning, if any, took place.

If there is a problem with any of the above this can be considered a legitimate item to be placed on the current session's agenda.

In terms of the homework review, some typical questions for consideration are:

'Can you recap the headlines or main points from your completed homework?'

'Tell me about your homework in detail. I would like to hear how you thought it went.'

'Was there anything that requires clarification?'

'Was there anything you found useful?'

'How do you think the completed homework addressed the goals and targets we have set?'

'Can you tell me if/how the homework moved us forward towards your goals?'

'If you had difficulty in completing your homework task, could I suggest it would be important to review the homework again in this session's agenda?'

There are a variety of questions to be asked; here it is important to use questioning which can deal both with successful and unsuccessful homework completion. It must be made clear that there is no such thing as 'failure' for the client, in terms of homework, just opportunities for new learning experiences.

As previously indicated, homework or 'self-therapy' is an essential part of the treatment process, both in the promotion and maintenance of change. In terms of ensuring treatment is successful, it is important that new skills learned during the treatment session are tested by the client in their own environment. If this is not successfully accomplished, it is unlikely the treatment will achieve the desired outcome.

Set agenda

The agenda will contain the main issues for the current session, and will be directly linked to the client's problems and goals, set at the beginning of treatment. Times should be agreed and allocated to each agenda item, and the number of agenda items will depend on the time available.

The functions of the agenda are:

- to agree the main areas to be discussed in the current session;
- to prioritize the level of importance of those areas and therefore determine item order;
- to determine those areas for discussion which will best move treatment forward, in line with the client's goals. It is important that within each session the client's goals and targets are referred to, as this ensures both the practitioner and client remain goal-focused.

In terms of setting the agenda, the following questions can be useful:

'Having reviewed the problem list, discussed the goals for treatment and reviewed homework, what problem issues or situations would you think are important for today's session?'
'What issue/s do you think could move us forward in terms of your goals?'
'How may discussing this help us move forward?'

If more than one issue is highlighted, this can be addressed with the following question:

'We have two issues for discussion. Which do you think is the most important in terms of moving treatment forward?'

These questions are focused upon getting the most out of the agenda and therefore collaboratively moving the client towards recovery.

Setting homework

The functions of setting homework are:

- to ensure the client understood the purpose of the current session;
- to ensure the task has been set collaboratively and the rationale has been understood;
- to ensure the task is 'doable', identify and resolve any potential barriers to successful completion;
- to ensure the plan is in line with the client's problems and goals.

It is important to start the homework in session; 10–15 minutes at the end of each session need to be allocated to setting homework in a one-hour session. For example, the client may need to practise what has been agreed with the guidance of the practitioner (e.g. in the form of role play or the completion of appropriate forms).

In terms of homework setting the following questions may be of use:

'Given what has been discussed in today's session, how may this be carried forward in terms of homework or self-help task?'
'What could we learn by doing this?'
'How may this move us forward in terms of meeting your goals?'
'On a scale of 0–100, with 100 being the most confident, how confident do you think you are in terms of homework completion?'
'What would make your confidence score higher?'
'Is there anything we need to do in session, prior to you going out and doing this as homework?'

'Can you think of any barriers which may get in the way of you successfully completing your homework?'

'Have you any ideas on how we may overcome these barriers?'

Again, examining any potential barriers to successful homework completion allows the homework to be truly collaboratively set, thereby putting the client in the best possible position for successful homework completion. As this is an essential part of treatment, this will again facilitate a move towards successful treatment and recovery.

Final summary

> The function of the summary is:
>
> - to ensure both the practitioner and the client review what has been learned during the current session;
> - to identify and clarify any potential misunderstandings;
> - to note the key learning 'headlines'.

It is advisable that the practitioner elicits feedback from the client during the final summary. This ensures that the client has fully understood the session content. In addition, this is also an opportunity for the practitioner to learn how they are being perceived by the client, which allows the practitioner to reflect and improve on their own practice. Finally, any items on the agenda that were not covered due to time constraints must be acknowledged and it should be agreed that these will be moved to the next session.

For the final summary at the end of the session, suggested questions include:

'Can you briefly summarize the main learning points from today's session?' (Prompt if required).

'What would the main headlines/main points from today's session look like?'

'Could we note down the main learning points from the session?'

'Is there anything which upset you or that you didn't understand that may be useful to put on the next session's agenda?'

In the initial sessions, there will be greater direction by the practitioner, however, as the client gets used to the format, sessions should increasingly become client-led. It is also advisable to agree approximate times for each step and for the discrete elements within each step. As a rough guide, if you have one hour available, agree five minutes for the mood check, five minutes for the bridge, five minutes for homework review and 15–20 minutes for each agenda item. Then allow at least 15 minutes for homework setting, practice and final summary. For shorter sessions, you will need to adjust the times accordingly but we do recommend covering these areas. The session structure should apply, whether the contact is conducted face-to-face or via telephone.

Clients, understandably, often wish to tell their entire story repeatedly throughout treatment due to the high levels of distress they have been suffering, sometimes for a significant period. This may lead to therapeutic drift and therefore unproductive digression, and this can, as a result, lead to unsuccessful treatment. The client can be assisted to get back on track through the artful use of summary. In fact, the practitioner should provide frequent summaries throughout the session, as well as opportunities for the client to do the same. This enhances collaboration, lets the client feel heard and understood and ensures the session remains focused.

If, despite the practitioner's best efforts, the client presents with new problems every session or repeatedly revisits their story session after session, the practitioner needs to review and discuss with the client whether the current level of treatment can meet the client's needs. It may be that the client will need to be stepped up to a more experienced practitioner and a more intensive form of treatment. In our experience, many of the above difficulties can be adequately addressed through the use of good goals and targets, established at the beginning of treatment, and socializing the client as a partner in the process of treatment.

Conclusion

In conclusion, there are a number of stages that contribute to a good quality cognitive behavioural assessment. Following these steps will enable you and your client to develop a shared understanding of what the problem or problems are and what the triggers and maintaining behaviours might be. It is important to conduct this assessment within a framework to create the optimum conditions for successful treatment. In the following chapters, we outline problem identification, which includes a section on goal setting, and then, in subsequent chapters, discuss two clients with common mental health problems: anxiety and depression. We will then explore how the information gained from a detailed cognitive behavioural analysis, such as that described in this chapter, can be put to good use in terms of informing treatment.

Summary

- Obtain detailed information about the client's main problems.
- Identify triggering and maintaining factors.
- Perform a basic mental state examination including assessment of risk.
- Determine the suitability of low-intensity treatment for the client (consider stepping up to high intensity, if necessary, after discussion with your supervisor).
- Include the client in *all* decisions.
- Adhere to a specific structure in session to guide both the assessment and treatment sessions.

Recommended reading

Antony, M.M. and Barlow, D.H. (2010) *Handbook of Assessment and Treatment Planning for Psychological Disorders*. New York: Guilford Press.

Beck, A.T., Rush, A.J., Shaw, B.F. and Emery, G. (1979) *Cognitive Therapy of Depression*. New York: Guilford Press.

Beck, J.S. (1995) *Cognitive Therapy: Basics and Beyond*. New York: Guilford Press.

Clark, D.M. (1999) Anxiety disorders: why they persist and how to treat them. *Behaviour Research and Therapy*, 37: S5–S27.

Hawton, K., Salkovskis, P.M., Kirk, J. and Clark, D.M. (eds) (1989) *Cognitive Behaviour Therapy for Psychiatric Problems: A Practical Guide*. Oxford: Oxford University Press.

Lambert, M.J. and Hawkins, E.J. (2004) Measuring outcome in professional practice: considerations in selecting and using brief outcome instruments. *Professional Psychology: Research and Practice*, 35(5): 492–9.

Martin, D. and Hamilton, S. (2006) How to use non-verbal signs in assessments of suicide risk. *Nursing Times*, 102(2): 36–8.

Richards, D. and Whyte, M. (2009) *Reach Out: National Programme Educator Materials to Support the Delivery of Training for Psychological Wellbeing Practitioners Delivering Low Intensity Interventions*, 2nd edn. Rethink Mental Illness. Available at: www.cedar.exeter.ac.uk/iapt/iaptworkbooksandresources (accessed 23 May 2014).

Salkovskis, P.M. (1991) The importance of behaviour in the maintenance of anxiety and panic: a cognitive account. *Behavioural Psychotherapy*, 19: 6–19.

Salkovskis, P.M., Clark, D.M., Hackmann, A., Wells, A. and Gelder, M.G. (1999) An experimental investigation of the role of safety-seeking behaviours in the maintenance of panic disorder with agoraphobia. *Behaviour Research and Therapy*, 37: 559–74.

Simon, R.I. (2009) Suicide risk assessment forms: forms over substance? *Journal of the American Academy of Psychiatry and the Law*, 37: 290–3.

Simmons, J. and Griffiths, R. (2009) *CBT for Beginners*. London: Sage.

Trepka, C., Rees, A., Shapiro, D.A., Hardy, G.E. and Barkham, M. (2004) Therapist competence and outcome of cognitive therapy for depression. *Cognitive Therapy and Research*, 28(2): 143–57.

Westbrook, D., Kennerley, H. and Kirk, J. (2011) *An Introduction to Cognitive Behaviour Therapy: Skills and Applications*, 2nd edn. London: Sage.

3 Problem identification and goal setting

Introduction

This chapter aims to look in detail at how we can use assessment information to clearly define client problems. Once problem areas are agreed, the practitioner and the client can then collaboratively consider possible solutions. We will also consider the factors that make change more likely and the role of motivation – what it is and how it can be harnessed to move treatment forward. This sounds straightforward; however, very often practitioners may come across barriers. These barriers often emanate from the practitioner's mistaken belief that clients will automatically 'buy into' the professional practitioner's expert opinion about what needs to change and how that change can be best accomplished. This is essentially a problem of collaboration. When treatment begins, it is tempting for the practitioner to prescribe or dictate what changes are to be made and if this doesn't work, practitioners sometimes then say the client 'isn't motivated'. Collaboration requires a partnership: a partnership of equals with one partner aware of clinical conditions, their nature and what maintains them and the other aware of their own illness and all it brings to their life.

Problem identification

It is possible for the practitioner to lose sight of this partnership and fall into the trap of setting goals meaningful to *them* and then blaming the client when the plan doesn't work for them. How many times do we think or hear colleagues state: 'My client just isn't motivated!'? This is an interesting assessment, but what does it actually mean? If we assume that all human behaviour is purposeful (i.e. there is always a reason for why we act or don't act), then every action or inaction is purposeful and therefore all behaviour is motivated by something. As health care practitioners we are charged with understanding the purpose and motivation for current behaviour even when it does not at first appear obvious. If we notice clients behaving in a way that in our view is counterproductive or unhealthy, our first task is not to challenge the client but to work out how this particular behaviour is adaptive in terms of what that client believes.

Let's use an example. Imagine you've just returned from a rather over-exuberant but highly enjoyable holiday, paid for in part with a credit card, now full to capacity. You push it out of your mind and then suddenly four weeks later the postman brings you the dreaded credit card bill. How many of us are likely to be enthusiastically motivated to tear open the statement, reach for our cheque book at the same time and gleefully pay it all off there and then? Many of us will want immediately to put it away and hide it out of sight. What motivates such behaviour, and how might this be adaptive? By immediately removing oneself from the toxic statement and all that it brings (regret, self-criticism and self-reproach), we are (temporarily) trying to feel better, or at the very least we are trying to remove ourselves from the emotions that accompany regret, self-criticism and self-reproach – to return to a mood state pre-credit card bill arrival. Two possible explanations for this behaviour are available to us. Are we just simply not motivated to face up to our responsibilities? Perhaps an alternative explanation is that we temporarily dispose of the credit card statement because we are in fact highly motivated to avoid the pain of opening the letter. We are actively trying to avoid the self-criticism that follows on from recognizing how careless we have been with our finances on holiday! The truth is, it may actually work in the short term and allow us to temporarily feel better. Therefore this is highly motivated behaviour, which may work to some extent in the short term.

We often consider this temporary avoidance of pain as normal, but don't consider that our clients are doing exactly the same thing; however, the pain our clients are avoiding is often much more intense and includes an attempt to avoid a sense of fear, panic and despair. Therefore, in order to truly understand and then help them, the first thing we need to do is explore in some detail the type of avoidance used by our clients. Once we've explored how a client has managed so far to deal with their fears and worries, we need to feed this back as understandable and show a real appreciation of the effort and hard work the client has put into trying to address their problems so far. The fact is many clients view their avoidance as nonsensical and stupid and if you can convey the logic behind current behaviours you help foster the therapeutic alliance and encourage the client to join you in helping to change.

We can clearly see that in all the examples in Table 3.1, each person engages in the avoidant behaviour in order to try to help themselves. The amazing thing is that these behaviours do indeed work. They do what they claim to do – they help the client stop feeling so bad, reduce distress and therefore become quite addictive and repetitive. Once used, even if they bring minimal relief, the avoidant behaviour is reinforced. Negative reinforcement refers to the increased use or frequency of a behaviour if it is reliably followed by the removal of an aversive or unwanted stimulus or experience (Skinner, 1938). Negative reinforcement represents very powerful learning and is perhaps linked to an evolutionary survival propensity that promotes the easy recall of those things that we think protect or save us from fear, panic and perhaps ultimately death.

The problem is that learning to jump out of the way of an oncoming speeding car is an adaptive and useful avoidance strategy, while not going out of the house for fear of something bad happening, and all the disability this brings, is ultimately harmful in the long term. When we avoid situations where the fear is real but the danger is not, we can suffer unnecessary and unconsidered long-term consequences.

Avoidance may work in the short term, but it brings a multitude of problems in the long term. We've seen it restricts life and limits client choices but you can also see from Table 3.1 that it promotes another maintaining factor, which is the increased

Table 3.1 Types of avoidance

Condition	Behaviour	Perceived function	Consequences
Over-exuberant holiday – spending more than you have	Don't open credit card statement on return	Avoid or postpone the pain of realizing I was foolish for spending so much. Avoiding the pain of budgeting my way back to financial equilibrium	Feel better in the short term, as it is pushed out of my immediate awareness but as each day passes the amount of interest increases and the potential future pain mounts
Agoraphobia with panic	Not going out when panicking	Preserve life – reduce the chances of provoking a perceived catastrophic physical or mental breakdown (heart attack/go crazy)	By avoiding going out, feel better instantly but become trapped and unable to leave home, which allows even more time to check for signs of physical or mental danger
Depression	Stay in bed until 3.00 pm	Avoid messing life up even more or from being rejected for being useless. Prevent others from seeing how pathetic I am and thereby trying to feel better. Trying to feel less tired	Temporary relief that the pressure of having to keep going is removed. However, this leads to pondering or ruminating on how bad things are and how useless and pathetic I feel. The less I do, the less I feel like doing and the more tired I get

scanning (internally and externally) for signs of further danger or trouble. This increased scanning for danger both inside our bodies and in our environment leads to our client's focus of attention remaining fixated on further danger and trouble, which can maintain worry or fear and can reduce activity in other areas of the client's life. This fixation may also lead to further misinterpretation of benign changes or events as confirming the client's negative beliefs about self, others and the world in general. Negative changes in mood can act like a negative filter on a camera and tinge new benign or coincidental events as also dangerous or may confirm the client's current negative beliefs about themselves, others and their future.

To recap, before the practitioner and client identify and label client behaviour as pathological and harmful, they must first look at it in terms of its short-term benefit. Only when current behaviour is explored for its adaptive function should you and the client then explore what the longer-term effects have been of using avoidance. Has it helped or has it worked by removing distress permanently in the longer term?

The practitioner and client can begin this process by analysing the function of current behaviour and comparing short-term and long-term benefits (see Table 3.2).

Once the practitioner and client have analysed the effect of the current behaviour and the client agrees that the current behaviour is not so functional in the longer term, they can set about looking at what they need to consider doing about it. Before this there is just one more important task. In order to cement the client's belief that change is necessary we need to tap into what is important or valuable to the client.

Values are the things the client views as important. They are more than goals or targets; they are who we would like to be, despite where we are in the world or our

Table 3.2 Behavioural consequences analysis

Behaviour	Purpose	Does it work in the short term?	Does it work in the long term?
Not going out or returning home quickly when anxious	Preserves life – reduce chances of provoking a perceived catastrophic physical or mental breakdown (heart attack/go crazy)	Yes, feel better, recover quickly	No, it leaves me trapped and despairing and so guilty that I can't go out with the kids
Stay in bed until 3.00 pm every day	Avoid messing life up even more or from being rejected for being useless. Prevent others from seeing how pathetic I am and thereby trying to feel better. Trying to feel less tired	Well, I don't have to face things and if I don't do anything well then, yes, I can't mess up any more and it is a relief. Now I don't have to go to work and I feel that relief at 9.00 am each morning	By 9.10 am I feel even worse and then guilty and think how I'm going to lose my job and all that will bring and I guess I then am sure I've messed up even more. I try to sleep to take away the pain and when I do get up I'm exhausted

current experiences. An important value may concern how the client wants to be as a son, a father, a brother, an uncle, and so on. It defines the way we want to be.

An example of an important value might be to be a good father. This is not a goal; it cannot be ticked off in the future making you forever a 'good father'. It is a journey: a lifelong (and beyond life) aspiration, which represents how you want to be with your children. Values bring with them goals that service the value, for example, making sure your diary is cleared every Tuesday evening to enable you to share with your son his mini-league football coaching or stopping smoking because you want to be around longer to see your daughter grow up. The servicing of values is not straightforward. In the example in Table 3.3 we look at things that will get in the way: work, time, emotional well-being, tiredness and even illness. If a client can't leave the house due to a fear of panic and that client values being a good father to his children, how may his agoraphobia hamper or get in the way of this important value?

In Table 3.3 we can see that the client's agoraphobia effectively prevents him from attending to the things he views as important and valuable: in this case, being a good dad. Without dealing with what blocks or gets in the way of this important value, the client is at risk of remaining distressed and anxious and eventually becoming depressed.

There are a number of ways of establishing a client's values. You can simply ask for three or four things in the client's life that they value or consider very important. You can ask what they would like their life to stand for. An alternative

Table 3.3 Valued goal analysis

Value	Goal servicing value	Goal blocking factors	What will we do about it?
Being a good dad	Take son to mini-league football every Tuesday evening	1. Anxiety, tension and palpitations when away from home	a. Learn about what these sensations mean
		2. Believing I will die or stop breathing	b. Test this out and see what really happens
		3. Quickly returning to the house when I start to feel (1)	c. To really test (b) I need to stay away from the house longer and travel further without returning home at the first sign of (1)
		4. Fear	d. Test whether fear always equals danger

solution is to simply apply the following questions: How do your current beliefs and behaviours affect or interfere with your life? What limitations and restrictions do your current beliefs and behaviours place on your life? The client can then complete the following statements:

My current beliefs and behaviours affect or interfere with my life in the following ways . . .

Follow this up with this statement:

If I didn't carry my beliefs so strongly or behave the way I do currently, I would be able to attend to the following important areas of my life . . .

Identifying important and valued areas of a client's life is perhaps the first step towards setting appropriate goals (Veale and Willson, 2007; Veale, 2008) and ensures all treatment is truly client-centred and this guards against the practitioner setting goals that are not agreed. One method includes asking the client if all who knew them were to erect a monument to their life, what they would most like to see on that monument. This requires the client to look beyond the current limitations of their life and envisage what life could or should be. If a client is frightened of panicking, they may believe panic might indicate they will suffer some catastrophic physical or mental breakdown in the future when away from the safety of home or family.

By concentrating on what is important to the client we can more clearly highlight the devastating impact of holding on to a belief that panic equals impending doom and avoidance equals safety. We are expanding the client's understanding of the disadvantages of maintaining their current beliefs and behaviours. This, in turn, introduces and reinforces the need to ensure these beliefs are actually accurate and whether, therefore, their protective avoidant behaviours are actually helpful, or if they in fact maintain the problem.

In addition to the 'monument' question or as an alternative to it the practitioner can also consider formally administering an adapted form of Kelly Wilson's Valued Living Questionnaire (Wilson et al., 2010) (see Figure 3.1).

Importance:		Area	Consistency over the past week:	
Not at all	Extremely		Not at all	Extremely
1 2 3 4 5 6 7 8 9 10		1. Family, other than marriage or parenting	1 2 3 4 5 6 7 8 9 10	
1 2 3 4 5 6 7 8 9 10		2. Intimate relations	1 2 3 4 5 6 7 8 9 10	
1 2 3 4 5 6 7 8 9 10		3. Care giving (parenting and other forms of caring)	1 2 3 4 5 6 7 8 9 10	
1 2 3 4 5 6 7 8 9 10		4. Friends/social life	1 2 3 4 5 6 7 8 9 10	
1 2 3 4 5 6 7 8 9 10		5. Work	1 2 3 4 5 6 7 8 9 10	
1 2 3 4 5 6 7 8 9 10		6. Education/training	1 2 3 4 5 6 7 8 9 10	
1 2 3 4 5 6 7 8 9 10		7. Recreation/fun/sport/music, etc.	1 2 3 4 5 6 7 8 9 10	
1 2 3 4 5 6 7 8 9 10		8. Spirituality/faith	1 2 3 4 5 6 7 8 9 10	
1 2 3 4 5 6 7 8 9 10		9. Citizenship/community life	1 2 3 4 5 6 7 8 9 10	
1 2 3 4 5 6 7 8 9 10		10. Physical self-care (diet, exercise, sleep)	1 2 3 4 5 6 7 8 9 10	
1 2 3 4 5 6 7 8 9 10		11. Mental health/mental wellbeing	1 2 3 4 5 6 7 8 9 10	

Figure 3.1 Assessing important areas of the client's life

This identifies 11 valued life areas and the client is first asked to indicate in the left column (Importance) how important that life area is to them (if at all). Second, you ask the client to rate in the right-hand column (Consistency) how much time, effort and perseverance they have attended to this particular valued living area. This represents a very interesting definition of what mental illness is. Having unrealistic and even irrational thoughts are not in themselves indicative of mental illness. This has already been recognized by a number of authors who reviewed the prominence (and normality) of apparently irrational intrusive thoughts among the non-clinically ill population (Rachman, 2003). Having bizarre and weird thoughts is not therefore pathological; it is how rigidly we buy into them and the impact they have on our lives that defines mental illness. In other words, the importance of a mistaken or irrational belief is defined by how much it diverts us from what we really value and how much it distracts us from attending to important areas of our life.

It is our behavioural responses to those beliefs that are pathological. For example, imagine someone believes every flight they take is doomed to crash or believes that when their trousers are washed the waistband shrinks, thus accounting for why their clothes are getting gradually tighter. These are clearly irrational beliefs. Yet, they are not rigidly held, and therefore, so far, have not prevented the person catching a flight or changing the brand of washing powder every time their clothes don't fit as they once did. These beliefs, although clearly irrational, have not so far interfered with the individual attending to those things that are important in his life.

To recap, once the practitioner and client have identified why and how a client's current beliefs and behaviours are established and maintained, attention turns to the impact of the client's current beliefs and behaviours on their identified important values.

Questions to ask the client about current illness and its impact on valuable areas of their life

1   *How do your current difficulties impact on your identified values?*
2   *Does your current behaviour help or get in the way of you pursuing your values?*
3   *What might you be willing to try (with the full support of your practitioner) in order to test these beliefs, change your behaviour and eventually overcome these barriers to a meaningful and productive life?*
4   *Are you willing to join with your practitioner and to put up with an increase in distress and anxiety or depression, if it means following your identified values?*
5   *Are you prepared to test out your negative automatic thoughts even if it means struggling with feeling fearful, uncertain and distressed, if it is in the service of those things that are important or valuable to you?*

While discussing the above questions, it is important to compassionately convey to your client the fact that although many people (ill and not ill) want to change, they are also understandably apprehensive or frightened of the prospect of change. Change entails moving into a territory the client may be unfamiliar with and, although an illness can be limiting, it is an experience the client is at least familiar with. Breaking out of thinking and behaving in a particular way that has at least worked in the short term can understandably seem risky to those trapped in avoidance.

Client apprehension should be treated with empathy, with the practitioner conveying that the client's concerns are fully understandable, and in fact normal.

It is important that the practitioner reinforces to the client that all change brings some degree of distress, discomfort and uncertainty. You can't get a job without the hassle of an interview and the fear of rejection; you can't learn to ride a bike without the fear of falling off; you can't give up chocolate or alcohol without a period of craving for the taste of chocolate or alcohol; you can't give birth to a child without the pain or discomfort of childbirth; and you can't present a piece of work without the fear of being criticized and it being failed. The aim is not to trivialize the client's concerns or invalidate their distress, but to let the client appreciate that the practitioner understands all change is difficult. The client staying the same is obviously not comfortable but may be perceived as less frightening than risking change and the unknown.

To recap, once you have established what the client's current beliefs and behaviours are that maintain the client's problems, you then need to fully acknowledge and normalize their use of short-term, but ultimately unhealthy, strategies. The practitioner and client then turn their attention to the client's important values, which may have been sacrificed or put on hold due to their reliance on avoidance strategies. Finally, you must acknowledge that change is universally difficult and therefore any journey from illness to wellness will necessarily be difficult and uncomfortable. It is at that this point that the practitioner can discuss with the client whether they imagine that the discomfort of change will be anywhere near as terrifying or damaging as the pain inflicted by their illness.

Goal setting

Once there is recognition that current patterns of behaviour are not so helpful and realization that the client may have sacrificed or put on hold valuable areas of their life, the next question for the client and practitioner to address is what it may be possible to change. If the client agrees and is willing to change, then the initial area of change needs to be related to an identified valued life area that is currently not being attended to. For example, imagine a female client who suffers panic symptoms and has grown to believe they are a sign of impending catastrophic physical illness (collapse and heart attack). After her assessment she recognizes her way of dealing with this belief (not going out, depending on family and friends for reassurance and tending to her children) has helped in the short term only. She also recognizes through looking in detail at her values that she has sacrificed being the mother she wants to be.

This means that due to her beliefs about having a heart attack, she misses out on taking her young children to school, feeding the ducks in the local pond and taking her children cycling to the local play park. In addition, you have established that by doing little and not going out, she never really tests her belief. By spending a lot of time indoors doing very little, for fear of provoking another panic attack, she now has an enormous amount of time to excessively scan and check her body and ponder endlessly on what might be physically wrong with her. This constant body scanning and endless worry mean that even routine changes in her body scare her even further and reinforce her belief that something is wrong.

You should hopefully see that this client is trying her best to cope with a catastrophic misinterpretation of what anxiety symptoms actually mean. More importantly, imagine how important it is to help bring her attention to the fact that the things she has put in place to protect her actually maintain her focus on possible danger from physical symptoms of anxiety. Once all this is understood by the client and the practitioner, what we need to ask is, how we could both test whether what she tells herself is actually true. This means setting a goal.

Practical goal setting

By approaching practical difficulties one step at a time, it is possible for the client and practitioner to begin to deal with problem areas and instil hope. We need to remind ourselves and our clients that everything cannot be dealt with at once and it may be necessary to prioritize and focus on changing just one area to begin with. This means that other problems may need to be put to one side initially. When deciding on what needs attention the golden rule is to choose something that is related to a client value and will bring initial success to instil hope and generate an increase in confidence that things can change for the better.

Prioritizing what targets to address is normally a collaborative process, but the clinician may need to take the lead if there is a particular behaviour which may lead to harm or a crisis in the near future, if it is not addressed (e.g. someone using high daily doses of painkillers to avoid distress). When there is a potential risk, the clinician will need to prioritize this and give a full and detailed rationale about why it is important to deal with this particular problem first. Risk behaviour should also be discussed in supervision at the earliest opportunity.

Questions to ask the client to help prioritize what problems to work on

Do we need to address any of these problems first to avoid a potential crisis in the near future?

Which problem is related to a particularly important value area of your life?

What particular problem area, if tackled, would make the most immediate improvement in your life and/or those important you?

Are there other small steps you need to take or is there another problem you need to deal with first before you can achieve your desired goal?

What precisely would we be testing if we completed this goal?

What precise belief are we testing by setting this goal?

What would we need to precisely change to test this belief once and for all?

How would we know if our goal was achieved?

If we use the example above, the client may answer these questions in the following way.

Client: *If I exert myself by leaving the house alone to pick up the children from their nearby school, I'll have a panic attack which will provoke a heart attack and I'll collapse and could die (belief currently 80 per cent). It is an important goal and is related to my values related to care giving.*

Practitioner: *Do we need to address any of these problems first to avoid a potential crisis in the near future?*

Client: *Well, I've noticed the less I do with the children, like pick them up from school or take them to the park, the more ill I feel and worry I'll never be able to take care of my children and be a real mother. I get down and cry often now (begins to get tearful in session).*

[From the client's response and emotional reaction it appears that the longer the client is unable to get out with the children, the more she worries that she'll never beat this and this seems to be making her sad and perhaps hopeless as well as anxious.]

Practitioner: *Which problem is related to a particularly important valued area of your life?*

Client: *Getting out and having fun with the kids is the most important thing to me. This is why I had children, to really be there for them but instead now I'm always making silly excuses for why I can't go to the park, feed the ducks or go cycling. I feel I'm really letting them down and would love to be the mother they want.*

[It is clear this is the most important area of the client's life and is affected by her mistaken beliefs about anxiety symptoms and her protective behaviours employed to keep her safe. This is therefore a good area for goal setting.]

Practitioner: *What particular problem area, if tackled, would make the most immediate improvement in your life and/or those important you?*

Client: *The kids always ask me why I can't leave them off to school and collect them from school any more. Their school is just a few blocks away, just a five to seven minute walk from home. They remind me everyone else's mum does it and I feel it is important to them and me. In addition, I have very dear friends who have always been important to me and since this panic started I feel like I use them to take the kids and this is not the kind of friend I'd like to be.*

[This answer clearly indicates the school drop off and pick up is an important value-related goal but it also may be related to another value. Friends are important and the client clearly believes that she is not being the friend she wants to be, by now having to rely on them primarily to attend to her children when they are out of the house.]

Practitioner: *Are there other small steps you need to take or is there another problem you need to deal with first before you can achieve your desired goal?*

Client: *I haven't done the school run for four months now, therefore I'm unsure if I could just do it in the middle of school drop off rush hour. I think I would have to make the journey first with my kids and my close friend just to familiarize myself with the route. I also have to get out of the habit of going back to bed for the rest of the day once the kids go to school. I'd probably need to prepare and have clothes ready to just slip on because again I have lost the habit of changing into outdoor clothes in the morning, as I don't go out.*

We can see that even a seemingly simple first target requires careful preparation and planning. Preparing to go out by acclimatizing herself to the route again after four months seems sensible, as is doing it accompanied by a friend at first, at a quieter time. However, ultimately the target has to be completing the drop off and pick up with only her children as company for half the journey. In addition, we now recognize the client has even got out of the habit of getting dressed for the outdoors immediately on getting up. This is important and can be initiated immediately, as homework. However, it is very important to remember that even doing something as straightforward as getting dressed in outdoor clothes again may provoke anxiety at the anticipation of going out in the future.

This may, in turn, provoke thoughts and even images of future collapse and death on the school run. This belief will feed the client's anxiety symptoms and a panic attack is possible. It is important to have this conversation beforehand, as it prepares the client and you can use it as a good example of how even the thought of doing something fearful can provoke a reaction. Remind the client again that it is the testing of these thoughts that is important and therefore every increase in anxiety affords us the chance to test the belief behind it. Willingness to experience the belief and its consequences is all part of treatment. You may remind her about the difference between fearful thoughts and real danger once but be very wary of reassurance once the testing of beliefs begins.

Think about these questions:

What precisely would we be testing if we completed this goal? What precise belief are we testing by setting this goal?
What would we need to precisely change to test this belief once and for all?
How would we know if our goal was achieved?

These questions can be incorporated into a method that helps practitioners and clients set goals in a very systematic way.

A SMART way to think of goals

The behaviour associated with both depression and anxiety, such as social withdrawal or avoidance, can lead to a gross reduction in the things a client does or believes they can do. Previous important areas of the client's life may be abandoned and any attempt at trying to regain those areas can appear unachievable when the client is lacking motivation or is paralysed by fear. The client may even begin to believe that they can no longer think about achieving anything again, as they put all their energy into trying to contain their anxiety or depression.

If the client agrees that yielding to their anxiety or depression has not helped, then the practitioner and client need to agree new goals that are related to those things the client may have lost sight of due to their illness. Goal setting is the first step in conquering the inertia of depression or the avoidance of anxiety; goal setting is the first step in the client reclaiming their life.

Setting goals is therefore one of the most important processes in treatment. Goals provide a map for treatment that give the practitioner and client an agreed direction in which to head and also should establish clearly when treatment has reached its destination. If goals map out the journey of treatment, then, like all successful journeys, it must be easily broken down into very succinct stages (going initially from A to B then C, etc.). A long journey taken all at once can often seem overwhelming. In addition, what the client gains from the first part of the journey may be necessary or essential for the client to successfully complete the later stages.

For example, a currently depressed client may express a desire to return to work. If work was an important valued behaviour in the client's life and brought a number of rewards, then this would seem a very important area of the client's life to reclaim. However, if that client isn't managing to get up from bed until 3.00 pm each day and then sits in their night clothes, trying to catch something on television which may lift their low mood, then work may appear a long way off. The 'journey' in this case may appear overwhelmingly long, unless the practitioner and client start to plot smaller journeys in the service of ultimately achieving a return to work. These smaller steps not only make attaining the main goal more likely, but also will introduce skills that will be vital to the client as they approach returning to work again. Those smaller steps may include the following:

1   Re-establishing a morning routine, which will include

- setting an alarm clock
- responding to the alarm clock
- getting showered and dressed

2   Starting to plan a daily routine – organizing what needs done

- in the morning
- in the afternoon
- in the evening

In the above example, the client and practitioner can systematically begin to set goals for each area, with the aim of both moving the client towards their valued goal and also beginning to practise essential skills that will be required if the ultimate goal is to be achieved (e.g. developing routine, establishing plans for the short and longer term and problem solving).

The next step is making sure that each goal is a SMART goal (see Table 3.4 and Appendix 2). SMART is an acronym for a process which ensures that goals set by the client and practitioner meet a standard that makes them more likely to be successful. Vague and woolly goals lead to vague and woolly outcomes (or no outcome at all, just endless talking treatment).

Table 3.4 SMART goal setting form (example)

Specific	Set goals that are as specific as possible. This means setting dates, times, identifying resources needed, etc.	*Starting on Monday, I will set the alarm clock for 9.00 am and get up as soon as it rings, have a shower within 10 minutes of getting up and get dressed in fresh clothes*
Measurable	The goal should be capable of being measured to allow you to know when you have met it	*I will record each morning what time I get up. I will record what time I get into the shower and will record when I get dressed. I'll also measure my mood as I do this each morning*
Achievable	The goals set should be achievable, therefore realistic, given the time available, not an exercise that risks setting you up to fail	*By next Monday, I should be getting up and dressed five times during Monday to Friday*
Relevant	Is this important to you, does it concern an activity you value, or will it help you achieve something you value?	*Yes, if I'm ever going to return to work then I need to start with restoring my morning routine*
Time limited	Set a time by which you hope the goal will be achieved. If it's longer than a week, then go back to the Achievable section	*Next Monday up at 9.00 am throughout the working week*

SMART means:

S = Specific –   The client and practitioner try to set goals that are as specific as possible.
This means setting dates, times, identifying resources needed etc.

M = Measurable –   Goals should be capable of being measured to allow the client to know when they have met them.

A = Achievable –   Goals should be realistic and challenging, but not impossible.
Equally, the goals the client set should be achievable, not an exercise that risks setting the client up to fail.

R = Relevant –   Goals should be directly relevant to the client's life and ideally be tied to an important area of their life (a valued area),

T = Time limited –   The practitioner and client agree on a time scale in which to achieve the goal.

Goals should be viewed initially as experiments. The practitioner and client need to be aware that initial early goals may have to be revised or indeed dropped and new ones developed, as the client and practitioner learn more about what is achievable and which goals are worth pursuing.

Once treatment goals are specified, the practitioner and client can decide how many problems can be tackled in the negotiated time available. As a guide, if you are seeing the client for between four and eight sessions, one or two goals would be a realistic outcome. If the person has multiple problem areas, be realistic about what can be achieved and agree how many of the problems can be tackled in the time available. One suggestion may be first to take a relatively new or easier problem, then agree on a medium-sized difficulty and, finally, the most prominent difficulty. This will, of course, require the practitioner and client to assign a level of difficulty to each individual problem area. Prioritization can be achieved in other ways. If the client is willing, the first target can be based on the client's accounts of the most distressing problem. Be careful, however, as the client may overestimate their own resilience and therefore may set themselves unrealistically high expectations, which may ultimately end in failure and therefore result in a loss of confidence by the client that change is possible. Whatever target is chosen, remember goals must be linked to client values.

The time taken in setting concrete goals is time very well spent. It is more than compensated for by:

• the resultant increase in client involvement;
• the decrease in time and effort wasted on peripheral topics;
• providing a focus for treatment and its conclusion.

Summary

- A problem list needs to be developed jointly by the practitioner and the client, working collaboratively.
- It is important for the practitioner and the client to understand the motivation behind current behaviour – what keeps the problem going?
- Linking goals to the client's values makes sure goals are relevant, motivates the client and helps collaboration.
- Developing SMART goals helps make the journey to recovery an achievable one, step by step.

Recommended reading

Antony, M.M. and Barlow, D.H. (2010) *Handbook of Assessment and Treatment Planning for Psychological Disorders*, 2nd edn. New York: Guilford Press.

Beck, A.T., Rush, A.J., Shaw, B.F. and Emery, G. (1979) *Cognitive Therapy of Depression*. New York: Guilford Press.

Beck, J.S. (1995) *Cognitive Therapy: Basics and Beyond*. New York: Guilford Press.

Hawton, K., Salkovskis, P.M., Kirk, J. and Clark D.M. (1989) *Cognitive Behaviour Therapy for Psychiatric Problems: A Practical Guide*. Oxford: Oxford University Press.

Martin, D. and Hamilton, S. (2006) How to use non-verbal signs in assessments of suicide risk. *Nursing Times*, 102(2): 36–8.

Richards, D. and Whyte, M. (2009) *Reach Out: National Programme Educator Materials to Support the Delivery of Training for Psychological Wellbeing Practitioners Delivering Low Intensity Interventions*, 2nd edn. Rethink Mental Illness. Available at: www.cedar.exeter.ac.uk/iapt/iaptworkbooks and resources (accessed 23 May 2014).

Simmons, J. and Griffiths (2009) *CBT for Beginners*. London: Sage.

Veale, D. and Willson, R. (2007) *Manage Your Mood: Using Behavioural Activation Techniques to Overcome Depression*. London: Robinson Press.

Westbrook, D., Kennerley, H. and Kirk, J. (2011) *An Introduction to Cognitive Behaviour Therapy: Skills and Applications*, 2nd edn. London: Sage.

4 Depression

Introduction

What is depression? The word depression is a common and often misused everyday word. Everyone feels fed up, sad or 'in a mood' at times. Sometimes people say 'I'm depressed' when they really mean 'I'm fed up' because they have failed an exam or had a row with a partner. These are the normal trials and tribulations of everyday life, and most of the time we recover very quickly. This chapter and the next aim to concentrate on specific cognitive behavioural approaches to depression and anxiety that should be delivered in conjunction with appropriate self-help material.

Defining clinical depression

Clients with clinical depression present with low mood or loss of interest or pleasure and other symptoms nearly every day for at least two weeks, and the symptoms are severe enough to have a negative impact upon everyday functioning. Clinical depression is diagnosed if at least two out of three key symptoms below have been experienced for most of the day, nearly every day, for at least two weeks. These key symptoms are:

- low mood
- fatigue or lack of energy
- lack of interest or enjoyment in life

Other symptoms may include:

- reduced self-esteem and confidence
- ideas of guilt and worthlessness
- pessimistic thoughts including ideas of self-harm or suicide
- disturbed sleep
- appetite changes
- agitation or restlessness
- reduced concentration/slower thinking processes

(American Psychiatric Association, 2013)

Clinical depression can be classed as mild, moderate or severe, depending on the number and intensity of symptoms such as sleep disturbance, appetite and weight change, agitation, poor concentration, irritability and suicidal thoughts.

Between 8 and 12 per cent of the UK population experience depression in any year. Across the globe almost 6 per cent of men and nearly 10 per cent of women will experience a depressive episode in a 12-month period, a total of about 121 million people (Singleton et al., 2001; WHO, 2001; NICE, 2003).

There is a growing recognition that effectively treating depression when it first presents is essential as depression tends to recur. Half of those who have one episode of depression will have another, while those who have a second episode have a further relapse risk of 70 per cent. A client who experiences a third episode has an increased relapse risk of 90 per cent (NICE, 2003). Cognitive behavioural techniques offer the client the opportunity to learn very practical self-help techniques that should not only assist with the current episode of depression but, if utilized early enough, help with future episodes of low mood.

A cognitive behavioural approach

Cognitive behavioural techniques for depression focus attention on the relationship between the following:

- life events/situations (what happens to us);
- cognitions/thoughts (what we think, how we appraise or interpret events and situations that happen to us);
- behaviour (how we actually react or what we do when we interpret a situation in a particular way);
- physiology/body (how our body reacts when we interpret a situation in a particular way);
- affect/mood (how we feel, the emotional consequences related to how we interpret a situation in a particular way).

As you will see, depression is a multifaceted illness involving problems with both behaviour (withdrawal, avoidance, loss of interpersonal contact, etc.) and cognition (worry, rumination, negative automatic thoughts, etc.). Rumination is where a client broods or has repetitive thoughts about the past. A reduction in behavioural activity and negative cognitions interact with and enhance negative affect which in turn interacts with and can contribute to physical symptoms. Cognitive behavioural interventions traditionally begin by addressing depressive behavioural symptoms as unhelpful patterns of behaviour that often leave the client stuck and unable to problem solve. Inertia and withdrawal also have a knock-on effect in terms of important areas of a client's life. Interpersonal relationships suffer, their job/career suffers, rumination increases and negative automatic thoughts cannot be tested (and therefore tend to grow in credibility). In addition, if someone has been depressed for more than a few weeks their concentration and fatigue can severely hinder cognitive capacity. The ability of the client to combat a relentless stream of self-derogatory thoughts may be limited at the beginning of treatment. Therefore the application of the more straightforward, easy-to-learn

Table 4.1   Model to guide the treatment of depression (Overholser, 2003)

Stage 1 Engagement	Stage 2 Behavioural Strategies	Stage 3 Cognitive Strategies	Stage 4 Maintaining Wellness
Develop therapeutic alliance	Target reduced activity	Target rumination	Relapse prevention
Complete assessment	Target loss of interpersonal contact	Target specific negative automatic thoughts	Maintain wellness and recovery
Ascertain maintaining factors	Target excessive non-rewarding activity	Target internal mental problem solving	
Consider solutions (goals)	Target problem spotting rather than active physical problem solving	Target ideas about self, others and the world in general	

and easier-to-retain behavioural monitoring and change techniques seems appropriate in the first instance.

Initiating behavioural change can be an effective way of engaging the client again in rewarding, mood-lifting activities and also a very useful way to begin challenging negative automatic thoughts. For example, when a client eventually masters a task they once thought impossible this can bring them a sense of reward and achievement. It also allows the practitioner to question the client's earlier automatic thoughts about not believing the activity would work out. Beginning an episode of treatment with behavioural methods seems logical. The focus on negative automatic thoughts can then be addressed when unhelpful beliefs begin to interfere with the progress of behavioural activation.

The treatment for depression therefore could be viewed as consisting of four distinct phases: engaging the client in treatment which permits an accurate assessment to be obtained; the use of behavioural activation in order to address the client's lack of activity; the use of cognitive techniques to combat rumination and negative automatic thoughts and, finally, addressing the important issue of maintaining wellness and recovery (see Table 4.1). We will review those techniques and explain how to apply them in Chapter 7.

To help with our understanding of the connections between life events, thoughts, behaviour, body and mood, we will look at a typical case example of a woman suffering low mood:

Case example

Jill is a 35-year-old engineer for a construction firm. She is married with two children, aged 6 and 9. Jill moves from her home town to take up a promotion in the city. She is now responsible for other staff and initially looks forward to the challenge. She finds a new house and a new school for her children. At first, things seem good for Jill. She has more money and a more challenging job. However, Jill's new manager tells all the staff that productivity is everything and constantly reminds them that their jobs are on the line if production deadlines are not met. This leads to endless rumours in the plant that jobs will go. Jill's 6-year-old daughter is homesick and misses her friends and finds the new school daunting. Mornings are hectic enough but now there is a crisis every morning persuading her daughter to get to school. Jill's husband is stressed by this and rows develop about how best to deal with it.

Jill's husband is also finding the move difficult. He gave up long-term friendships and work to move away with his wife because her career prospects are better and he wanted to spend more time with his children. Jill, fearful of being laid off, feels compelled to spend longer hours in the office. She is fearful of delegating in case things go wrong as she would be held responsible. Her workload therefore increases. Her long hours at the office leave her husband even more frustrated, isolated and alone in dealing with the house and children.

Jill starts to go into work earlier and leave later. Because her husband is having his own problems coping with the move she finds staying in the office a relief from the growing disharmony at home. Her fears about her job and the hassles at home mean that she starts to find sleep difficult. However, she discovers that a few drinks at night quell her anxiety and get her to sleep. However, the mornings become unbearable. She awakens tired and irritable and leaves for work quickly before the morning rush to get both children ready and off for school. Rows at home are now a constant feature of her life.

Jill gets irritated by her husband's refusal to understand that her job could be on the line. Because she tends not to delegate, her workload increases and some things get left undone. Her filing is months behind and she constantly worries this is going to be discovered. She tries to work even harder and starts going into work at weekends. She gradually gets more and more tired. Jill starts the day now dreading work but also hates coming home. She is constantly tired, irritated and anxious. Her drinking increases and Jill and her husband barely communicate. Her daughter is more and more homesick. Jill's tendency to try to do everything at work by herself has left major pieces of work half-finished. Her working day is chaotic and she spends more and more time looking for things in the mess that is now her office.

Eventually one morning Jill turns the alarm clock off and sits by the side of the bed and ponders all that has gone wrong and all that could go wrong in the future. She becomes first panicky and then tearful. For the first time in her career she rings in sick. She then spends the rest of the day in bed cursing herself for not being the wife, mother and employee she wanted to be. Although off work she lies in bed searching constantly for a solution for work issues. But her fears escalate and her thoughts now turn to what her boss will make of her ringing in sick. One day of lying in bed until midday and not getting dressed leads to another and another and another. At home she engages in nothing except constant thinking, brooding and worrying. She finds drinking even more useful. It quells her worry and helps her sleep for longer periods of the day. It blocks out her worry and helps her shut off from her husband's increasing anger and distress.

Assessment

In order to understand and ultimately help Jill understand what is happening to her we need to use the cross-sectional cognitive behavioural model to highlight the consequences of her current thinking and behaviour.

Ultimately the aim of any assessment is to establish:

- Why Jill? (What makes Jill vulnerable to low mood?)
- Why now? (What has triggered the current drop in mood? What has changed?)
- What keeps it going? (What maintains the current problem or problems? What prevents Jill from effectively dealing with this situation in a more helpful way?)

In order to obtain answers to all of these questions a detailed assessment needs to be completed. (Please refer to Chapters 2 and 3.)

Generating a problem list

As explained in Chapter 2 on assessment, the first step is to list the client's main problems. You might start by asking them: 'What kind of difficulties brought you to the GP?', 'What is it that you have difficulty with at the minute?' or 'What is it that perhaps you once were able to do and now struggle with?'

Defining problems in behavioural terms helps the practitioner develop a concrete picture of what is actually happening in someone's life. It helps establish what the client is doing too much of at the minute (isolating themselves, sleeping, avoiding work) and too little of (maintaining a routine, attending to relationships, engaging in previously valued activities). The practitioner can then explore the client's reasons for current behaviour and elicit the thinking that drives the current behaviour, for example, by asking 'If you did attempt to socialize again, what would be so bad about that?' or 'What would be the worst thing that you imagine would happen?'

Subjective descriptions of how someone feels are less helpful at explaining what is going on in the client's world, as feelings can mean different things to different people. What does a statement such as 'I feel utterly rotten all the time' actually mean? What does it actually tell you about what is going on in the individual's life? If a client starts with a series of emotional statements, it is helpful to obtain an example of specific times or situations in which the emotion occurred. It is also important to clarify what precisely the client means by 'utterly rotten'.

- What does this look like when it happens?
- Where does it feel like it is in your body?
- Describe a recent concrete example of when you felt 'utterly rotten'. Where were you? Who was there? What was happening? How did you read that situation?

All of these questions help the practitioner discover what 'utterly rotten' actually means to the client.

From what you know, how might Jill's problem list look if defined in behavioural terms? What is Jill doing or not doing at the minute? If she describes a series of emotions then we need to ask for specific examples of when they occur or when they are most prominent. Recent examples are more useful and more accessible so focus on these at the beginning.

Case example continued

Some typical difficulties which Jill may describe include:

- I stay in bed until the kids leave for school.
- I go back to bed when they arrive home.
- I drink alcohol to stop me worrying at night.
- I can't deal with the children or my husband's nagging so I stay away from them.
- In the morning I worry about the future and about losing my job, losing my house, losing my family and pull the duvet over my head to try to get back to sleep.
- I feel tired all the time.
- I put off everything such as getting dressed, washing, getting up and going out.

We can see from the list that Jill's problems include both problems with thinking and very clear difficulties with behaviour.

Evaluating current behaviour and its overall impact on mood

Once the practitioner has elicited current specific behaviour, the practitioner and client can then explore the reason for responding in this way. Once the reasoning behind current behaviour is analysed, it may actually begin to become apparent that Jill was working extremely hard to deal with her many problems. If she perceives her job is on the line she may see some sense in working harder and for longer hours. If home life distracts her from her work, she could view avoiding this as a useful strategy in order to keep her focused on work, avoid being laid off and allowing her to continue paying the mortgage and other bills. If sleep is disturbed, then drinking becomes a useful strategy to deal with this difficulty. Jill is fire-fighting and she may initially believe she is simply taking the best course of action to deal with the mounting pressure she feels.

The difficulty is that each action may initially seem helpful to the client but what may not be so obvious are the unexpected consequences. Working longer without rest can only add to her fatigue and tiredness. Avoiding attending to issues at home so she can concentrate on work, and ultimately maintain her job, may increase tension between her and her partner, increase her guilt and deepen her depression even further. In addition, drinking to chill out and help promote sleep may actually reduce the quality of sleep. The hangover effect in the morning may cause low mood and anxiety symptoms, exacerbate tiredness and further erode her motivation to continue to engage and attend to necessary family and work activities. Lack of motivation then promotes further withdrawal behaviour which allows even more time for Jill to worry about her problems and so depression deepens.

While Jill's decisions may initially seem reasonable in her battle with worry about work, difficulties with fatigue and growing family difficulties, she may be unaware of how each decision has a number of additional consequences. The reason for this is that during a client's struggle with depression the focus of attention may be concerned with just getting by and avoiding more pain (self-protection) rather than weighing up the immediate and longer-term consequences of current strategies in a clear and objective way.

The practitioner's task is certainly not to point out the client's lack of objective consideration of their current behaviours. The aim is to explore collaboratively all the consequences of current strategies used. This means acknowledging the client's attempts to manage their problems but also bringing attention to those unexpected effects that might actually be maintaining the problem. A decision on the effectiveness of current strategies is ultimately the client's call. The practitioner's role is to facilitate a collaborative exploration of all the consequences and allow the client to truly evaluate if their current strategies seem to be working for them in the long term.

Let's take a look at this in the context of Jill's recent work situation.

Case example continued

What is the possible unexpected impact on Jill's mood in choosing to work longer hours and being too worried to delegate work to other staff?

What is the potential impact on Jill's mood in choosing to completely avoid work due to tiredness and fatigue and instead stay in bed for much of the day?

As already described in Chapter 2 on assessment, the client's cycle of responding to worrisome thoughts and the emotions they produce are captured in the generic maintenance model, which is also known as a cross-sectional formulation (Figure 4.1). This should be drawn up collaboratively with the client. The specific problem formulation draws the client's attention to the important connections between an event, the interpretation of that event, the emotions generated due to that interpretation and ultimately the client's current behavioural method of coping with those thoughts and emotions. Secondy, the model draws the client's attention to the full consequences of current behavioural responses to depression.

It is important that the client, through the above analysis, has an opportunity to explore the fact that mood is often related to or strongly influenced by both how we perceive and interpret certain situations and can be even further influenced by how we react or change in the face of certain situations (behaviour). It's also important to always remember that mood can equally generate negative automatic thoughts as the person attempts to understand and make sense of their emotions.

It has been established that when a client experiences a negative shift in mood, negative thoughts can be generated as the shift in mood makes information (thoughts and images) available to the client. These thoughts and emotions may be related to that particular mood state experienced in the past (Teasdale and Fogarty, 1979). Past experiences of low mood may be associated with many negative thoughts and associated negative moods that burst forth when the low mood is experienced again.

For example, imagine a client with a past experience of depression or guilt in childhood related to beliefs about failing a high stake examination (beliefs about not succeeding or letting others down). If those beliefs are reactivated in a current situation the person will likely experience the same emotion. Likewise if the

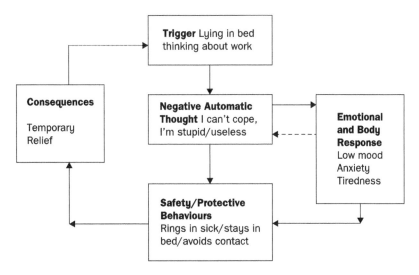

Figure 4.1 Generic maintenance model

emotion is provoked again in the future, then this shift in mood in turn may produce a stream of past beliefs that may maintain the negative emotion and shape current behaviour. The aim of low-intensity treatment is not to explore the client's past experiences (emotions, beliefs and behaviours) but to understand how current and previous beliefs and associated emotions are played out in the here and now.

Exploring current behavioural responses

The primary aim of exploring current behavioural responses is to reach a shared, informed consensus between the practitioner and client on whether change in current behaviour is worth considering. At this point we need to help the client establish whether current ways of responding (behaviour) work in the short term and the long term. Client behavioural change is based entirely on evidence obtained objectively by scrutinizing current effects of behaviour and deciding if current strategies work. If the client agrees, then behavioural change becomes a target for treatment. If the client concludes that current strategies don't work so well in the long term, then the priority is to help the client avoid continuing to engage in behaviour that they agree doesn't work.

The practitioner and client are then tasked with testing whether targeting changes in the client's behaviour can improve thinking, mood and overall quality of life. Although we may initially be concentrating on behaviour we cannot ignore thinking and emotions. However, there is compelling evidence that negative thinking and emotions may be amenable to change when more positive, productive and rewarding events and consequences are experienced by the client. It is important to point out to clients that engaging in life more fully will not immediately stop depression. However, what is clear is that staying inactive or engaging in unhelpful, short-term protective behaviours are potent maintaining factors in depression. In other words it is important to convey to the client that it is difficult to remain depressed if they regularly engage in activities that bring with them a sense of accomplishment and/or pleasure.

The principle of targeting the client's activity levels has always been advocated in CBT and more recently addressing behavioural change has been developed further by the renewed interest in Behavioural Activation (Jacobson et al., 1996; Martell et al., 2001). Lejuez et al. (2001) outlined the process by suggesting that if clients increased rewarding behaviours (behaviours that bring a sense of achievement or pleasure), and by doing so decrease depressive maintaining behaviours (behaviours such as withdrawal and interpersonal avoidance), they are more likely to access rewarding experiences. These more positive rewarding experiences facilitate greater access to both improved mood and thinking.

This sounds simple, however, it is important always to remember that from the client's perspective there are often clear benefits that can be derived from depressive behaviours including avoiding something unpleasant (or something perceived as unpleasant) and avoiding overwhelming responsibilities, or possible criticism from family, friends and/or the local community. The benefits of depressed behaviour are sometimes rapid and if they work in the short term, they may become reinforced and therefore repeated. As depressive behaviours become more frequent, non-depressive (helpful behaviours) may become less frequent. If helpful behaviours stimulate activity, drive and motivation, then depressive (self-protective) behaviours promote withdrawal, avoidance and putting things off. Gradually helpful behaviours are replaced with unhelpful avoidant behaviours and depression deepens. Through exploring the global consequences of their current depressive behaviours we can hopefully focus the client's attention to the benefits and costs of their current behavioural choices.

One possible way to conceptualize depression and the importance of behaviour and activation for clients is to consider using a pictorial representation of how drive and human motivation works. We have replicated a patient information sheet on behaviour and depression in Appendix 3.

In order to identify more fully behaviours which are causing the client difficulty we can begin to obtain a baseline activity diary. These tools will enable us to assist the client to break behaviours down into helpful and unhelpful activities, and from this we will be able to generate a more detailed goal list.

The use of a daily diary (see Table 4.2) helps to outline what the client does hour by hour and can help them identify any positive lift in mood associated with specific behaviours as well as any less helpful emotional shifts tied to specific behaviours. Once this has been completed in conjunction with the client, the practitioner is now in a position to further refine where change might need to occur.

The client is encouraged to complete the diary outlining what precisely they do and the impact of that activity on their mood. A checklist of moods (see box below) should be provided as clients may often have difficultly precisely differentiating moods.

Checklist of moods/feelings

Negative:

Depressed	Useless	Tense
Sad	Angry	Embarrassed
Despair	Annoyed	Irritated
Fear	Guilty	Disappointed
Terror	Shameful	Hurt
Anxious	Concerned	Disgusted
Nervous	Worried	Panicky
Hopeless	Helpless	Humiliated
Worthless	Frustrated	Shy
Suspicious	Paranoid	Sorry

Positive:

Happy	*Tranquil*	*Excited*
Joyous	*Peaceful*	*Fine*
Stable	*Strong*	*Relieved*
Content	*Cheerful*	*Interested*
Relaxed	*Aroused*	*Proud*
Calm	*Loving*	

Table 4.2 Daily activity diary

Time	Activity	Mood rating
4 am–5 am		Rating (1–10)
5 am–6 am		Rating (1–10)
6 am–7 am		Rating (1–10)
7 am–8 am		Rating (1–10)
8 am–9 am		Rating (1–10)
9 am–10 am		Rating (1–10)
10 am–11 am		Rating (1–10)
11 am–12 am		Rating (1–10)
12 am–1 pm		Rating (1–10)
1 pm–2 pm		Rating (1–10)
2 pm–3 pm		Rating (1–10)
3 pm–4 pm		Rating (1–10)
4 pm–5 pm		Rating (1–10)
5 pm–6 pm		Rating (1–10)
6 pm–7 pm		Rating (1–10)
7 pm–8 pm		Rating (1–10)
8 pm–9 pm		Rating (1–10)
9 pm–10 pm		Rating (1–10)
10 pm–11 pm		Rating (1–10)
11 pm–12 am		Rating (1–10)
12 am–1 am		Rating (1–10)
1 am–2 am		Rating (1–10)
2 am–4 am		Rating (1–10)

The client is taught to rate their mood on a 0–10 scale with 0 = no distress and 10 = maximum distress. The client is also taught to map their behaviour during a typical week and monitor their mood. This must be started in session and then ideally completed for homework. It is important to stress that all behaviour is captured and that there is no such thing as doing nothing. Therefore staring at the television for two hours while not really watching what is on is not 'doing nothing'. Ask the client to record that they sat and stared at the television for two hours and the impact this had on their mood. The client is then asked at the next session what they have learned by doing the exercise.

Particular attention should be drawn to behaviours associated with a lift in mood and behaviours that seem to be associated with a deterioration in mood. This can bring the client's attention to a number of factors. These include activities that seem to be associated with an increase in positive mood and specific activities or time periods that are more associated with a deterioration in mood. Patterns of behaviour may emerge that the client may not be aware of. This may indicate that certain behaviours consistently produce a negative shift in mood. These time periods then become the practitioner's and client's target area.

If a client is engaging in an activity that consistently produces a negative shift in mood, then this may again highlight a behaviour that initially seems helpful in the short term but ultimately maintains depression. For example, if Jill's tendency to remain in bed and avoid the hustle and bustle of the morning routine leads to feelings of guilt and further depression, then the practitioner and the client need to ascertain if this is a priority goal area. If this particular behaviour has shown to consistently increase depression, then a conversation has to be had about why the client might continue with a behaviour that doesn't seem to work. What are the benefits? What are the disadvantages?

The client is then asked to engage with the practitioner in designing ways in which to modify their response during this time frame. This is agreed not because the practitioner thinks it is a good idea but because the client agrees their current behaviour simply doesn't work (i.e. any benefits of this behaviour are outweighed by longer-term negative consequences). The client and practitioner can then reopen a discussion about how their activity has changed since becoming depressed. Old, previously more healthy behaviours can be discussed and the client asked if they would be prepared to engage in an experiment that would involve reinstating alternative behavioural responses or previously employed behavioural responses. No assumption is made about the outcome.

It is the client who will determine whether the modified behaviour is more useful than their current depression-driven behaviour. Start small and change only a few things. This is then documented and set as a homework experiment. Both the practitioner and client need to document precisely what changes are planned and perhaps what preparation is needed beforehand. For example, a client who agrees to get up one hour earlier, have a shower, get dressed and make breakfast may first need to plan to have clean, fresh clothes washed and ironed before the morning of the experiment. Any potential barrier to the new behaviour must be addressed.

In addition, the client could be advised to inform their family of the experiment so that the entire family understands its parameters. Otherwise the family may suddenly overwhelm the client on getting up with numerous additional demands and the experiment could fail. Discussing the experiment with family can be very helpful as they can then offer encouragement. Framing the new behaviour as an experiment is important as it may be seen to succeed or fail, *not* the client.

Once a detailed description of the experiment is agreed, the client can then choose a start date and prepare for it. Again it is important to reiterate to the client that the process is one of experimentation and this is done for a very good reason. The experiment will either be wholly or partially successful or indeed may need further fine tuning, however, it is the experiment that succeeds or doesn't succeed, not the client. Once the experiment is completed, it is evaluated by the client and the practitioner. Permission for things not to work out is agreed beforehand and success should be measured in degrees not in absolute terms. Again, re-emphasize that modifying discrete areas of behaviour will not 'cure' depression but may help make that particular time less depressing. Ask the client how you might both find out.

Remember change is difficult! As mentioned in Chapter 3, change can be viewed as frightening, therefore prepare the client for some distress or anxiety before the experiment by reiterating that change can initially be very difficult. The use of metaphors can be useful at this stage. You could remind the client of a previous skill they learned and how difficult it may have been to start with, for example, learning to drive for the first time or preparing an assignment for marking. We can't successfully learn to drive without the fear of crashing or hurting ourselves and we cannot submit an assignment paper without the fear of potential failure or rejection. The application of new skills or the reinstatement of old skills will naturally be difficult and therefore must be done one step at a time.

Once the identified areas of change are agreed, following a review of the client's activity diary, a goal or change list can be generated and the practitioner and client can begin to construct an action plan. In doing this we are effectively converting the client's problem list into a list of goals or targets (see Chapter 3).

To recap, the first aim is to generate a baseline measurement of current activity (using the activity diary) which should clearly indicate what the client is doing more of or not doing enough of currently. It should also indicate very clear areas of time when depression is most prominent. These problem areas may indicate what behaviours have changed or stopped due to illness and the client and practitioner can then collaboratively establish manageable and realistic targets. These target behaviours should be elicited by asking the client what their behaviour consisted of when they were not depressed.

Linking behaviour change to values

In Chapter 3 we looked at the importance of eliciting important or valued areas of the client's life and how goals and targets need to be set in the context of these identified values. This is therefore true of any agreed planned behaviour change. Targeting behaviour change should involve negotiating a behaviour that is consistent with the client's values. For example, if being a good mother is an identified value for your client, it would be important to design behavioural activities that move the client in the direction of being a good mother.

This might, for example, mean scheduling some regular but limited time with the client's children every day starting with half an hour and gradually increasing this. Choosing activities with the children that were enjoyable before the client became depressed is important. If a client identifies their career as a value, then asking the client to gradually get up earlier in the morning and add some routine such as washing, dressing and attending to their appearance may seem a necessary first step in moving in the direction of that valued behaviour. Although a return to work for the client may be some way off, the ability to establish an early routine could be viewed in the context of eventually re-establishing the routine necessary to return to work. If the client can't establish an early morning routine, then a return to work and career will remain unobtainable.

Case example continued: Jill's problems converted into targets

Jill's goal: Getting more active and helping my husband with the children and engaging more fully with what is really going on at home rather than what has gone before (brooding) or what might happen in the future (worry).

The next step is to specify precisely what 'more active' means to Jill in very concrete terms. What might she want to do? When might this happen and for how long and with whom? Jill and the practitioner need to establish what the real and perceived barriers are to her becoming more active. The client and practitioner then need to agree collaboratively on how to best manage each of the barriers identified. In addition, Jill and her therapist need to establish how to measure the outcome of any change.

Standardized outcome measures for depression and anxiety are now very common and easy to administer. The most commonly used are PHQ–9 for depression and the GAD–7 for anxiety (Kroenke et al., 2001; Spitzer et al., 2006). They allow you and your client to obtain a baseline measurement of illness severity and permit the session-by-session measurement of progress and change throughout the rest of treatment. If administered every session they should indicate if treatment is working or not and this will be one of the practitioner's key indicators that the client needs to be 'stepped up' to more intensive formal CBT.

Case example continued

Jill's activity diary suggests that although lying in bed in the morning brings temporary relief from watching her husband struggle alone with the children, that relief is short-lived and, once the family depart for school and nursery, she is left feeling even more depressed and guilty. Therefore the initial target for behavioural change is tackling the pattern of lying in bed longer and avoiding the things she used to do when well. This includes getting up with her husband, showering, getting dressed and helping get the children dressed and with the breakfast routine. This included an enjoyable shower to the sound of her favourite music and a discussion with the children around the breakfast table about what the children were doing in school that day. It also previously included planning after-school activities for the children.

Jill agrees with her husband that in the short term he will manage the after-school activities. However, we immediately see that tackling the morning routine leads Jill to actively thinking about what is the next target for change, for example engaging the children in fun after-school activities (going to the cinema, going to the park, a special trip to get ice cream or agreeing to a family game). Jill and her practitioner had established that these once brought enormous happiness and allowed time for the family to simply be together. Targeting additional behaviour change, however, must be put on hold until the first morning experiments are completed.

In preparation for changing Jill's current behaviour in the morning, Jill and her practitioner agreed in fine detail how this would be best achieved.

Targeted change includes reducing the amount Jill drank the night before the experiment as she considered this left her more tired and groggy in the morning. Second, Jill selected a few clothes from the growing number in her clothes basket and washed and ironed them the night before the experiment. She set her alarm clock and it was agreed that regardless of how well she slept she would practise throwing the duvet off as soon as her alarm clock went off and head straight for the shower. She planned the night before to have her MP3 player and speakers fully charged and in the bathroom, ready to be turned on while she was having her shower. Jill also agreed that she would aim to help plait her younger daughter's hair as they had both enjoyed this previously. Finally Jill would have breakfast with the family and would kiss and hug the children before they headed off to school.

Jill's task has within it a number of minor tasks which are all framed as experiments. It is important to remember that Jill's example may have included too many tasks and therefore some may have had to be postponed if she was overwhelmed.

Case example continued

Jill felt the above was doable and this was measured beforehand using a confidence rating scale of 0–100 (with 0 = not confident at all she could achieve it and 100 = fully confident that she could achieve it). Jill's confidence rating was initially 60 per cent and when asked by her practitioner how this might be increased, she suggested that initially she would not agree at breakfast to take part in after-school trips as she felt this would put pressure on her for the rest of that day. In conjunction with her husband it was agreed any after-school activity would be managed by him initially. This increased her confidence level to 70 per cent.

This demonstrates the need to involve others in the planning of the experiment. By including her husband and explaining in detail what Jill hoped to achieve he could then fully support her in the early stages of trying to reclaim her life. If her husband had not been briefed about the experiment, then this could have led to him expecting too much or even to be confused about why Jill suddenly wanted to be engaged again in a morning routine he has struggled with alone for many months.

Case example continued

The experiment was set and Jill picked a morning to begin. It was emphasized to her that we were not trying to lift her entire mood by engaging in one experiment but instead that we were simply measuring whether changing her morning routine in this way had any effect on her mood in the morning. This required Jill to continue to complete her diary and to measure her mood on the morning of the experiment and compare this with previous mornings when she remained hidden away in bed. Any further changes in her routine would have to wait until the practitioner and Jill could analyse the results of this experiment.

Overall any single experiment may be viewed as one step towards a much larger goal (e.g. getting back to work again). The rationale for starting with small steps is that they are likely to be more achievable and, ultimately, if the client can't engage in initial early steps, then larger goals are unlikely to succeed. Research has shown that success builds success so achievement of one small goal may spur Jill on to try to achieve another (Robertson, 2011). In Jill's case, if she first couldn't master her morning routine again then it is unlikely that more demanding goals such as getting back to work would be achievable. Sometimes it is useful to prime the client for staging experiments in a very systematic way by using metaphors.

One example is using the metaphor of planning a holiday. If the client dreams about embarking on a driving holiday across Europe and views this as an exceptionally good way to spend the summer but has yet to pass their driving test, then ask them what steps need to be taken first. Should they book their ferry tickets before their driving test? Systematically planning an imaginary task and breaking down each step into manageable targets or goals will hopefully help prime the client to think sequentially when planning their route out of depression. In tackling the problems of depression in this way we are in effect 'kick-starting' the client's problem-solving abilities. This is important as arrested problem solving is a key feature of depression and other mental health disorders, particularly social and interpersonal problem solving (Goddard et al., 1996; Bell and D'Zurilla, 2009).

Let's recap a little. When clients experience low mood/depression for whatever reason they may experience negative thoughts a lot of the time, and with each subsequent negative thought the feelings of low mood/depression are likely to increase. As a result their behaviour is likely to change; in other words this combination of negative thoughts and feelings stops them from engaging in activities they would normally engage in.

The client may view this as a rational self-protective behaviour in order to avoid feeling more depressed. In addition, any activities they would normally have gained pleasure from reduce or even stop. In any event they do not get as much enjoyment from these activities as they used to. What happens next? With more time available to worry, unsurprisingly thinking may become even more negative, they may get thoughts about being stupid/useless/lazy, which in turn makes them feel even worse. In other words they get caught up in a self-defeating, negative vicious cycle.

Not all behaviours are created equally. Research has discovered that particular behaviours may produce a 'double whammy' effect. Physical inactivity alone may be associated with the development of mental health problems (Motl et al., 2004). Research has shown exercise to be efficacious as a stand-alone treatment and exercise is now included in the American Psychiatric Association's treatment recommendations for depression (Rethorst and Trivedi, 2013). Therefore if a client valued exercise before they became depressed, this may be a doubly rewarding behaviour to target as a treatment goal. The most important issue before initiating a gradual exercise plan is for the client, practitioner and the client's GP to work in conjunction.

When behaviour change isn't enough

Having started to test whether current behaviour is useful or not, we can then reflect again on other aspects of the cognitive behavioural cycle of depression. This should further enhance our understanding of the links between events, thoughts, behaviour, body and mood (see Figure 4.2).

As has already been mentioned, when clients first attempt to replace negative depressive behaviours with new helpful behaviours, this will feel uncomfortable and awkward. However, persistence and a graded approach to new healthy behaviours will eventually work if the client can be encouraged to truly engage in the new behaviour and realize that previous depressive behavioural strategies may help in the short term but lead to additional problems in the long term.

However, trying new alternative behaviours will produce little change if while engaged in the new behaviour the client continues to ruminate about past failings or future worries. Rumination occurs when the client repeatedly engages in asking themselves (or others) questions that cannot be answered. Focusing intently on the new and helpful behaviour is therefore vital. Remember it's important the problems can be dealt with in the here and now. Clients who are depressed often brood about events in the past which cannot be changed or worry about events in the future over which they have little or no control. It is important to gently guide the client back to the 'here and now'. Remind the client that it is only in the 'here and now' that actual change can occur.

If the client has recurring thoughts that cannot be easily answered such as 'Why am I like this?', 'When will I feel better?' and 'Why is this happening to me?'

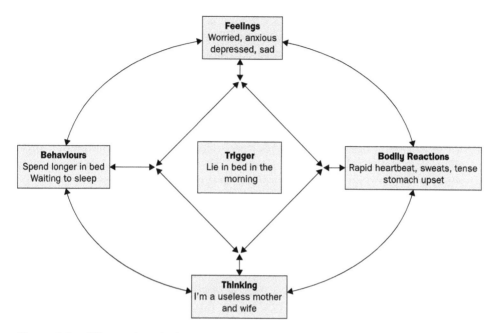

Figure 4.2   Jill's cognitive behavioural model

then ask the client whether engaging in this style of thinking helps lift their mood or causes a deepening of low mood. If the answer is that it depresses mood further, then gently ask them to refocus attention onto what they are doing. The practitioner must never try to encourage the client simply to 'think more positively'. This can be viewed by the client as extremely invalidating and displays a gross misunderstanding of the automatic pernicious nature of negative thoughts. Negative automatic thoughts are as much an unavoidable symptom of depression as seizures are a symptom of grand mal epilepsy.

The practitioner can, however, bring the client's attention to the impact of focusing attention on negative automatic thoughts. This may include drawing up a list of advantages and disadvantages of continuing to concentrate attention on these types of unanswerable cyclical questions. This involves joining the client in investigating the usefulness of paying attention to negative ruminatory thoughts. The practitioner and client can achieve this by using a simple cost benefit analysis sheet (see Table 4.3).

The aim is to draw attention to the fact that ruminatory negative automatic thoughts have a very real and sometimes devastating impact on how the client feels. The more attention we give to them, the more depression increases and the less time we spend in tackling real current problems or on more productive, healthy behaviours. If the client has difficulty in identifying whether a thought or worry is a rumination thought (a thought that has no immediate benefit or solution) or not, then a 'Rumination thought record' can be used (see Figure 4.3).

Identifying time spent by clients on rumination can also be elicited via the daily activity diary. This can be achieved by instructing the client when filling in an activity diary that it is important to remember that there is no such thing as doing nothing. If the client stares at the television, not watching but ruminating, then this behaviour (staring blankly at the television screen) needs to be treated as any other behaviour. You and the client must collaboratively explore and question whether this behaviour is helpful and, if not, then you and the client can plan to experiment by changing the behaviour at these times. The rumination thought record (Figure 4.3) can be a useful tool not only in identifying rumination type brooding or worrying thoughts but can also direct the client in actively shifting attention and behaviour onto more productive problem-solving tasks.

Non-rumination specific negative automatic thoughts

Other negative automatic thoughts can occur in relation to more specific situations. These don't take the form of endless rumination-style worries but are more directly related to a specific situation, person or event. They appear in the form of derogatory self-statements and may suggest to the client that they are specifically

Table 4.3   Cost benefit of spending time on negative automatic thoughts

Negative automatic thought	Benefits of spending time on this thought? Was it useful in terms of helping you out of low mood?	Cost of spending time on this thought? What did it bring in terms of helping you solve problems?	What would have been more helpful at this time than spending time on this thought?

defective in some way. Again this type of thinking can have a profoundly disabling effect not just on the client's mood but also their behaviour. These more specific negative automatic thoughts are to be found initially by reviewing the client's daily diary. If it is clear from the daily diary that the client is engaged in an activity that is purposeful, and which in the past would have given the client a sense of achievement or pleasure, but the mood remains low at this time, then you need to investigate what precisely the client was telling themselves at this time.

What am I thinking about or worrying about now?

Negative automatic thought or worry:

A. Is this a thought or worry that I can answer or resolve right here and right now?
Yes/No

If no, is it worth spending more time on it (move on to B section)?
If yes, then what (practically) can I do to resolve my worry now?

B. Questions to ask when brooding or worrying thoughts occur. If the answer to the above question is no, then am I BROODING or WORRYING? Note: worry or brooding thoughts cannot be answered or resolved immediately. They are questions about the past or future that have no immediate answer. Is spending time on this thought helping my mood or lowering it? Is spending time on this thought or worry bringing me closer to feeling better or dragging me further into feeling low?

If I CANNOT resolve or respond to the worry or thought immediately, does thinking about it make life better for me or not? If not – what else could I constructively tackle? Are there problems that I should be tackling that will give me either a sense of pleasure or achievement?

Figure 4.3 Rumination thought record

Case example continued

For example, in the later stages of treatment Jill plans an experiment to invite friends and family over for a weekend so she plans and executes a dinner party. This is agreed as an experiment as Jill identified this as a previously pleasant experience. If, however, after completing the weekend experiment, mood remains low or even deteriorates further, then a closer analysis is warranted. What we might find is that during the actual dinner party Jill appears engaged but for the duration of the party is subjected to a barrage of thoughts about no one liking her and everyone at the dinner party believing she is a failure for not seeing them sooner.

In addition, Jill and her practitioner also discover that she tells herself that everyone at the dinner party must think her weak for taking time off work. Therefore what may appear as a perceived gain (achieving and carrying off a dinner party) is actually converted to a horribly depressing and worrying event due to what Jill is telling herself. Jill's increased behavioural activation is derailed by a stream of specific negative automatic thoughts about herself and the way she perceives others see her.

These negative automatic thoughts lead Jill to negatively evaluate the party, reduce her enjoyment of the party and actually deepen her depressed mood. Initiating a previously pleasant behaviour in this instance is not sufficient to reduce depression and lift mood. The exercise is sabotaged by the stream of negative automatic thoughts (or appraisals) about the event and those attending the event.

The client and practitioner can begin by investigating whether these thoughts are helpful or not. If following your assessment you can identify possible mistakes in the client's evaluation, then the next step is to introduce the notion of testing the validity of thinking in this way. You can first establish the impact of these specific negative automatic thoughts and their effect on mood and behaviour and then explore with the client how awful it might be if they were condemning themselves over something that may or may not be true.

The practitioner can begin by identifying some common thoughts and beliefs that eventually turn out not to be true, for example, the belief in Santa Claus when we are children or the beliefs people hold about a vast array of situations that turn out later not to be true. Examples may include thoughts about never passing an exam which is eventually passed or predictions about people or events that turn out to be mistaken. The examples will be more meaningful if you use personal client data.

Any initial improvement in treatment can also be used to highlight how wrong we can get things. For example, if Jill was dubious about early behavioural activation experiments but they turned out to be helpful, then the practitioner can bring Jill's attention to this and she can use this as an example of how our thoughts and beliefs can be mistaken. The aim is to introduce the notion that often our thoughts and beliefs can easily be distorted and therefore a sense of scepticism in what we tell ourselves is helpful.

Negative automatic thoughts are a stream of rapidly flowing, critical, self-disparaging thoughts that take the form of a running commentary in the client's head and can also contain quite vivid negative images. Automatic thoughts are common to us all, but they tend to be more negative in depression. They are neither wanted by the client nor deliberately created by the client but instead are an involuntary, common manifestation of depression that have their roots in the client's early experiences. They may be connected to a time when perhaps the client felt particularly vulnerable or lost in childhood and early adolescence. Remember that pursuing the possible origins of negative automatic thoughts is not the target of low-intensity treatment. Instead we remain focused on current negative automatic thoughts and their impact on the client in the 'here and now'.

When triggered by current adversity and low mood, these dysfunctional earlier-held beliefs temporarily re-emerge and can generate previously dormant and mistaken ideas about how fragile or defective we are. These thoughts temporarily dampen our awareness of our strengths and exaggerate our perceived weaknesses. At their most extreme they generate three fairly global and credible patterns of thinking (Beck's Negative Triad; Beck, 1967).

- Negative and pessimistic ideas of self. These ideas relate to the client's subjective evaluation or view of themselves (I'm useless and weak).
- Negative and pessimistic ideas about the client's world. This involves the client's perceived negative beliefs about their world and not being able to meet the demands of their current situation or environment (I'll never cope with the demands of the job).
- Negative and pessimistic ideas about the client's future. This involves the client's negative beliefs about the future and strongly held predictions that current depression will persist. It includes the client's evaluation that they are powerless to do anything to change their predicament (I'll never be the mother, wife or employee I should be).

When clients experience low mood/depression they are often cognitively trapped in Beck's negative triad and these negative and pessimistic ideas are maintained by a number of unhelpful extreme thinking styles (see Table 4.4).

When negative automatic thoughts interfere with the client's progress towards becoming more behaviourally active, the practitioner and the client need to collaboratively elicit those negative automatic thoughts. Then, in the same way as the client and practitioner tested the usefulness of dysfunctional depressive behaviour, they now have to set about exploring the actual credibility of these often very vicious and depression-maintaining negative automatic thoughts.

When considering thoughts, our minds could be seen as a busy traffic roundabout; cars (or thoughts) keep whizzing through, the minute one car whizzes past another arrives to take its place. Like cars whizzing past on a traffic roundabout some cars are beautiful and pleasant to watch but some can be noisy old bangers from the past that stink. Sometimes while observing the cars as they pass through the roundabout our attention can become fixed on the old bangers or we only notice them as they are so loud and seem to dominate our attention. This is what can happen to negative thoughts in depression. Many of our thoughts will focus on what is happening around us, what has already happened to us or what we think may happen to us in the future. They can also be concerned with how we think other people see us and indeed with how we see ourselves.

Table 4.4   Unhelpful thinking styles

Unhelpful thinking style	Typical thoughts	
1.	Dichotomous thinking, sometimes referred to as black and white, all or nothing or polarized thinking	Client categorizes experiences in either/or extremes. Either something works out perfectly well or it is viewed as a complete disaster. The client doesn't think in terms of grey or partial success
2.	Arbitrary inferences	An arbitrary inference refers to an error whereby a client jumps to a conclusion but doesn't provide evidence that relates to the conclusion they draw, e.g. thinking of the absolute worst scenario occurring without clear and relevant evidence
3.	Selective abstraction	The client forms a conclusion based on one or two isolated random details of an event, e.g. one person yawned so the whole dinner party was a disaster
4.	Over-generalization	Extreme beliefs extracted from a single situation and held by the client as indicative of all future events. The client predicts a similar occurrence in all future situations
5.	Personalization	The client relates external events to them personally without basis or connection. A client may attribute a group of people sharing a laugh as indicating they are laughing at them
6.	Labelling and mislabelling	The client sums up their entire identity on the basis one mistake or one event, e.g. I'm a loser. Judging others on the basis of one event, e.g. he is completely heartless and doesn't care

Let's think about negative thoughts in a little more detail. Negative thoughts tend to be automatic, in other words they seem to just appear rather than being created. Often at the time they arrive they seem entirely reasonable and rational, but as mentioned above, once we are depressed, they may be arrived at through faulty, depression-generated logic. This process makes the client prejudiced against themselves. The net effect of this is that when depressed, the client homes in on and exaggerates their errors and mistakes and absolutely discounts any successes. They are effectively blinkered and attention is reduced to the point that all that is visible are experiences that feed the depressed state.

It's also important to note that even if the client doesn't actually make a mistake, once in a depressive mindset, anything at all, no matter how insignificant the event, may appear to support the client's depression-generated, negative beliefs. Such is the level of reality distortion in depression, even the most benign event may be seized upon and used as concrete evidence to support whatever negative belief is predominant at that time.

Beck (1972) observed that when something negative happens to someone experiencing depression, that individual invariably interprets the experience as representing a personal failing or defeat. They ascribe this defeat to some personal innate defect. The perceived tendency to fail is viewed as intrinsic and if this is accepted by the individual, then there may be a secondary belief that there may be no hope of their circumstances changing.

Case example continued

For example, Jill's friend – who may have had a very busy and trying day and then failed to telephone Jill when she said she would – may be seen by Jill as evidence that: 'I knew they didn't care about me'; 'They obviously see I'm a loser' and 'Everyone can tell how useless I am'. We can therefore see the impact that this kind of grossly distorted thinking can have on a client's mood and on future behaviour. Is Jill likely to ask this friend to call again?

Jill's temporarily narrowed, blinkered and distorted thinking (created by depression) prevents her from accessing or retrieving other less devastating alternative explanations for her friend not contacting her. She is only accessing what she feels to be true, therefore if she thinks she is worthless, her thinking is biased towards supporting this belief.

Our aim then in low-intensity treatment is to begin to explore all the information available to the client: information which may not be attended to by the client due to the effects of distorted thinking, information that may allow the client to better appraise the accuracy of negative automatic thoughts. In doing so, we enable the client to consider alternative, more realistic appraisals of what is actually happening. This involves the practitioner and client reviewing all the information available in a particular situation rather than the client relying solely on feeling-based judgements that are contaminated and biased due to the client's depressive mood.

The first step in this process is introducing the client to the idea that there are two factors involved in experiencing a thought. The first is the content of the thought itself. What does it tell us? Is it in the form of a comment about us or others or about our situation? Second, we need to consider how credible or believable it is at any one point in time. An example is the belief that flying is dangerous and that the next flight taken will crash and that will be the end of you! When there is no flight imminent, the thought may be there but not be credible to any large degree. An individual with this thought may even scold themselves for how ludicrous the thought is. The thought at this point in time is obviously less credible or believable. If the individual were asked to rate how much they believe the thought out of 0–100 per cent, with 0 per cent = not credible and 100 per cent = certain to happen, therefore totally credible, then the person may decide it is not so credible (20 per cent). However, if we were to ask how credible the thought is when the individual is strapped into an aircraft about to be hurtled into the sky, then in this situation the credibility of the belief that the aircraft will crash may increase. It is the content of a thought that impacts on what emotion we experience and the credibility of a particular belief that impacts on how intense that emotional reaction is.

Automatic thoughts, therefore, are the rapid monologue (or images) in which all of us are constantly engaged. We normally have little conscious awareness of these thoughts, but they can easily be brought into conscious awareness by specifically drawing our attention to them.

As already mentioned, in depression, automatic thoughts are negative in nature and reflect deeper levels of cognitive activity, such as the activation of beliefs regarding inadequacy and failure laid down during early development. It is vitally important to note that accessing those more deeply held beliefs from childhood is not the task of low-intensity treatment. This task should always be reserved for those who are fully trained and accredited cognitive behavioural psychotherapists.

However, helping the client to modify the more accessible, currently available thoughts has definite therapeutic value in its own right. Clients are taught to monitor these thoughts, and once they can be monitored, the practitioner teaches the depressed client to test whether their credibility rating of those thoughts is warranted. The practitioner facilitates the client challenging how credible the thought actually is by bringing the client's attention to alternative information that might contradict their automatic conclusion.

The client's belief in a thought might initially be amenable to being modified by teaching the client to examine the evidence for and against the thought. Negative automatic thoughts are rapid mood-driven conclusions and they often go unexamined by the depressed client. Depressed mood may also lead to the client's biased selection of information that supports the emotion-generated thought. This reflects the extreme negative thinking styles noted earlier. When an extreme negative thinking style is activated, it can result in the client discounting or ignoring any information that runs counter to the client's negative automatic thought. Therefore, negative automatic thoughts are not simply a benign side effect or symptom of clinical depression; they are a very potent and powerful maintaining phenomenon (Hollon and Kendall, 1980; Kendall, Howard and Hays, 1989).

The first step in the process of helping the client to test the validity of their negative automatic thoughts is to teach them how to separate their thoughts from their emotions. Negative emotions are obviously prominent in depression and it is the emotional reaction that clients experience very readily. A useful way of helping clients distinguish between emotions and the thinking that may drive them is to begin by using a general scenario. The client is asked to consider the scenario in Table 4.5 and to establish what any individual might feel emotionally and how they may react or behave, given a range of automatic thoughts.

The example can then be used to ask clients to consider that although the situation is exactly the same, what is different are the thoughts or how this imaginary individual interprets their situation. You can then engage the client in trying to collaboratively link a specific emotional reaction to each hypothetical thought (see Table 4.6).

We can now try to help the client build up an association between what happens to us (situation), how we read or interpret that situation (thoughts) and how these

Table 4.5   Thought record to illustrate negative automatic thoughts

Situation	Thought	Mood	Behaviour
Sitting in a bar alone having a quiet beer on the way home from work when a very heavy-set, extremely drunk and unsteady man starts heading towards where you are sitting	1. *Oh, my goodness, he looks really out of it. He looks like he could do anything, he is so out of control and here I am all alone in this quiet part of the bar*	?	?
	2. *Poor bloke, he is so drunk he is a danger to himself. How could the bar staff have allowed anyone to get into that state? If he leaves this bar and gets out on to the street, he'll end up falling in front of a car or something*	?	?
	3. *Oh, my goodness, you can't even pop into a bar by yourself for a quick, quiet drink without some idiot, who can't control their own behaviour, hassling you. He is a disgrace and a fool and should be barred from being around good decent people*	?	?

Table 4.6 Thought record to illustrate the effects of negative automatic thoughts

Situation	Thought	Mood	Behaviour
Sitting in a bar alone having a quiet beer on the way home from work when a very heavy-set, extremely drunk and unsteady man starts heading towards where you are sitting	1. Oh, my goodness, he looks really out of it. He looks like he could do anything, he is so out of control and here I am all alone in this quiet part of the bar	Fear, anxiety or apprehension	Move to a part of the bar where help might be more easily sought
	2. Poor bloke, he is so drunk he is a danger to himself. How could the bar staff have allowed anyone to get into that state? If he leaves this bar and gets out on to the street, he'll end up falling in front of a car or something	Compassion, concern	Help the man get a taxi and ensure he gets safely home
	3. Oh, my goodness, you can't even pop into a bar by yourself for a quick quiet drink without some idiot, who can't control their own behaviour, hassling you. He is a disgrace and a fool and should be barred from being around good decent people	Annoyance and anger	Get bar staff to remove him immediately from the bar for annoying customers

thoughts can have an impact not just on our emotions (mood) but also directly on how we react (behaviour).

It is then vital that the practitioner moves quickly on to an example relevant to the client to reinforce the learning and to transform a generic teaching example into a personally meaningful example (Table 4.7).

Once again we can use this real lived example to investigate the impact of one negative automatic thought and one alternative thought on Jill's mood and behaviour. A recap on the emotions checklist used for the activity diary might be helpful

Table 4.7   Jill's thought record example

Situation	Thought	Mood	Behaviour
Sitting at 3.00pm waiting by the phone because Jan said she was going to call you back by 2.30pm	*1. I knew she was tired of me and my pathetic problems. She is sick of me and obviously thinks I'm a total loser and waste of space. I'm alone and will always be alone – no one understands*	Depressed and lonely	Take phone off hook and avoid seeing Jan in case Jill burdens her even further
	2. Jan is the kindest friend I know and has helped me a lot. There must be a very good reason if she can't call – we can catch up later. I'm glad I have someone in my life at the minute who genuinely cares about me. Jan is a mother with three kids of her own and this must be school pick up time	Content and happy	Get on with what needs done and ring Jan later to see if she is OK

and agreement reached on what each emotion word means to the client so you are both clear what the client means by being depressed, lonely, and so on.

The alternative second thought is reached by exploring all Jill knows about Jan and her past experience of being Jan's friend. It is not based solely on one moment in time when Jill is feeling down and depressed. The next step is to rate the belief in each thought and to connect the credibility of the thought to the intensity of the emotion felt. A discussion also needs to take place on the longer-term consequences of believing a particular thought and then acting as if that thought were true. What impact might Jill's initial negative automatic thought, mood and her consequent behaviour have on the long-term maintenance of her friendship with Jan?

Cutting out one more source of companionship and support when Jill is already feeling alone can only compound her feelings of depression. Again we can see that negative automatic thoughts are not just a benign side effect of depression but also a potent maintaining factor.

The above example also allows us to demonstrate to the client that negative automatic thoughts can be labelled in terms of the kinds of biases or negative, unhelpful, thinking styles that may be negatively impacting on the way the client is processing information. For example, Jill – who is upset because she believes Jan didn't ring her because she thinks Jill is a loser – may be engaged in 'mind reading'. This is a form of the unhelpful thinking style 'arbitrary inference'. Jill is also predicting, 'I'm alone and always will be alone', which is effectively 'fortune telling' in a catastrophizing way, related to the unhelpful thinking style overgeneralization. It is important not to challenge these thoughts at this point in time as they may be accurate. Instead you would begin to help Jill investigate whether there is a pattern of negative thinking styles emerging.

The aim at this stage is to encourage the client to stand back or distance themselves temporarily in order to more objectively scrutinize what precisely is going on when mood shifts in a negative direction.

Once the client's attention has been brought to the presence and impact of negative automatic thinking and the practitioner is assured the client understands, then the next stage is to teach them how to scrutinize their own thoughts. In order to do this, the practitioner can introduce the client to a thought recording form (Thought Record). The thought record can help the client identify those thoughts which appear negative and what type of unhelpful thinking style they are engaged in. In Table 4.8 we can see an example of a typical thought record. The most upsetting prominent thought is important. This 'hot thought' is the negative automatic thought which has high credibility and appears to be linked to the key negative emotion.

The client is initially asked to list all negative automatic thoughts and the 'hot thought' is then picked from this list. This is done because we can only work on one thought at a time. Picking out the most upsetting thought is only the first stage; the second stage is the collection of evidence to show how accurate their thoughts really are, and finally the client is encouraged to re-evaluate their thoughts in light of the new evidence they will have collected. Thoughts are reappraised and alternative thoughts created.

First, we help the client identify the very specific situation which can be done using the five 'W' questions (Who, What, Where, When, Why?), then the client is helped to identify their feelings and rate them (out of 0–100 with 100 being

Table 4.8 Jill's thought record

Situation	Feeling (0–100%)	Thought (belief 0–100%)	Revised thought taking in to account all the evidence (belief 0–100%)	Feeling (0–100%)
9.00 am in bed, alone, not going to work, avoiding family	Depressed (90%) Fearful (50%) Anxious (85%)	I am stupid and useless. I am a bad wife and mother. My children don't love me (95%)	My children do love me they just can't really understand what's going on (65%)	Depressed (85%) Fearful (50%) Anxious (75%)

indicative of major distress and 0 of no distress). The practitioner then helps the client identify the thought or thoughts they were experiencing at that time and in relation to that specific situation. We then need to explain to the client how to rate how much they believe each thought out of 100 per cent (with 0–25 per cent being not credible and 75–100 per cent being totally credible). If more than one thought is identified, it is important the client identifies the most upsetting prominent thought and focus on this.

These prominent upsetting thoughts can be identified by asking the client to think about what thought rings most true and seems to cause most psychological distress. Once the most upsetting thought is identified, the client can then go to the evidence sheet and list the evidence for and against this belief, finally re-rating their belief once this has been completed (Table 4.9).

The client can be informed that this is equivalent to putting the negative automatic thought on trial where all the factual evidence is considered, not just the first conclusion that might appear to be true. Would a judge accept a policeman standing in court saying that he had a hunch or a feeling that someone committed a crime, with no hard factual evidence? This process aims to help the client become aware of all the evidence, not just the evidence they are biased towards through negative, unhelpful thinking styles.

The importance of a good assessment cannot be emphasized enough at this point. The practitioner will have to use all they know about the client at this stage to help guide the client to additional information that they have access to but may be ignoring or discounting due to their depressed state. The practitioner, through the use of gentle prompting questions, is assisting the client to effectively kick start a fight-back against the unhelpful thinking style that so dominates depressive thinking. This is guiding the client to bring to light additional or alternative accurate information that has eluded the client due to their current illness.

Table 4.9 Putting the most upsetting or prominent thought on trial

My upsetting thought My children don't love me Evidence for (95%)	My belief 0–100% Evidence against (85%)
I don't play with my children. I don't take them to school. I should be out working and providing for them which I am not! A good mother wouldn't spend so much time in bed or be upset all the time. My children are always tiptoeing past my room. They don't come into the bedroom to talk to me any more	I made the move for the children for the new house and the school and I know the kids were happy with the new house. They always ask (my husband) how I am doing. They make me get well soon cards. The reason they tiptoe around the room is because they know I am not well and don't want to upset me. This shows they care and love me

This is not 'telling treatment' or a challenging approach. The overall aim is to facilitate the client to self-challenge their often biased appraisals. The practitioner's therapeutic stance during this stage is one of gently putting the client in touch with information they would readily have access to if they were not depressed.

Once the client has put the negative automatic thought on trial (Table 4.9) the client is asked to return to the thought diary (Table 4.8) and in the fourth column write down any new thoughts based on evidence identified which may challenge the original dominant negative thought. That belief is now rated again, taking into account any new information.

Now it is important the client compares columns two and four and notes any changes in their feelings and the intensity of those feelings. (Tip: One possible way of opening up the discussion as to possible alternative thoughts is by asking the client if their belief in the most upsetting prominent thought was 95 per cent, then what may make up the other 5 per cent?) Table 4.9 gives a short example of what Jill's thought record evidence sheet may look like.

It is very important that the practitioner is aware that the client who is depressed will not readily have access to alternative anti-depressant thoughts. This is part of being depressed so the practitioner must guide the client through this process in session and never just allocate both sheets for homework. If the client is struggling, break the process down further by helping the client to catch situations when their mood shifts and plotting together what thoughts may be present. This skill can then be built on until the client is able to practise alone between sessions.

Helping a client achieve an alternative perspective on their thinking can have a profound effect in terms of lifting mood but the practitioner needs to be patient. The process is akin to chipping away at the negative automatic thoughts and the underlying process which feeds them (unhelpful thinking styles). The consequences for treatment of facilitating access to alternative, more balanced thinking is that the practitioner and client now have two or more ideas of what is going on which can then be further tested out in the client's real world.

The practitioner and client can use this more balanced thinking to set up experiments to further test whether the negative automatic thoughts fit with reality. This is ultimately the aim of cognitive restructuring, to help the client see that their depressed interpretation of events is merely one way of viewing the situation. However, simply intellectually debating away a client's negative automatic thoughts may bring very transient relief unless the discovery of a new alternative way of viewing their condition is followed up with real and meaningful change in the client's behaviour.

The next stage is to ask the client how we may test and gather further information to strengthen the alternative belief. This is best done by introducing the concept of behavioural experiments. Behavioural experiments take the form of utilizing the negative automatic thought and the alternative thought derived from thought recording to set about testing each in a real-world experiment.

Case example continued

For example, Jill may test the belief that her children don't like her against the idea that they still care for her but don't understand what is going on.

An experiment could be conducted whereby Jill specifically engages with the children for an agreed and specific period of time and during this interaction Jill can further test whether the belief is valid or not.

Such an experiment may look like this . . .

Negative automatic thought to be tested

The kids have grown apart from me; they hate what I've become. They won't want to be with me (70 per cent).

Alternative thought

I'm just worried they don't want to be with me because I haven't been able to be around so much (30 per cent).

Experiment

Set aside 45 minutes to spend making cupcakes with them and observe how I feel and how they behave. Count smiles and note laughter.

Ask at the end whether they enjoyed the activity and how they feel.

What needs to happen first

Get materials in to bake, set a time that doesn't interrupt any other routine they have, prepare aprons and let them know when baking will occur.

Complete experiment and reflect on the result

Spent more than 45 minutes, girls had a ball. Smiles and laughter all round and they said they really loved it at the end and felt really happy. Plus buns were delicious. Agreed to do the same next week. They were a bit sad when it was over and I went to sit down to rest.

Re-rated negative automatic thought to be tested

The kids have grown apart from me, they hate what I've become. They won't want to be with me (40 per cent).

Re-rated alternative thought

I'm just worried they don't want to be with me because I haven't been able to be around so much (60 per cent).

What does this tell me about the way I'm thinking?

I'm still imagining things are blacker than they are but when I test these ideas out, I'm surprised how wrong I can get things. The kids loved being with me. I need to do more experimenting and less thinking things over!

The above behavioural experiment gave Jill access to real-world evidence and from that she was able to challenge further the beliefs that had dominated her depressed state for so long. Behavioural experiments ultimately bring real behavioural change and it is this that should offer the best hope of enabling someone with depression to eventually reclaim their life.

Our journey has, in a way, taken us full circle. We began by helping the client establish whether current behavioural patterns were helping in the long term. The next step included changing that behaviour and noting any improvement in mood. We then elicited negative automatic thoughts that got in the way of effective behavioural change. We helped the client test whether their thinking was accurate and, in doing this, introduced the notion of alternative, less harmful explanations for what might actually be going on. Finally, we tested these new alternative thoughts in the real world. In doing so we helped the client move from a state of inertia and depression to someone more able to problem solve their way out of the cycle of depression. Maintaining wellness and recovery is the next step in treatment, which is covered in detail in Chapter 7. The 'golden rules' for completing a thought record follow.

---

12 golden rules for completing a thought record

1 When does the client complete a thought record? When you notice a negative shift in mood.
2 Situation – needs to be precise and coincide with the time the mood shifted – record where, when, with whom, time and what the client was doing.
3 Mood – choose from the checklist – rarely one mood occurs.
4 The client should pick or decide on the dominant mood.
5 The client must rate their mood (level of distress) out of 0–100.
6 Thought – what went through the client's mind at the moment of mood shift? Where was their attention at that moment? If necessary, practise with the use of imagery.
7 The client must record all thoughts regardless of how superficial, silly or stupid they may think they are.
8 The client should rate their believability of the thought (in other words, how much they believe what they tell themselves is true). The balanced/rational thought should also be rated, e.g. if you believe something 90 per cent, what alternative thoughts make up the other 10 per cent? (It is this that we need to strengthen.)
9 The client chooses a hot thought and draws this down to analyse the evidence.
10 Once evidence is gathered, choose an alternative thought based on all the evidence analysed.
11 Re-rate the original thought in terms of credibility and impact on mood.
12 Ask what the client has learnt from doing the exercise and what they need to do next to build on that learning.

Self-help: supporting the client with more than words

In low-intensity treatment as much emphasis is placed on how the treatment is delivered as on what is actually delivered. Improved access to cognitive behavioural treatments means developing methods of delivery that can maintain the efficacy of the modality while reducing the amount of time the client spends in face-to-face treatment. This has led to a reinvigorated exploration of bibliotherapy as well as the exploitation of new technology in order to find new and novel ways of delivering treatment to more people. Formal CBT always has had, at its heart, a self-help treatment philosophy, therefore it lends itself to being delivered using less one-to-one practitioner contact time.

However, accurately assessing the efficacy of low-intensity self-help treatments has been incredibly challenging because of the wide range of self-help materials available, the numerous potential delivery methods, the unique characteristics of the client population to be treated and the variable degree of practitioner guidance recommended.

Self-help cognitive behavioural treatment can be delivered by books, computers and via the internet. A number of studies reviewing different methods of delivering self-help treatment of depression conclude that a range of delivery methods can be effective but only as long as the self-help material is accompanied by a supportive practitioner (Gellatly et al., 2007; Spek et al., 2007).

If CBT-facilitated self-help can be effectively delivered in fewer sessions or with minimal practitioner contact, this opens up new opportunities in terms of increasing access to more people. The benefits may include:

- The client has speedy access to interventions that work.
- The client can work at their own pace.
- Information materials are always available for easy reference and top-up information.

What becomes crucially important to consider is: how easy the self-help material is to comprehend; how closely it mirrors the original evidence-based formal CBT protocols; how much supportive contact is necessary for each client; how competent the practitioner delivering the programme must be and, finally, who oversees the care in terms of effective clinical governance.

Regardless of the treatment approach used (face-to-face self-help or limited contact facilitated self-help), it is vitally important that the practitioner delivering or facilitating the delivery of treatment has appropriate knowledge of the evidence-based therapy on which self-help treatments are based and is competent to deliver treatment. Practitioner competence has clearly been associated with improved treatment outcomes in formal therapy (Waller, 2009; Webb et al., 2010; Ginzburg et al., 2012). In addition, Keijsers et al. (2000) noted that the client's perception of the practitioner as being self-confident and skilled indicated a fairly moderate and consistent impact on treatment outcome.

If minimal practitioner contact at any level of care is achievable, then this is good for the client and an efficient use of health care resources. Mansell (2007) outlines positive and negative aspects of self-help guides but rightly reminds all practitioners that a self-help approach alone cannot provide the client with the experience of being listened to and understood in a compassionate way. He goes on to highlight that for many clients it is this experience that makes change more likely to happen. Therefore giving the client the option of face-to-face contact with a practitioner skilled in CBT treatment techniques is important at all levels of care.

There are a multitude of self-help materials for the practitioner to choose from; however, one of the most well thought out, comprehensive packages incorporating on-line support and bibliotherapy is the Living Life to the Full programme devised by consultant psychiatrist, Dr Chris Williams. This is a CBT approach designed to help the individual use some of the skills described in this book. It is free to use and includes the impact of reduced activity and how to treat this, how to better understand and deal with negative thinking as well as many more life skills that are designed to improve and enhance the user's mental health and general wellbeing. It has been identified as one of the top four mental health portals by *The Times* newspaper.

Williams has also produced a comprehensive set of structured self-help workbooks for use by people experiencing depression called *Overcoming Depression and Low Mood: A Five Areas Approach* (Williams, 2012a). The material's reading age is approximately 14 years and therefore aims to be jargon-free and accessible. How the person thinks and reacts is addressed, and it dovetails perfectly with the on-line programme. There have also been attempts to empirically test the book's effectiveness (Williams et al., 2013).

Williams has gone on to use the same format to produce a series of self-help workbooks for those suffering from anxiety. *Overcoming Anxiety, Stress and Panic: A Five Areas Approach* (Williams, 2012b) is designed to help individuals suffering mild to moderate levels of anxiety and panic. The reader is encouraged to explore a number of self-help materials best suited to their particular client and circumstances.

Medication

Although cognitive behavioural interventions are increasingly the treatment of choice for depression and anxiety disorders, antidepressant medication is still often prescribed as first-line treatment for depression (Anderson et al., 2008). This is despite current guidelines that assert that psychological therapy, for example, CBT, behavioural therapy/activity scheduling (BT/AS) or interpersonal therapy (IPT) can be as effective as antidepressants for mild depression. Antidepressants are not contraindicated when employing psychological interventions; in fact, it has been shown that combination treatment of CBT and antidepressants is more beneficial for moderate to severe depression. Cognitive behavioural therapy in combination with medications is particularly useful if there are residual symptoms or a higher risk of relapse (e.g. more episodes of depression).

Selective Serotonin Reuptake Inhibitors (SSRIs), for example, fluoxetine, are most commonly prescribed first line as they are generally well tolerated and relatively safe in overdose in comparison to older antidepressants such as tricyclic antidepressants and monoamine oxidase inhibitors, which are usually reserved for second- or third-line treatment in secondary care. Serotonin Noradrenaline Reuptake Inhibitors (SNRIs), for example, venlafaxine, are also quite commonly prescribed in secondary care.

It is most likely that you will encounter clients on SSRIs so it is important that you know some facts about them. SSRIs do the following:

- take at least two weeks to show significant benefit (sometimes longer trials are required);
- only work if taken as prescribed – they do not work on an as required basis;
- may have common side effects of increased anxiety, nausea or stomach upset in the first couple of weeks, which should settle down;
- are not known to be addictive;
- may have a discontinuation syndrome if stopped abruptly (this mimics anxiety);
- should be continued for at least six to nine months following remission to reduce the relapse rate (longer is required if there has been more than one episode of depression);
- are not associated with an increased rate of completed suicide (in fact there is a lower rate of suicide overall) but individuals may react differently.

(Anderson et al., 2008)

The role of psychological wellbeing practitioners with medication

Psychological wellbeing practitioners are not expected to advise on medications, for example, stopping medication or changing doses, but need to be informed about the role of medication so that they can provide support to clients to make informed choices (Richards and Whyte, 2009). It is therefore important to gather information about:

- medication type and dose;
- if medication is taken as prescribed (concordance);
- any potential side effects;
- other over-the-counter medications/alcohol or illicit drug use which may interfere with treatment.

It can be useful to know the evidence base for medications, common side effects and misperceptions about antidepressants in order to help your client make the best decision for them. It is a matter of them being able to weigh up the pros and cons in an informed way. If you have any serious concerns about medications or side effects, you should discuss with your client the following:

- making an urgent GP appointment;
- informing the GP
- informing your supervisor.

The client should always be encouraged to discuss any decisions about medication with their prescribing doctor. It would not be considered ethical or good practice to suggest a client stops their medication to see if they can 'do without it' while undergoing psychological treatment. It would, however, be important to discuss with your client, their GP and your supervisor if you are concerned that medications are being misused, not being taken appropriately or if alcohol or illicit drug use may be interfering with treatment.

Summary

- All of us can experience sadness but clients with clinical depression are those who present with low mood or loss of interest or pleasure and other key symptoms nearly every day for at least two weeks, with a resultant negative impact upon everyday functioning.
- The likelihood of reoccurrence increases with every subsequent episode of depression, therefore successful early intervention is important.
- Depression has a distinct effect on behaviour and thinking, leading to withdrawal and loss of social contact and can lead to a stream of critical, self-derogatory, negative automatic unhelpful thoughts about self, others and life in general.
- The less engaged in life the person suffering depression becomes, the less access they have to rewarding activities and the more time available to concentrate on negative automatic thoughts.
- Assess for specific, recent examples of low mood, detail triggers and physical effects and elicit negative automatic thoughts, changes to behaviour and their effect on the client in the short and long term.
- Use a cross-sectional formulation to plot the links between negative automatic thoughts, emotions, physical sensations and behaviour.
- Feed back the formulation until the practitioner and client agree it is accurate and then explore with the client the utility of current behavioural responses.
- Introduce psycho-education on depression and focus on the role of behaviour and unhelpful thinking styles in maintaining depression.
- Behavioural activation needs to be linked to valued stepped goals and focus on reinstating pleasurable, rewarding activities.
- Thought records are an excellent way of testing existing unhelpful thoughts and also generating alternative, more balanced thoughts.
- Test both possibilities using a series of behavioural experiments.
- It is important to measure progress in terms of the client's clinical outcome measures, level of distress and belief in unhelpful and alternative thoughts.

- Self-help needs to be tailored to the client's needs and resources.
- If progress is limited or the client's mood deteriorates, consider stepping up to formal cognitive behavioural psychotherapy at supervision.
- Medication and psychological treatments can work well together; practitioners need to have a basic knowledge of the evidence base and likely medication-related issues.

Recommended reading

Antony, M.M. and Barlow, D.H. (2010) *Handbook of Assessment and Treatment Planning for Psychological Disorders*, 2nd edn. New York: Guilford Press.

Beck, A.T., Rush, A.J., Shaw, B.F. and Emery, G. (1979) *Cognitive Therapy of Depression*. New York: Guilford Press.

Beck, J.S. (1995) *Cognitive Therapy: Basics and Beyond*. New York: Guilford Press.

Hawton, K., Salkovskis, P.M., Kirk, J. and Clark, D.M. (1989) *Cognitive Behaviour Therapy for Psychiatric Problems: A Practical Guide*. Oxford: Oxford University Press.

Lejuez, C.W., Hopko, D.R., LePage, J.P., Hopko, S.D. and McNeil, D.W. (2001) A brief behavioral activation treatment for depression. *Cognitive and Behavioral Practice*, 8: 164–75.

Martell, C.R., Addis, M.E. and Jacobson, N.S. (2001) *Depression in Context: Strategies for Guided Action*. New York: Norton.

Richards, D. and Whyte, M. (2009) *Reach Out: National Programme Educator Materials to Support the Delivery of Training for Psychological Wellbeing Practitioners Delivering Low Intensity Interventions*, 2nd edn. Rethink Mental Illness. Available at: www.cedar.exeter.ac.uk/iapt/iaptworkbooksandresources (accessed 23 May 2014).

Simmons, J. and Griffiths, R. (2009) *CBT for Beginners*. London: Sage.

Veale, D. and Willson, R. (2007) *Manage Your Mood: Using Behavioural Activation Techniques to Overcome Depression*. London: Robinson Press.

Westbrook, D., Kennerley, H. and Kirk, J. (2011) *An Introduction to Cognitive Behaviour Therapy: Skills and Applications*, 2nd edn. London: Sage.

Williams, C.J. (2012) *Overcoming Depression: A Five Areas Approach*. London: Hodder Arnold.

5   Anxiety

Introduction

This chapter will explore the difference between the normal anxiety response and anxiety as an illness. A brief overview of the main cognitive themes in specific anxiety disorders will be described before focusing on an explanation of what panic disorder is from a cognitive behavioural perspective. We will demonstrate how to treat panic disorder using cognitive behavioural interventions and an illustrative case study. Several client worksheets and information sheets are included to guide treatment. The role of the practitioner in helping clients make informed decisions about their treatment, including medication, is highlighted throughout.

Understanding anxiety

Anxiety is a normal response to threat or danger and a vitally important part of normal human experience. It is the anxiety response that helps us avoid an oncoming car while crossing the road or to respond instantly when confronted with a dangerous life-threatening event. It provides us with an instant physical response to threatening and dangerous situations and ensures that we survive another day. Even in non-life-threatening situations our anxiety response system gears us up to meet the demands or stresses of everyday life (an exceptionally busy period in work, preparing for a high stake exam or performing well at a job interview). In adult learning and education theory it has long been accepted that to effectively learn we require an optimum level of anxiety. Create a learning environment that is boring and unchallenging and the trainee learns little; likewise, make the learning experience too stressful and you generate high levels of anxiety, induce panic and learning capacity reduces. Therefore for human learning to occur, a degree of anxiety is necessary and essential (Yerkes and Dodson, 1908; Csikszentmihalyi, 1975).

However, anxiety can become a mental health problem if the response is exaggerated, lasts more than a few weeks and begins to interfere with daily life. When exaggerated or lasting for long periods of time, anxiety is often associated with apprehension about the future and is often accompanied by very rapid, dramatic physical body changes such as rapid breathing, a fast heartbeat or hot and cold sweats. Anxiety is best thought of as our own personal alarm system and 'body guard', which when activated helps us deal with internal or external sources of threat and stress. Its role is to respond instantly to danger and then check internally and externally for that danger returning (Craske, 2003). It is a sophisticated evolutionary wonder but is highly sensitive and always reacts even if danger is minimal (the 'better safe than sorry' rule). False alarms are common. How many times does someone wonder whether they've locked their car, think about it a bit too long, pick up a threat signal in the form of thoughts about the car being stolen, which then activates anxiety and sends them back to check if their car is still where they left it?

No matter how sophisticated humans become, we still essentially share the same alarm system our ancestors had 80,000 years ago. Anxiety is sometimes referred to as the fight, flight, freeze system and this is very apt. Anxiety prepares us for three possible responses to stress: gearing us up to confront and overcome stress and threats (fight), preparing our body to quickly escape from threatening and potential dangerous situations (flight), and finally preparing our body to remain perfectly still until danger passes (freeze).

Anxiety disorders are common; for example, in a lecture theatre of 100 adult learners on average:

- 1–3 people will suffer from persistent panic attacks;
- 5–11 people will suffer a specific phobia;
- 11–15 people will suffer social anxiety disorder;
- 3–5 people will suffer generalized anxiety disorder (GAD) ;
- 2–3 people will suffer from obsessive compulsive disorder (OCD);
- 7–8 people will suffer a post-traumatic stress disorder (PTSD).

(Overbeek et al., 2001)

The systematic study of all the major anxiety disorders has established a number of common dominant cognitive themes (Clark and Beck, 2010):

- Clients suffering panic disorder appear to misinterpret benign physiological sensations as a sign of imminent catastrophic physical disease or imminent catastrophic mental 'breakdown' such as going crazy or losing control.
- Those suffering agoraphobia link the development of high levels of anxiety with specific situations. These situations are viewed thereafter as threatening and this leads to avoidance. Typical situations include those where escape may be viewed as difficult or where help may be difficult to elicit. Agoraphobia means literally fear of a gathering place (derived from Greek) but can refer to any situation perceived as dangerous.
- Clients with specific phobia associate high levels of anxiety with a specific triggering object or situation. This object or situation is therefore perceived as threatening and avoidance is employed.
- Clients with obsessive compulsive disorder display an overdeveloped sense of responsibility and experience beliefs about possibly harming others.
- Those with generalized anxiety disorder tend to overestimate the dangerousness of situations and underestimate their ability to cope with aversive or unexpected situations. There is an overall intolerance of uncertainty.

- Clients with social anxiety report an avoidance of situations where they perceive they may be negatively evaluated. The individual fears doing or saying something that may be embarrassing, humiliating or breaching social etiquette. This may include looking anxious.
- Those with post-traumatic stress disorder become highly sensitive to physiological sensations related to a real traumatic event. Any reoccurrence of these symptoms provokes flashback memories to the actual traumatic event. The key feature is that the 'here and now' emotional response mimics the actual emotional and physiological response suffered during the trauma.

It is beyond the scope of this text to comprehensively explore all of the major anxiety disorders. In addition, specialist skills are required to treat severe levels of anxiety and more complex anxiety disorders (e.g. post-traumatic stress disorder and generalized anxiety disorder). The competencies required to treat severe or more complex conditions are best acquired through specific (high-intensity) Postgraduate Diploma Cognitive Behavioural Therapy training. However, it is possible to treat less complex anxiety disorders, such as mild to moderate panic disorder and agoraphobia, in routine mental health care using brief interventions and that is what this chapter will concentrate on. The delivery of treatment can be negotiated with the client and may range from very minimal practitioner telephone contact supporting the client's use of self-help material through to negotiated time-limited face-to-face contact with the emphasis on self-help material as the basis of reinforcing what is taught in session.

Regardless of the type of anxiety disorder, a key element of the client's presentation is the tendency to misinterpret benign physiological symptoms as catastrophic (or indicating some warning of impending doom) and an attentional bias towards threat cues from within the client's body or from some external source (McNally and Foa, 1987; Clark et al., 1997). Individuals suffering from anxiety can display a gross aversion to any increase in autonomic arousal (anxiety symptoms) and can scan for signs of danger if they view autonomic arousal as a signal that something is threatening or potentially dangerous. It is this scanning process and the aversion to anxiety that lead the individual to employ strategies designed to control that arousal and avoid the perceived feared consequences (Salkovskis, 1988).

Panic disorder

The anxiety disorder that captures this process most concisely is panic disorder. Out of all the anxiety disorders, panic disorder is often considered the clearest manifestation of human fear (Barlow, 2004). In panic disorder the client suffers recurrent unexpected surges of concentrated fear or intense distress that can last a number of minutes. The increased autonomic arousal can develop out of the blue with no warning or can occur in someone who is already stressed or in response to specific triggers.

Panic symptoms

These include the following:

- palpitations, pounding heart, or increased heart rate;
- sweating;
- trembling or shaking;
- sensations of shortness of breath;
- dry mouth and throat and a feeling of choking;
- chest pain;
- nausea or other gastrointestinal distress;
- feeling dizzy, unsteady, light-headed, or faint;
- over-heating or suffering from chills;
- numbness or tingling sensations;
- derealization (feelings of unreality) or depersonalization (being detached from oneself);
- fear of losing control or 'going insane';
- fear of collapse and/or dying.

The client suffering from panic attacks may also experience a range of other physical sensations such as ringing in the ears, shoulder and neck pain, headache and uncontrollable observable distress, including crying.

Once the acute phase of a panic attack is resolved, the client may experience persistent concern or worry about possible future panic attacks or their consequences (e.g. losing control, having a heart attack or 'going insane'). In response to these alarming symptoms the client may suffer a significant change in behaviour related to the attacks (e.g. engage in behaviours designed to avoid having a future panic attack, such as avoidance of exercise or avoidance of unfamiliar or distant situations).

As one-off panic attacks are common, with community surveys suggesting up to 28 per cent of the general population can experience panic attacks (Wilson et al., 1991), the practitioner needs to ensure during the assessment phase of treatment that the client's symptoms are not due to an isolated one-off incident (panic attack not panic disorder), or a panic attack directly related to the physiological effects of a substance (e.g. withdrawal from alcohol, caffeine use, drug misuse or medication), or a medical condition (e.g. hyperthyroidism – overactive thyroid gland) or cardiac problems.

The question that must be at the forefront of the practitioner's mind during assessment is 'Could these symptoms be better explained by another physical or mental disorder?' For example, do the panic attacks occur only in response to: feared social situations, as in social anxiety disorder; specific phobic objects or situations, as in specific phobia; disturbing intrusive thoughts, as in obsessive-compulsive disorder or reminders of traumatic events, as in post-traumatic stress disorder (APA, 2013)? Because the client's bodily sensations in panic often mimic real physical health difficulties, it is important that the client has been initially assessed by a medical practitioner to rule out any physical cause of symptoms. This is the first rule in treating mental health problems. If there is any doubt, discuss with your supervisor before implementing treatment.

The cognitive behavioural theory of panic disorder suggests that clients who suffer from recurrent panic attacks tend to do so because they interpret particular bodily sensations as an indication that they are suffering from, or are about to suffer, an imminent catastrophic physical or mental illness. The symptoms mentioned above that are misinterpreted as harmful are actually benign (therefore harmless) bodily changes associated with normal stress or anxiety symptoms (e.g. heart palpitations, breathlessness, dizziness). The catastrophic beliefs associated with noticing these changes involve perceiving the sensations as potentially dangerous and a threat to normal physical and mental functioning. This in turn further activates the body's anxiety response system (fight/flight/freeze reaction) and the misinterpreted symptoms escalate, thereby feeding the client's belief that physical or mental breakdown is imminent. The fight, flight, freeze reaction is an excellent response system when the danger is external and real (confronting a vicious dog or fleeing from a burning house) but when the threat is imagined and generated by a thought that is false but credible to the client at the time, it can appear to confirm the client's misinterpretation of danger. As the threatening thoughts are internal, they tend to last longer and escape is difficult.

The situation is further compounded if the panic symptoms occur in, and are then associated with, a particular external situation (such as being on a bus or in a supermarket). The client may then avoid these situations for fear of having another attack and gradually over time their freedom to venture from the safety of their home becomes limited. When this occurs repeatedly, the client may begin to develop phobic avoidance of a number of situations and places for fear of provoking another attack. The client's life can dramatically shut down and agoraphobia develops. Eventually both external, situations and internal sensations or stimuli can provoke a panic attack.

In summary, Clark (1986, 1989 and 1991) suggests that the primary critical event is the person's initial misinterpretation of bodily sensations, caused by stress, anxiety or other sources of increased arousal such as exercise. If interpreted as dangerous, this then creates a heightened state of awareness of these symptoms and a growing sense of apprehension. If these bodily sensations are interpreted as indicating a catastrophic physical or mental event, apprehension increases further, producing even more bodily sensations. This leads to a vicious circle that spirals the individual into a panic attack.

Let us now take a look at a specific client who displays all the typical signs and symptoms associated with panic disorder.

Case example

Clare is a 25-year-old teacher. She is married with two children, aged 4 and 6. Clare is also taking night classes and has recently been promoted. She is Acting Head of the English department of a local comprehensive school. She has found the job rewarding but challenging.

During a recent school inspection she found her workload increased considerably. Over a two-week period she was required to work longer hours and also take more work home. The fortnight was dominated with meetings and ensuring all the staff in her department were up to speed on the criteria of the forthcoming inspection. Clare engrossed herself in work and rose to the challenge. She focused all her attention on getting the job done. The inspection occurred and her department was praised for the standard of work they presented.

On the last day of the inspection her headteacher approached her when she was packing up to leave and suggested that she should seriously consider applying for the permanent post of Head of Department. As she cleared her desk and prepared for a restful and relaxing weekend her attention shifted onto her chest. She felt her heart flutter for just a second. She stopped and focused on it more, thinking the sensation strange. As she focused more on her body, she also noticed that her breathing was 'a bit off'.

She tried to take a deep breath and fill her lungs, however, the more she tried, the less she felt comfortable. By now, she started to feel slightly hot and the fluttering in her chest began to increase. She sat down and tried to gain control of her breathing, however, the more she tried, the more difficult breathing became. Then she began to contemplate that something was wrong with her physically. As she grew more and more focused on these changes in her body, her thinking turned to her father who had died of a heart attack, aged 56, two years earlier.

Clare now began to notice an increase in sweating and felt tense and shaky. The fluttering in her chest turned to tightness and she was now gasping for breath. The more she tried to regain control over her body, the more she failed and the more convinced she was that she was suffering a heart attack. Instead of driving home she called her husband who took her straight to her GP's open surgery. The symptoms settled once she arrived but her GP organized tests and reassured her that they felt sure it was just 'stress'.

Over the next two weeks the tests indicated nothing abnormal and Clare returned to work. However, one morning while running to catch a bus she noticed, as she settled into her seat, that her heart began to flutter again. She immediately found it difficult to breathe and this time also found it difficult to swallow. Again the more she tried to control the changes in her body, the more she felt she was losing control. She got off the bus at the next stop and walked slowly home and lay down. She rang her husband at work and talked to him for over 20 minutes. The symptoms slowly subsided and she was left feeling exhausted and dozed off to sleep.

By the time Clare arrived for treatment she was suffering three to four panic attacks per week, she was off work and called her husband four to five times per day. She kept her mobile phone and water by her side and had given up most activities for fear of another attack.

Consider for a moment if Clare had noticed the initial flutter of her heart and instead thought to herself that she was excited to be offered a promotion. What would have possibly happened then? Beck (1975) stated it is the interpretation of the event that is important, rather than the actual event itself. Clare interpreted the heart flutter as having a negative significant meaning for her – impending heart attack (probably because she lost her dad to a heart attack) – which then started a cascade of negative emotions and unhelpful behaviours.

As for most anxiety disorders, Clare's symptoms presented her and her practitioner with a puzzle. Despite numerous panic attacks, which were frightening and stressful, she had not gone on to suffer a heart attack. Yet the thought dominated most of her thinking. Common sense should tell us that perhaps after five to ten attacks Clare should learn that they are uncomfortable but harmless. Instead, the thought 'I'm going to have a heart attack' grew in strength, it did not diminish.

The reason for this is now well established. Clark (1991) describes a number of processes that prevent learning when individuals suffer anxiety. These maintaining factors effectively block learning and maintain unhelpful thinking. In panic disorder they include:

- safety-seeking behaviour
- attention bias.

Safety-seeking behaviours

Safety-seeking behaviours are protective behaviours employed in order to prevent or reduce the effect of a feared catastrophe (Salkovskis, 1991). They may work incredibly well in the short term but at a cost of long-term learning (Gelder, 1997; Salkovskis et al., 1999). While Clare relies on sitting down, not exercising, ensuring her mobile phone is charged and with her, and keeping water by her side, she temporarily reduces the impact of her symptoms in the short term. However, these very measures keep her attention squarely fixated on having another panic attack and also prevent her from learning that a panic attack, although distressing, is harmless.

Three main types of safety behaviour have been identified in panic and other anxiety disorders. These are:

- direct avoidance of situations;
- escape from situations;
- subtle avoidance while in the anxiety-provoking situation.

(Salkovskis et al., 1996)

Safety behaviours are best viewed (and conveyed to clients) as the client's attempt to avoid sensations or situations previously linked to panic symptoms, which are therefore understandable given the client's belief of what is happening to them. This type of behaviour, following an initial panic attack, may be viewed by the client as a rational response to prevent the perceived catastrophic disaster (e.g. a heart attack or impending insanity).

Safety behaviours may include gross avoidance of situations associated with panic symptoms or situations where the client anticipated an impending panic attack (e.g. Clare avoiding the bus). It may also include more subtle forms of safety behaviours such as having assistance instantly available (an ever-charged mobile phone) or the use of water or a handheld fan to quell a dry mouth and prevent sweating.

Other forms of safety behaviour include trying to actively curtail any activity that might provoke internal bodily sensations which may be different but sufficiently similar to the symptoms suffered during a panic attack. This may include avoiding any activity that might provoke feared internal bodily changes, for example exercise to avoid increased heart rate or avoiding entering a warm room to avoid feeling too hot. Some people take more alcohol, which may initially reduce anxiety symptoms but can provoke bodily sensations similar to anxiety the following day.

It is important to note if the client has been prescribed any sedative medications, for example, diazepam, or is using any over-the-counter remedies or illicit drugs, for example, cannabis, to manage their anxiety. These can be potent safety behaviours. Removal of the unpleasant feeling (anxiety) by use of safety behaviour, for example, diazepam, results in this behaviour being strongly associated with improvement in symptoms in the short term, and therefore makes it more likely to occur again.

Focus of attention (attentional bias)

Once Clare's first attack occurred it was sufficiently traumatic and terrifying that even after she got the all-clear from her GP, she had already began to monitor her body intensely for signs of another attack. The body's aim is to be prepared should it happen again. However, once we begin to scan our bodies for any internal changes, we may begin to notice an array of normal physiological sensations that have been there a lifetime, but are now viewed as potentially threatening and further indication of imminent physical catastrophe or total mental breakdown.

Essentially the initial catastrophic misinterpretation of bodily sensations (if terrifying for the client) may produce heightened awareness (hypervigilance) for future internal bodily changes. As our body is in a constant state of change, persistent scanning by the client sets up a vicious cycle of looking for and finding bodily sensations. If these new-found bodily changes are further misinterpreted as a sign of imminent danger, this may increase physical arousal and further reinforces to the client that their catastrophic appraisal is correct.

Let's return to a phenomenon we looked in Chapter 2. Try this experiment: concentrate on your swallow reflex and then try to swallow three times in rapid succession. What do you notice? Something you have done automatically up to this point in time, and which has not been noticed by you, now feels strange and abnormal. The more we scan our bodies, the more we notice physiological processes. The more we interfere with normal benign bodily processes, the more symptoms we perceive.

Any physiological change that resembles or replicates the horrible symptoms first experienced by Clare now may be perceived as dangerous and a warning sign of a further attack. Clients with high levels of anxiety will selectively attend to internal bodily (or somatic) changes. The catastrophic misreading of these bodily sensations increases the client's level of anxiety and so fear escalates. Clare may notice that escalation of symptoms and then interpret them as confirmation that another 'attack' is returning. This then convinces Clare to employ safety-seeking behaviours in order to quell her distress and so the problem continues.

Ultimately the feared appraisal of what the body sensations mean results in the person acting in such a way as to prevent the worst happening (Salkovskis, 1991). Taylor (2000) described how specific bodily sensations could be misinterpreted and we present a few examples in Table 5.1. However, practitioners need to be cautious about assuming a specific symptom means anything to the client. Let the client tell the practitioner what they make of their symptoms. The practitioner will also have to consider the cross-cultural differences in the perception of bodily sensations during emotion (Philippot and Rime, 1997).

Table 5.1   Bodily sensations and common associated cognitive themes

Bodily sensations	Possible cognitive appraisal
Dizziness/unsteadiness	'I'll lose control, pass out, faint'
Palpitations and chest/heart symptoms	'I'm having a heart attack'
Difficultly getting a breath/over-breathing	'I'll stop breathing, suffer respiratory arrest, collapse and die'
Dry mouth/difficulty swallowing	'My throat will close over and I'll suffocate'
Pins and needles in extremities	'I'm having a stroke'
Butterflies in stomach/nausea	'I'm going to vomit now'
Muscle tension/trembling	'I'm losing control of my body and I can't stop it, therefore I could do anything, go berserk'
Losing focus of attention	'I'm losing my mind, I'm going insane'
Sense of unreality/perceptual disturbance	'I'm losing a grip on reality. I'm permanently losing my mind'

The overall aim of treatment is therefore to help the client realize what is happening to their body and help them to identify that continuing to scan for more evidence of serious physical illness is actually maintaining their symptoms. In the case example above, we need to help Clare recognize her negative automatic thoughts about dying and give her the tools to begin to modify faulty thinking. As safety behaviours effectively block Clare from learning that her symptoms are *not* a sign of catastrophic danger, the practitioner will need to bring Clare's attention to this through effective questioning.

The process begins by the practitioner inviting Clare along to an interview or arranging an interview at Clare's home or via telephone. A home visit may be necessary if the client is unable to leave home due to panic attacks (agoraphobia). An eventual home visit is an excellent idea anyway as it allows the practitioner to fully assess the impact of panic symptoms on the client's day-to-day functioning.

Whether carried out in a clinic setting, the client's home or via telephone, the initial assessment will follow the process laid out in Chapter 2. Begin by eliciting a comprehensive problem list then draw down those problems using a cognitive behavioural maintenance model (eliciting specific recent situations when a panic attack has occurred and analysing the situation in minute detail focusing on the trigger, physiological changes, subjective description of mood and current behavioural responses).

As you progress through each problematic situation you will be attempting to understand what the client's current thoughts are, what is going on in her body and what she currently does that helps her cope with the symptoms of panic. Even at this very early assessment stage, you should be analysing the client's thoughts about whether her current methods of responding work for her, both in the short and the long term. For example, you could ask, 'Have you ever used any methods that help reduce or remove the symptoms and has it worked for a substantial period of time?' The aim is to bring the client's attention to the short-term relief offered by avoidance.

An important factor to be aware of is that some clients who are disabled with panic learn how to avoid any stimulation which might provoke bodily sensations that produce catastrophic negative automatic thoughts. The client may be symptom-free in terms of panic attacks but trapped in a cycle of avoidance.

If this is the case, you can use information from previous panic attacks or simply ask the client to imagine they were going to engage in avoided activities, such as going out alone or walking to and entering a busy supermarket. Asking a phobic, avoidant client to even imagine breaking out of their illness-induced prison may provoke anxiety symptoms which can then be mapped on to the cognitive behavioural generic maintenance model.

Another reason that the client may be symptom-free is if they are using medication or drugs such as sedative medication (e.g. diazepam) to prevent panic attacks. This is important to establish at assessment and discuss with your supervisor or the client's medical practitioner. As already mentioned, the use of medication like diazepam can be a potent safety behaviour and can interfere with treatment.

Case example continued

Clare's problem list consists of the following:

- worry I'll stop breathing or that I'll collapse and die of a heart attack when I feel my heart rate increase;
- heart races fast when I leave the house alone therefore I can't leave the house alone;
- gasping for air when I leave the house alone therefore I can't leave the house alone;
- need to have a supply of cold drinking water within arm's reach to cool me down;.
- have to have mobile charged and with me at all times to call for help;
- ring husband four to five times per day when I'm at home and he is at work;
- check my pulse on wakening, late morning and early afternoon to check it is not racing;
- have a paper bag with me at all times in case I get out of breath (heard this works after seeing it used on TV programme *Casualty*) but never have used it as it seems too frightening to try it by myself but I like it nearby just in case;
- have stopped going to work because I can't leave the house alone;
- can't leave home without husband;
- can't travel on bus (even with husband) for fear of having a heart attack.

Once a problem list has been completed, then the practitioner and client can think about drawing down a specific problem area and investigating it more thoroughly using a cognitive behavioural analysis. Clare selects her inability to travel on the bus as a major disability; this is drawn down and Clare and her practitioner begin to analyse what created the problem. As Clare is no longer travelling by bus, they select the event which sparked off the fear (Clare's last bus journey). Careful questioning focusing on precisely what caused Clare to avoid travelling by bus is necessary: questioning that is focused and purposeful:

Practitioner (P): *What had you been doing just before the panic attack on the bus?*

Clare (C): *I was rushing to catch it and eventually I did. I sat down and began to notice my heart wildly pumping like it was trying to burst out of my chest.*

P: *What was going through your mind when you noticed your heart racing?*

C: *Well, I thought there was definitely something very wrong – why was my body feeling like it was about to burst? I was feeling awful!*

P: *What did you make of it? Tell me more about what you imagined was happening.*

C: *It happened so quickly I thought I was very ill and I needed to get off that bus.*

P: *What was the worst thing that you imagined might happen if you had stayed on the bus?*

C: *I thought my heart was going to explode, then I was convinced I wasn't getting in enough air. I was just waiting to collapse and die at any moment (tearful).*

P: *I can see from your reaction that it was a very difficult situation for you. I notice you are a bit tearful now. Could I ask what is going through your mind right now, here in the office?*

(An emotional shift is a good opportunity to empathically establish the driving thought/image.)

C: *I'm just remembering how awful it was and I'm having that feeling again. I can't get enough air (client tries a large sigh).*

P: *That's perhaps an interesting observation we could note. Even when you think about that time on the bus (sitting here in my office), your body seems to react or respond again. We could just note that and come back to it. Are you OK to go on?*

C: *Yes.*

P: *When you had that thought that you were having a heart attack and were going to die on the bus, then could I ask how much do you think you believed that at the time out of 100 per cent, with 100 per cent meaning you were absolutely certain?*

C: *I was pretty sure or I wouldn't have got off the bus or rang Bill. I would have said 90 per cent.*

P: *OK, so there you are on the bus and you notice your heart speed up and you notice that it seems you can't get enough air into your lungs and you begin to have the thought that you are having a heart attack and are going to die and this seems real at 90 per cent credible. Could I ask, when you began thinking that, did you notice any further changes in your body?*

(Notice the practitioner uses present tense – this can make the discussion of the situation feel more real and may help get the client back in the situation and therefore able to access more readily thoughts, feelings and behaviours.)

C: *I tried to take deep breaths, I felt my heart pounding even more, pins and needles in both hands, I felt hot and sweaty, dizzy and when I got up to leave, my legs were shaking like they were about to give in.*

P: *So let me see if I can get all that – you tried to take deeper breaths, you felt your heart beat harder, pins and needles, hot and sweaty and dizzy and when you tried to get up to walk from the bus, you noticed your legs shaking. What effect did these changes have on the belief you were dying?*

C: *Well, by then I was sure of it – that's the point I rang Bill and left the bus.*

P: *So these changes really confirmed that you were having a heart attack and were going to die. Could I ask what word would best describe your mood or your feelings at that moment?*

C: *I was terrified, absolutely petrified, in fact.*

P: *When you were absolutely petrified, were you aware of any thoughts or images in your head? Sometimes people think in pictures.*

C: *Yes. I had this picture in my head – I was lying on the ground dying and Bill was there. It was awful.*

(During anxiety, people can often experience disturbing images which represent their worst fears.)

P: *So that was a really distressing image – Bill being there with you lying on the ground. You've already mentioned you rang Bill – can you tell me a bit more about what happened at that time, did you do anything else?*

C: *I rang Bill to come and get me immediately and asked the bus driver to just stop the bus. I told him I felt sick. I then just steadied myself against a wall and waited for Bill.*

P: *So you got off the bus and phoned Bill to come immediately. How did that work for you?*

C: *Yes, well even the cold air seemed to help and leaning against the wall also helped a bit but my body didn't really settle down until I got home and lay down.*

P: *OK, so what you did seemed to work then, how about now? What is it like when you think about getting the bus again?*

C: *Oh, I can't even think about it for too long or I feel an attack come on even before I leave the house. Just like I felt a bit here today, describing this earlier, but much worse. I can't even think about getting back on a bus.*

P: *So getting off the bus seemed to help immediately but in the longer term you haven't been able to get on a bus since.*

The practitioner then summarizes all of the above to ensure they have an accurate understanding of the incident. Notice that the practitioner constantly feeds back and paraphrases throughout the interview to make sure that they have got a good understanding of what specifically happened.

While questioning, the practitioner maps out the feedback the client gives onto a generic maintenance cycle. Note that the practitioner's questioning is guided by the generic maintenance model (Figure 5.1).

This maintenance model is useful in a number of ways, as it highlights:

- the links between the trigger and the client's appraisal of the trigger;
- the impact of thinking on emotion and bodily changes;

- the reverse impact of increasing emotion and bodily changes reinforcing and strengthening the client's negative automatic thoughts (a classic vicious cycle or feedback loop);
- the client's behavioural responses to escalating catastrophic thinking, negative emotion and seemingly overwhelming bodily symptoms;
- the impact of the client's behavioural response on how they feel in the short term;
- the realization that although those safety or protective behaviours work in the short term they promote avoidance or withdrawal behaviours that reduce the individual's life and block learning (i.e. testing out the credibility of the negative automatic thoughts).

The cognitive behavioural generic maintenance model captures the links between trigger, thinking, mood, physiology and the role of safety behaviours. It also brings the client's and practitioner's attention to the 'workability' of current safety behaviours in terms of their short-term and long-term consequences. The

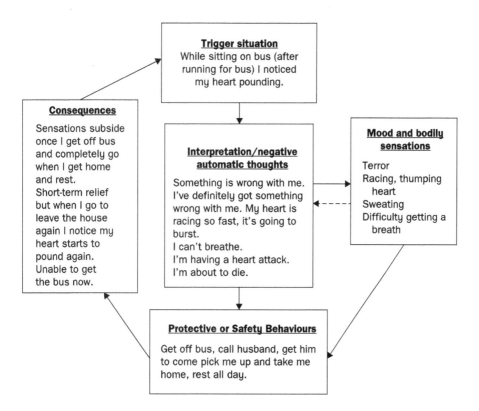

Figure 5.1 Generic maintenance model

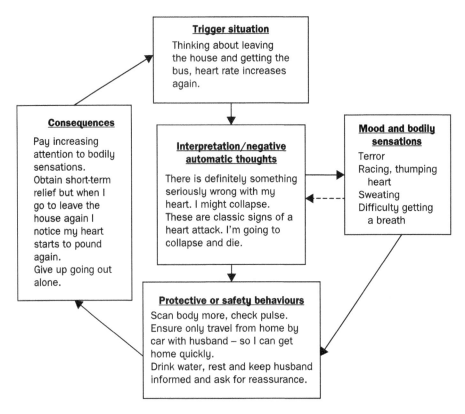

Figure 5.2   Generic maintenance model example 1

practitioner can then plot other situations onto the generic maintenance model (see Figures 5.2 and 5.3).

These examples give the practitioner and the client a very clear outline of what is actually happening and highlight the links between triggers, apprehensive thinking, changes to anxiety, how they are misinterpreted and the client's reactions to those catastrophic predictions. The practitioner can bring the client's attention to the fact that by avoiding or trying to control or stop the anxiety, the client prevents testing out the negative automatic beliefs and then remains convinced that she has repeatedly just about cheated or escaped death by seconds.

The practitioner now starts to bring the client's attention to the fact that the use of safety behaviours is not merely a side effect of distressing thoughts, it is in fact a very powerful maintaining factor in the client's condition. In addition, through the practitioner and client drawing out a number of maintenance cycles we can bring the client's attention to the realization that, although the triggering situations are different, the negative appraisal remains the same – 'I'm going to have a heart attack and die.'

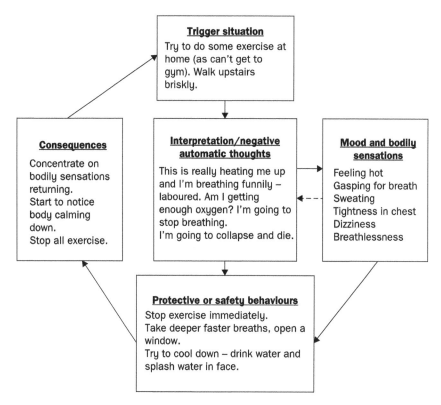

Figure 5.3   Generic maintenance model example 2

These examples act as a series of 'cross-sectional formulations'. They don't just describe what happens to the client, they begin to explain the relationship between different components of the problem. The arrows in the model are equally as important as the description of the symptoms; it is the arrows that explain the connections. The client may come to treatment with just an overwhelming awareness of their emotions. The act of deconstructing an incident where a panic attack has occurred into specific components (some of which are amenable to change) can have an incredibly reassuring effect that treatment might work.

These cognitive behavioural maintenance cycles are fed back to the client and checked for accuracy and then used to demonstrate the importance of negative catastrophic predictions, and the client's use of particular behavioural strategies in maintaining the problem. The client and practitioner then jointly investigate how those maintaining patterns of current thinking and behaviour can be adjusted. If the client accepts they are trapped in the type of cognitive and behavioural cycles described above, then the next questions must be: How could we break out of these patterns? What is it the client and practitioner need to understand and then test?

This brings us to a discussion on the client's goals for therapy. Early in treatment Clare identified her longer-term goal as wanting to return to work. Her medium-term goals were to take the children for a walk and resume being able to eat out once a week with her husband. Clare also identified short-term goals of travelling independently on a bus, travelling independently to treatment appointments, going to the corner shop near to her home unaccompanied, taking exercise and going to the supermarket again.

We can compare her current reactions to her problems associated with believing she is going to die and discuss how her current behavioural reaction to these ideas, of heart attacks and dying, are the behaviours that prevent her carrying on with a normal life and returning to travelling on the bus and going shopping, and so on.

This discussion then should move on to how we might start to initiate previously rewarding behaviours. What would we need to test? As the behaviours are an attempt to prevent the thought that the client is vulnerable to a heart attack, then this thought needs to be further tested. If testing a thought is to be viable, then the client needs their attention drawn to other possible explanations for the rapid rise in autonomic arousal, rather than the one strongly held now about having a catastrophic cardiac event and dying.

The creation of an alternative explanation begins by first ascertaining the client's knowledge about heart disease, heart attacks and panic attacks (or going crazy and mental illness for those clients who predict insanity when they panic). The practitioner should try to understand if there are any gaps in the client's understanding about the physical or mental catastrophe they predict (e.g. heart disease, schizophrenia, etc.). The client and practitioner can then begin to help the client fill in those gaps with good quality, accurate information. The practitioner needs to source and assign clear and readable information on what a panic attack is and how easy it may be for someone to misinterpret the sensations as a sign of imminent physical or mental ill health.

If the client's medical practitioner has clearly not diagnosed heart disease or some severe form of mental illness, the client's continued scepticism of medical tests and investigations needs to be explored. Assess the client's existing knowledge about panic attacks and heart disease (or mental illness).

Treatment

Psycho-education

As mentioned already, the first task in formal treatment is to establish what the client already understands about the nature and maintenance of anxiety and their current knowledge of their feared catastrophic predictions. In panic disorder the feared consequences of remaining in a high state of anxiety broadly consist of two themes: suffering some imminent catastrophic physical illness (heart attack, stroke, respiratory arrest, etc.) or imminent catastrophic loss of control mentally (development of schizophrenia, loss of sanity, or going crazy, etc.). Access to the client's negative automatic thinking allows access to their catastrophic predictions. If the client is aware of anxiety's fight, flight, freeze response, then the practitioner can capitalize on this and bring the client's attention to how their symptoms may actually be an anxiety response.

The practitioner must appreciate that even if the client can see that their catastrophic predictions are irrational and that there is an alternative belief – a stress and anxiety explanation – this will have little impact on behaviour change until the client actually tests out both explanations experientially. If the client is fairly fixed on one catastrophic explanation for their symptoms, then the practitioner's first step is to teach the client that anxiety is a normal reaction whenever we feel threatened. The client needs to know that mild and moderate anxiety feelings are useful and prepare us for challenges or are protective and allow a rapid response to occur in really dangerous situations when our wellbeing is truly under threat.

The practitioner could use examples of when the client's anxiety system responded in the past (driving test, exam, avoiding getting bitten by a dog, etc.). The practitioner can then begin an explanation of the body's natural ability to prepare to fight off danger, run (or flee) from it, or freeze until the threat subsides. Clients are informed this is an evolutionary response that has generally been very adaptive and is an excellent response whenever we are confronted with a real external threat. It is protective, not harmful. The client needs to know that the only problem with the system is that it is our only defence against all threats.

The practitioner explains that as humans we do not have to be physically in a real threatening situation to feel fear; as humans we only need to imagine or think about a threat and the system is activated. This tendency for our bodies having an anxiety response to false alarms is the price we humans pay for having a very vivid imagination. This can be explained using an imaginary example. Ask the client to imagine that they are woken by a loud bang at 3.00 am. What might they make of it? If they jump to the conclusion that there is a burglar in the house, what might they feel? If the belief seems real at that time, what bodily sensations might they notice? What might they then do? Going down and confronting the imagined burglar is a 'fight' response, calling for help or planning your escape from the house is the 'flight' response and finally pulling the duvet up over your head and waiting for the burglar to go is the 'freeze' response. Now remind the client that at this stage there is no burglar, there is just the thought that there is a burglar.

The idea that there is a burglar is generated in the client's head. However, even an imagined burglar can instantly fire off the fight, flight, freeze response. It prepares us for action in order to protect us. Now ask the client to imagine that shortly after the loud bang the client hears their cat meow and they suddenly remember they hadn't let the cat out for the night. What new thought arrives? What happens to their fight, flight, freeze reaction in response to this new thought?

The next step is to take each of the symptoms presented by the client and explore its purpose in terms of our fight, flight or freeze response. This is best done by engaging the client and asking questions rather than didactically lecturing. The following explanation is only one suggested way in which the practitioner could explain the fight, flight, freeze anxiety response to a client.

When we come across either real danger or perceived or imagined danger, our body will prepare itself for some form of physical action. Unsurprisingly, this is called the fight, flight, freeze response. When this occurs, we may notice a number of physical changes which can include some or all of the following (see also Figure 5.4):

• butterflies in the stomach, nausea
• increased startle response
• shortness of breath
• palpitations or raised heart rate
• light-headedness, dizziness, feeling faint
• urge to go to the toilet
• sweating
• dry mouth, difficulty swallowing
• tense muscles (including muscles in legs, chest, neck and shoulders)
• churning stomach
• muscle tremors.

If we are responding to a real, external, threatening situation or trigger, then once that triggering event is over, or the situation has been avoided, we will report an easing of these symptoms, and the body will very quickly return to a state of rest.

Again the practitioner can use real examples of any previous actual threatening situations the client has experienced to emphasize the useful role anxiety plays in preparing us for threat. Then the practitioner returns to anxiety symptoms generated when the threat is perceived as real (e.g. a false alarm situation such as imagining a rapid pulse is a sign of heart disease or racing thoughts a sign of madness). Explore with the client that although they thought they were going to suffer some major catastrophic physical or mental breakdown, what actually happened? Also explore the following: if anyone held the beliefs they hold as strongly as they do when suffering high levels of anxiety, how might others feel as a result of this? Normalize their reaction in terms of their response being understandable, given their excessive and relentless focus on the symptoms and the (mistaken) conclusions they jump to. It can be useful to use analogies such as an alarm system that is designed to alert us to burglars or potential attackers being set off by a gust of wind. There is no imminent danger from the gust of wind, but the alarm sounding is still frightening. Should we continue to behave as if there is an attacker? What should we do about the alarm's sensitivity?

Our own protective fight, flight, freeze 'alarm' mechanism can become a perceived source of threat itself. When this happens, the client is effectively

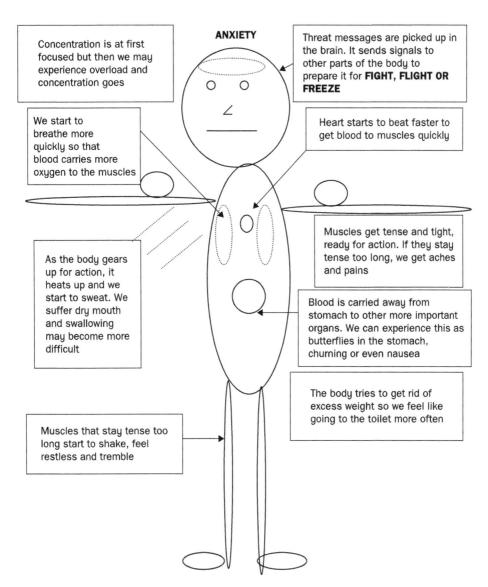

Concentration is at first focused but then we may experience overload and concentration goes

ANXIETY

Threat messages are picked up in the brain. It sends signals to other parts of the body to prepare it for **FIGHT, FLIGHT OR FREEZE**

We start to breathe more quickly so that blood carries more oxygen to the muscles

Heart starts to beat faster to get blood to muscles quickly

As the body gears up for action, it heats up and we start to sweat. We suffer dry mouth and swallowing may become more difficult

Muscles get tense and tight, ready for action. If they stay tense too long, we get aches and pains

Blood is carried away from stomach to other more important organs. We can experience this as butterflies in the stomach, churning or even nausea

The body tries to get rid of excess weight so we feel like going to the toilet more often

Muscles that stay tense too long start to shake, feel restless and tremble

The above response is harmless and is designed to FIGHT off danger or helps us escape from danger (FLIGHT) or stay perfectly still and allow danger to pass (FREEZE). This is very helpful if the danger is external, i.e. a savage dog or a mugger. However, if the fear is imagined or simply a frightening thought, the system may stay 'switched on' too long and lead to stress, severe anxiety or even panic. These bodily sensations may then be mistakenly perceived as a source of danger.

Figure 5.4 Physical effects of anxiety disorders

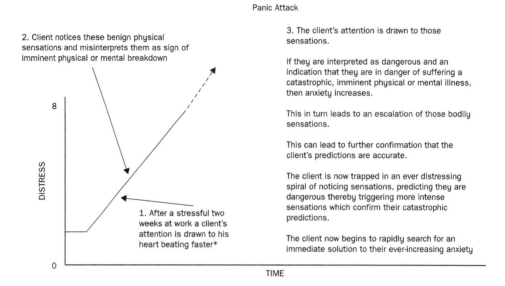

Panic Attack

2. Client notices these benign physical sensations and misinterprets them as sign of imminent physical or mental breakdown

3. The client's attention is drawn to those sensations.

If they are interpreted as dangerous and an indication that they are in danger of suffering a catastrophic, imminent physical or mental illness, then anxiety increases.

This in turn leads to an escalation of those bodily sensations.

This can lead to further confirmation that the client's predictions are accurate.

The client is now trapped in an ever distressing spiral of noticing sensations, predicting they are dangerous thereby triggering more intense sensations which confirm their catastrophic predictions.

1. After a stressful two weeks at work a client's attention is drawn to his heart beating faster*

The client now begins to rapidly search for an immediate solution to their ever-increasing anxiety

DISTRESS

TIME

* alternatively the client might notice a sense of detachment or thoughts racing and perceive they are experiencing some kind of catastrophic mental 'breakdown'

Figure 5.5 The panic trap

trapped in a cycle of fear and anxiety. We are left with a situation where the fear is real but the danger isn't (see Figure 5.5).

A client information sheet on bodily changes during stress can be used (see Appendix 4) that explains how our own protective fight, flight, freeze 'alarm' mechanism can become a perceived source of threat itself.

The practitioner can go over the explanation in session with the client and practitioner both reading sections of the sheet and then discussing it, verbally drawing on client examples. This ensures that both the practitioner and client both agree on the meaning of the information. In addition, it can be assigned as client homework.

If the information is assigned for homework, then the practitioner and client should agree the precise times the sheet could be read and what main points should be considered after reading the information sheet and both client and practitioner should set questions that the client can ponder and answer once the sheet has been read. The aim is to ensure that the client understands the information and that both understand and agree what it means in terms of the client's problems.

Many client self-help resources are available for the practitioner to suggest, reinforcing the message that panic may be distressing but ultimately harmless. Two excellent self-help examples are the National Health Service IAPT booklet, *Coping with Panic* (Young et al., 2011) or the equally excellent Northumberland, Tyne and Wear NHS Trust guide, *Panic: A Self Help Guide* (Maunder and Cameron, 2013).

Anxiety diary

Once the client and practitioner have agreed an alternative possible explanation, (high levels of anxiety versus major catastrophic imminent illness), the client can then track future attacks using an anxiety diary (see Figure 5.6). This will enable the client and practitioner to monitor specific trigger situations, their physical symptoms, their appraisals or beliefs about what is happening and the actions they take when confronted with anxiety. Clare's completed example of an anxiety diary is shown in Figure 5.7.

Clare's anxiety diary shows that she is beginning to identify the internal triggers and indicates that she is aware of her immediate catastrophic negative automatic thoughts. It also highlights that she is at least beginning to consider an alternative explanation (this is anxiety and not early warning signs of an imminent heart attack). This indicates that psycho-education has been helpful in generating an alternative perspective.

It is important to note that simply bringing the client's attention to the possibility of an alternative, non-catastrophic explanation is not sufficient in itself to effect dramatic improvement in panic symptoms and associated avoidant behaviour. However, offering a credible alternative explanation can act as a springboard into discussing how the practitioner and the client can now test which explanation is more valid. One suggestion is that the practitioner brings the client's attention once again to the role of safety behaviours in blocking learning. When the client engages in safety behaviours, they cannot effectively test whether their frightening negative predictions are accurate or not.

The practitioner can revisit the list of all the client's safety behaviours including gross avoidance and more subtle forms of avoidance, such as having a charged

Date/Time Situation	Changes in body	What you thought was happening	Is there another explanation for what is happening?	What did you do immediately?	Did it help?
	Palpitations, pounding heart, or increased heart rate, sweating, trembling or shaking, shortness of breath, dry mouth and throat and a feeling of choking, chest pain, nausea or stomach churning, feeling dizzy, unsteady, light-headed, or faint, over-heating or suffering from chills, numbness or tingling sensations, feelings of unreality being detached from oneself.	How much did you believe this at the time? 0 = not at all 100 = totally	How much did you believe this at the time? 0 = not at all 100 = totally		

Figure 5.6 Anxiety diary

Date/Time Situation	Changes in body	What you thought was happening	Is there another explanation for what is happening?	What did you do immediately?	Did it help?
2.00 pm making bed	Breathless Heart pounding	Can't get enough air heart is stressed I'm going to pass out or have a heart attack if I go on 70%	This could be me just noticing these bodily changes, they might be my harmless fight, flight, freeze response 30%	Stopped making bed and lay down	Yes, it passed but I was frightened to do anything for the rest of the day – lay and rested.
	Palpitations, pounding heart, or increased heart rate, sweating, trembling or shaking, shortness of breath, dry mouth and throat and a feeling of choking, chest pain, nausea or stomach churning, feeling dizzy, unsteady, light-headed, or faint, over-heating or suffering from chills, numbness or tingling sensations, feelings of unreality being detached from oneself.	How much did you believe this at the time? 0 = not at all 100 = totally	How much did you believe this at the time? 0 = not at all 100 = totally		

Figure 5.7   Clare's anxiety diary

mobile close by or a bottle of water at hand in order to counter the fear of being alone with no one to help or nothing to counter a dry mouth. The usefulness of these can be discussed in terms of what they each do to prevent the client testing their catastrophic predictions. This could be thought of as interrogating the client's safety behaviours. Remember this is best done by the client and practitioner, never by the practitioner alone.

Interrogating the effectiveness of current strategies employed (the workability criteria)

Once a list of all safety behaviours is constructed, then ask the client to slowly, step by step, analyse each safety behaviour, focusing on the effectiveness of each method. Acknowledge that safety behaviours are completely understandable given the client's current beliefs. However, we also then focus on whether the safety behaviour has brought real and lasting relief or temporary relief without any clear additional information on the actual dangerousness of the situation.

By using the workability criteria (does your current response really work at permanently quelling anxiety?) we can ask clients then to consider trying new approaches, other than those that both of you agree do not seem to work. The client can be asked, 'What have you done not to be here?' It is important that the practitioner reinforces that the client has actually worked very hard at dealing

with their problems so far, but it's also important to guide the client to the conclusion that although escape and avoidant behaviour are totally understandable, in
the end, these strategies do not seem to bring lasting relief.

The client is then invited to join with the practitioner in considering experimenting with alternative strategies rather than continuing to employ strategies
that do not seem to work in the long term. The client's ability to really scrutinize
whether all safety behaviours work or not is an exercise that will pay dividends in
the long term when clients may be inclined to revert to old strategies as treatment
progresses. Old tried and tested methods are difficult to leave behind, especially
when they work in the short term. The practitioner must always remember that a
life organized around avoidance is at least organized and therefore reverting to
old avoidant behaviour is not resistance, just a desire to return to the familiar. The
practitioner can then quickly review with the client whether any old avoidant
strategies are really worth pursuing. Once the futility of safety behaviours is
established, then the client and practitioner are in a position to explore new
approaches designed to test the client's negative predictions.

Cognitive behavioural interventions offer two highly effective anxiety treatment methods. The practitioner can ask the client to agree to provoke the anxiety
response (e.g. by going to an avoided place or putting up with a rise in anxiety)
and remain in a state of anxiety and simply notice what happens to their level of
anxiety if they do not use safety behaviours (exposure). Or the client and practitioner can elicit specific negative catastrophic predictions and systematically test
those beliefs (behavioural experiments).

An exposure-based approach

Behaviour therapy asserts that if we approach a situation or provoke sensations
that are fearful but ultimately harmless or benign, our body will adjust or acclimatize to the situation automatically (habituate to that situation or sensations). The
client is informed that anxiety is 'self-limiting' and will reduce automatically if we
just stay put in the fearful situation long enough (Rosqvist, 2005).

We prepare the client by explaining that habituation is a natural adjustment
response and by highlighting other common examples of habituation (e.g. the
initial presence of strange or annoying noises when we move into a new home
which then cease to be a problem once we've acclimatized ourselves to our new
surroundings). The practitioner can explain that by being prepared to experience
the sensations of anxiety often enough and for long enough (without the use of
safety behaviours), then anxiety will initially increase, then peak and then fall. To
do this we need to establish with the client a method to measure levels of anxiety.
Traditionally this is done using a Subjective Units of Distress Scale (SUDS).

Subjective Units of Distress are created by the therapist and the client to try to
capture or measure the fluctuations of anxiety from worst sensations to relative
calm or no anxiety. They are completed collaboratively and initially the therapist
and client anchor the scale by detailing the client's worst experience of anxiety so
far and assigning a number (0–100, 0–10 or 0–8). Traditionally the upper number

indicates extreme or severe levels of distress and the lower numbers indicate reduced levels of distress. The second task is to establish a cut-off point for normal moderate anxiety such as that experienced when sitting an exam or taking a driving test, for example. This reinforces to the client that at mild and moderate levels, anxiety is normal and in fact adaptive.

Now we ask the client to approach the feared situation or we begin to provoke a feared sensation and with the client measure the rapid increase in distress by recording their SUDS rating throughout the procedure. It is important to establish that the client will remain in the situation until they record that their anxiety has reduced by half. It's also important to reiterate that their usual safety behaviours are not deployed.

Feared situations include any situation that may provoke anxiety or bodily sensations that precede a rise in anxiety (increased respiratory rate, palpitations, sweating, muscle tensing, etc.). This may involve visiting a previously avoided place where the client experienced a panic attack (such as a supermarket, or travelling on a bus, etc.). It may also involve doing something that the client has avoided such as walking further and further from the safety of their home.

The overall aim of exposure is to habituate or acclimatize the client to heightened anxiety and therefore learn that by approaching anxiety-provoking situations often enough and long enough the anxiety reduces. This is important and the client's consent is sought beforehand that they will agree not to end the exercise until anxiety levels reduce by half.

If the situation is considered too fearful or there are numerous trigger situations then a graded approach to exposure may be employed. In reality, clients with anxiety often also present with agoraphobic avoidance to a number of situations.

A hierarchy of feared situations is collaboratively constructed and each item on the hierarchy is graded from least anxiety-provoking situation to most anxiety-provoking situation (see Appendix 5). The aim is to systematically work through each situation on the hierarchy using the principles above. The client begins by first tackling the least distressing situation and then moves up through the hierarchy. The aim is to not move on to the next item on the hierarchy until the client masters the preceding situation. The exposure to each feared situation continues until anxiety reduces by half. Initially exposure can be completed jointly, however, ultimately the client must complete exposure alone without using safety behaviours. The results are recorded in an exposure diary (see Appendix 6).

NOTE: if the client is suffering from blood or needle phobia this should not be treated as above as there is a risk of collapse. Instead the practitioner should discuss with their supervisor regarding possible referral to a more experienced practitioner.

Behavioural experiments: putting catastrophic predictions to the test

In essence, the cognitive approach to treating anxiety involves setting up a very precise behavioural experiment to test the client's catastrophic belief. A behavioural experiment is therefore just that: an experiment designed to obtain new information which the client can use to test the validity of an existing belief they may hold about themselves, the world or others (see Figures 5.8a and 5.8b). It can help create or test new beliefs, and will be used to update the client's appraisal of what is actually happening to them. The important aspect for the client to grasp is that a behavioural experiment is about testing the catastrophic belief that drives the client's anxiety. An experiment is constructed by following these rules:

- What belief does the client want to investigate and how much do they currently believe it?
- What might be an alternative explanation and how much do they believe it?
- How will the client and practitioner go about investigating the belief (what safety behaviour blocks learning or stops the belief being tested)?
- How will the client measure the results of the investigation?
- When and where will they carry out the experiment?
- What safety behaviours need to be dropped for learning to take place?
- What problems might adversely effect the experiment?
- After the experiment what did the client actually find?
- What new learning, if any, has occurred about the belief and its credibility?

If the client can create the experiment to test the distressing belief that is ideal, however, this is often not possible early on in treatment. As such, the practitioner should guide the client, in a collaborative way, in the development of

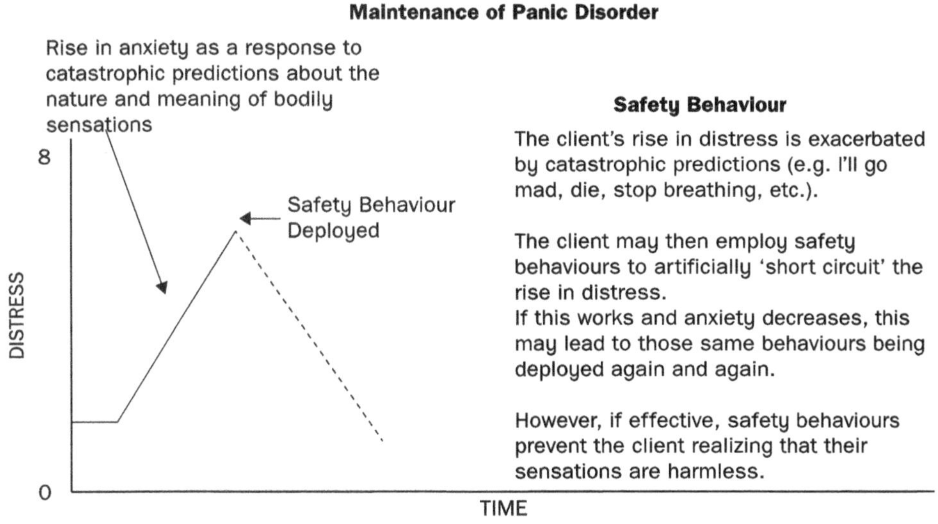

Maintenance of Panic Disorder

Rise in anxiety as a response to catastrophic predictions about the nature and meaning of bodily sensations

Safety Behaviour

The client's rise in distress is exacerbated by catastrophic predictions (e.g. I'll go mad, die, stop breathing, etc.).

The client may then employ safety behaviours to artificially 'short circuit' the rise in distress.
If this works and anxiety decreases, this may lead to those same behaviours being deployed again and again.

However, if effective, safety behaviours prevent the client realizing that their sensations are harmless.

Figure 5.8a   The function of a behavioural experiment

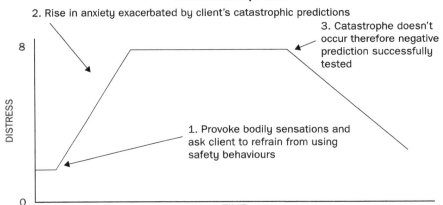

Catastrophic predictions can only be tested if all safety behaviours are removed and the client focuses on their threat appraisals and objectively observes what actually happens (i.e. no heart attack, madness, etc.)

Figure 5.8b   Testing catastrophic predictions

an appropriate experiment. It must be relevant, with a clear objective, and be measurable (using credibility ratings of belief and subjectively measuring levels of anxiety). Anxiety can be measured using a simple 0–10 scale with 0 = no distress and 10 = the worst distress the client has ever experienced. Finally there needs to be extensive reflection on the experiment outcome. Questions which should be asked are 'Did the outcome prove or disprove the belief?' and 'Have alternative beliefs been strengthened as a result of the experiment?'

Behavioural experiments are in fact the most potent form of cognitive restructuring (i.e. challenging the client's current beliefs and developing an alternative, more realistic appraisal of what is happening). The experiment is designed in collaboration with the client and the rationale is fully explained to them. Clare's behavioural experiment is given as an example in the box below.

Case example: Clare's behavioural experiment

What negative prediction is to be tested and how much do you believe this thought?
If I increase my heart rate or breathing rate for more than a few seconds, I will stop breathing then have a heart attack and die, 70%.

What is the alternative explanation for what is happening and how much do you believe this?
I've become frightened of changes to my body therefore I scan for any changes and when I find any changes, this scares me more and leads me to just worry

something more serious is happening. It is the worry that something is wrong that keeps the anxiety going – anxiety is harmless therefore I can experience being breathless and heart racing for more than a few seconds without dying, 30%.

How might I test this? What experiment could I devise to check out which belief is more accurate?
I will run up and down the 13 stairs where my health care practitioner works three times and make my breathing faster and my heart beat faster. I will do this on three occasions once with my practitioner and twice when he is at another part of the building.

What current safety behaviour/behaviours am I going to have to drop in order to truly test this belief?
I will not stop until I've done it three times and I will not carry my phone or water and will not leave the office and will not check my pulse or try to slow my breathing. I will do it once only with my practitioner and then twice alone without my practitioner.

What problems am I going to have to deal with and how may I overcome them?
1   *It will be very frightening I must not reassure myself that everything will be OK and instead allow the negative prediction to stay with me.*
2   *My practitioner will be with me for the first set and this may reassure me therefore I need to be aware of this and do two sets of running up and down the stairs on my own without my practitioner being directly with me.*
3   *I might get frightened with the experiment before it starts and call off the appointment. I need to remind myself, what do I learn from doing that?*
4   *I might try and deliberately do it so slowly to minimize the effect on my breathing and heart rate. I need to be clear, what do I really learn by doing that?*
5   *I might tell myself after the experiment that it wasn't enough and if I had done more then it would have killed me. The answer to this is that I can't even make a bed without the exertion leading me to believe I'll die. Running up and down 13 stairs three times will certainly test my belief.*
Set a time and date for experiment
   Tues 21st 3.00 pm next appointment with practitioner

Reflect on what actually happened after the experiment. What did doing this experiment tell you about both explanations? What does it tell you about your thinking?
I did the experiment and it was very frightening (even with my practitioner). I asked him for reassurance once but he didn't reply but just said let's see what happens!!! My breathing was so laboured I thought I would stop breathing and my heart pounded so much I thought it was going to burst out of my chest. I didn't leave or drink water and left my mobile at home. Although it was very frightening, I didn't

stop breathing and I didn't have a heart attack. I'm beginning to realize I'm very good at scaring myself but not really that good at predicting my own demise!!!! The getting breathless experiment lasted a total of 3 minutes. I now know I can have these feelings for 3 minutes and I haven't died.

Re-rate negative prediction
If I increase my heart rate or breathing rate for more than a few seconds, I will stop breathing, then have a heart attack and die, 40%

Re-rate alternative prediction
I've become frightened of changes to my body therefore I scan for any changes and when I find any changes, this scares me more and leads me to just worry something more serious is happening. It is the worry that something is wrong that keeps the anxiety going – anxiety is harmless therefore I can experience being breathless and heart racing for more than a few seconds without dying, 60%

As you can see from the above experiment, the belief that Clare would die if she remained breathless for more than a few seconds was tested by actually provoking the symptoms Clare feared most for more than a 'few seconds'. A three-minute experiment was chosen as it tested her specific belief that more than a few seconds of increased breathing or heart rate would kill her.

It needs to be remembered that the belief may now be modified but not completely disproven. Setting hyperarousal exercises for homework (using an experiment each time as set out in in Clare's example above) can then be extended to take into account increasingly longer periods of breathlessness and so test the belief Clare is vulnerable to a heart attack even further. The aim is not to simply have Clare get used to the symptoms of breathlessness but to continue to test her catastrophic beliefs about what the symptoms actually mean.

The test in the example is referred to as an interoceptive exposure experiment. Interoceptive exercises are designed to provoke the client's feared bodily sensations. The aim is to try as best as possible to replicate the sensations that the client misinterprets as dangerous. As mentioned above, the experiments described in this book should only be applied if the client's physician has ruled out any medical explanation for the client's symptoms.

Other methods of provoking the client's feared bodily sensations include:

- shaking head from side to side for 30 seconds;
- rapid shallow breathing (hyperventilation) for one to two minutes;
- rapid shallow breathing through a straw while holding nose for one minute;
- spinning round for one minute;
- jogging on the spot for one minute;
- staring at a spot or dot on the wall for three minutes.

The practitioner must first ensure the client is medically fit to participate, for example, that there are no medically diagnosed muscular problems with the neck, no history of severe or brittle asthma or ischaemic heart disease and no inner ear problems that may be causing balance problems. If in doubt, advice should be sought from the client's physician. The practitioner also must be prepared to demonstrate and then join in with the client when they are first introducing the method.

The technique recommended will depend on the sensation the client is most phobically avoidant of, that is, the bodily sensation that the client predicts is most dangerous. For example, head shaking and spinning are usually good at provoking dizziness for those who predict collapse, while hyperventilation or exercise can provoke cardiovascular sensations for those who fear a heart attack and hyperventilation through a straw can be used for those who fear respiratory arrest. For those clients who experience a sense of detachment or unreality (and who interpret this as a symptom of madness), staring at a black coloured spot on a white board or staring at their reflection in a mirror for two to three minutes may produce a sense of detachment or unreality (Taylor, 2000).

Situational behavioural experiments

Interoceptive exposure experiments are useful with all clients with panic disorder as all are fearful of bodily sensations. However, the practitioner and client may also need to design specific behavioural experiments with regard to visiting situations avoided because the client experienced panic or high levels of anxiety in those specific situations. Again an experiment is set as in Clare's example above, but this time the client is asked to remain in the situation for longer than the client perceives they can (without some catastrophic physical or mental illness occurring). This prediction is therefore tested and retested for longer periods with each exercise putting to the test the client's catastrophic prediction. Again the same procedure as before is used. An example of a behavioural experiment sheet to use is given in Appendix 7:

- negative prediction;
- alternative prediction;
- setting a specific experiment for a specified period of time (allocating enough time to test the negative prediction);
- agreeing to eliminate safety behaviours;
- predicting potential problems and adjusting for them;
- carrying out the experiment;
- reflecting on what was learned;
- re-rating both negative and alternative predictions.

Barriers to successful treatment

The most common barrier is perhaps an insensitive or hurried approach by the practitioner. Although the symptoms of anxiety are harmless, they are distressing and feel real to the client. Therefore a considerable amount of time needs to be dedicated to psycho-education and to ensure that at each stage of the process, the client remains a partner in the treatment process. This requires all the interpersonal skills outlined in Chapter 1 on interpersonal communication. The atmosphere in treatment should resemble two scientists, one who knows something about treating panic disorder and the other an expert in living with the symptoms of panic, working together to test a number of catastrophic predictions.

Second, often initial behavioural experiments are pitched at too difficult a level for clients and therefore they need to be further broken down into more manageable steps. If your client is not making adequate progress, then you should discuss the case with your supervisor, as the client may require high-intensity CBT.

Medication

Quite often a client will already have been prescribed medication by their GP or psychiatrist before attending for psychological treatment. There is also an evidence base for medication in the treatment of anxiety disorders so it is appropriate for both medication and psychological treatment to work alongside one another; there is grade A research (meta-analysis or randomized double-blind placebo-controlled trials) to support this. Antidepressant Selective Serotonin Reuptake Inhibitors (SSRIs), e.g. fluoxetine, are considered first-line treatment for many anxiety disorders and are generally well tolerated. Serotonin Noradrenaline Reuptake Inhibitors (SNRIs), e.g. venlafaxine, are quite often second-line treatments for anxiety disorders. When starting antidepressants, the most common side effects are nausea or stomach upset and a possible increase in anxiety symptoms, which often settles down within two weeks as the body gets used to the new medication. Older tricyclic antidepressants are much less commonly used due to side effects (e.g. blurred vision, dry mouth) but they do still have an evidence base, e.g. lofepramine for panic disorder or clomipramine for obsessive compulsive disorder (Baldwin et al., 2014).

Unfortunately antidepressants do not have an immediate effect and it can take a number of weeks to show benefit. If they are taken sporadically or in combination with alcohol or drugs of abuse, there is little chance they will work. For panic disorder, treatment periods of up to 12 weeks may be necessary to see an effect and it is recommended that clients remain on treatment for at least six months. Other anxiety disorders may require treatment of at least 12–18 months.

Benzodiazepines (sedative medication, e.g. diazepam) can be very effective in helping people with extremely distressing anxiety in the short term but can become an addictive safety behaviour in the longer term. Often a short course of benzodiazepines (one to two weeks) is added to SSRIs or SNRIs to allow time for the antidepressant to take effect and manage the possible side effect of an increase in anxiety symptoms.

Abrupt discontinuation of any of these medications may cause a withdrawal (benzodiazepines) or discontinuation syndrome (antidepressants), which may mimic anxiety symptoms. It is important to note that although benzodiazepines are known to be addictive, antidepressants are not thought to be. This can be a common misperception and may be a reason clients give for not taking their antidepressant as prescribed.

Propranolol (a beta-blocker medication, which slows the heart rate down) used to be commonly prescribed to clients with panic attacks to try to help reduce palpitations. This is no longer recommended (Baldwin et al., 2014). In fact propranolol can become yet another safety behaviour.

The role of psychological wellbeing practitioners with medication

Psychological wellbeing practitioners are not expected to advise on medications, for example, stopping medication or changing doses, but need to be informed about the role of medication so that they can provide support to clients to make informed choices (Richards and Whyte, 2009). It is therefore important to gather information about:

- medication type and dose;
- whether medication is taken as prescribed (concordance);
- any potential side effects.

It can be useful to know the evidence base for medications, common side effects and misperceptions about them in order to help your client make the best decision for them. It is a matter of them being able to weigh up the pros and cons in an informed way. If you have any serious concerns about medications or side effects, you should discuss with your client:

- making an urgent GP appointment
- informing the GP
- informing your supervisor.

The client should always be encouraged to discuss any decisions about medication with their prescribing doctor. It would not be considered ethical or good practice to suggest a client stops their medication to see if they can 'do without it' while undergoing psychological treatment. It would, however, be important to discuss with your client, their GP and your supervisor if you are concerned that medications such as diazepam are being used as a safety behaviour and are hampering psychological treatment. It is also important to establish if alcohol or illicit drug use may be interfering with treatment.

Further more detailed information is available at www.bnf.org (British National Drug Formulary) and www.bap.org.uk (British Association of Psychopharmacology). Useful information leaflets for clients about different mental disorders and the treatment are available at www.rcpsych.ac.uk

Summary

- Anxiety is a natural and in fact an essential response that has helped us survive as a species.
- Anxiety disorders occur when the anxiety we experience is out of proportion to the danger we face.
- Anxiety disorders are not uncommon. Panic disorder is caused by an individual paying attention to benign internal bodily sensations and becoming apprehensive of these sensations, which in turn increases the intensity of the sensations. This can lead the individual to appraise the growing sensations as an indication of imminent catastrophic physical or mental harm.
- Ruling out any real physical cause of those sensations is the first essential in psychological care; therefore ensure a client has been investigated beforehand by their physician.
- Assess for specific, recent examples of panic, detail triggers, exact physical sensations attended to, elicit negative automatic thoughts concerning those sensations, and elicit all behaviours employed and their effect in the short and long term to complete an individual formulation.
- Feedback the formulation until practitioner and client agree it is accurate and then explore with the client the utility of safety behaviours.
- Introduce psycho-education on anxiety, panic and the role of the fight, flight, freeze response. Does this offer a possible alternative explanation?
- If the client is engaged in this process, then collaboratively plan how to test the client's catastrophic predictions and the newly formed alternative explanation.
- Measuring the client's level of distress and the credibility of the client's catastrophic beliefs should be used to plot success.
- If progress is limited or the client's mood deteriorates, consider stepping up to formal cognitive behavioural psychotherapy at supervision.
- Medication and psychological treatments can work well together; practitioners need to have a basic knowledge of the evidence base and likely medication-related issues.

Recommended reading

Antony, M.M. and Barlow, D.H. (2010) *Handbook of Assessment and Treatment Planning for Psychological Disorders*, 2nd edn. New York: Guilford Press.

Barlow, D.H. (2004) *Anxiety and Its Disorders: The Nature and Treatment of Anxiety and Panic*. New York: Guilford Press.

Beck, A.T., Rush, A.J., Shaw, B.F. and Emery, G. (1979) *Cognitive Therapy of Depression*. New York: Guilford Press.

Beck, J.S. (1995) *Cognitive Therapy: Basics and Beyond*. New York: Guilford Press.

Clark, D.A. and Beck, A.D. (2010) *Cognitive Therapy of Anxiety Disorders: Science and Practice*. New York: Guilford Press.

Clark, D.M. (1999) Anxiety disorders: why they persist and how to treat them. *Behaviour Research and Therapy*, 37: 5–27.

Hawton, K., Salkovskis, P.M., Kirk, J. and Clark, D.M. (1998) *Cognitive Behaviour Therapy for Psychiatric Problems: A Practical Guide*. Oxford: Oxford University Press.

Richards, D. and Whyte, M. (2009) *Reach Out: National Programme Educator Materials to Support the Delivery of Training for Psychological Wellbeing Practitioners Delivering Low Intensity Interventions*, 2nd edn. Rethink Mental Illness. Available at. www.cedar.exeter.ac.uk/iapt/iaptworkbooksandresources (accessed 23 May 2014).

Simmons, J. and Griffiths, R. (2009) *CBT for Beginners*. London: Sage.

Taylor, S. (2000) *Understanding and Treating Panic Disorder: Cognitive Behavioural Approaches*. New York: Wiley.

Westbrook, D., Kennerley, H. and Kirk, J. (2011) *An Introduction to Cognitive Behaviour Therapy: Skills and Applications*, 2nd edn. London: Sage.

Williams, C.J. (2012a) *Overcoming Depression: A Five Areas Approach*. London: Hodder Arnold.

Williams, C.J. (2012b) *Overcoming Anxiety, Stress and Panic: A Five Areas Approach*. London: Hodder Arnold.

6   Sleep

Introduction

This chapter will review the human need for sleep and the way in which sleep changes over time and at stressful times. In addition, it will look at the role that worry and rumination play in poor sleep and will review the main approaches used to assist clients in improving the overall quality and amount of sleep they have.

Understanding the impact of sleep problems

Sleep difficulties impact upon a great many people and can be serious enough to negatively affect their overall quality of life. It's thought that between 5 per cent and 20 per cent of the general adult population and 20–30 per cent of those in primary care medical settings are affected (Buysse et al., 2011). Older adults are particularly impacted with a prevalence rate of 15–30 per cent and those with physical and mental disorders experience persistent insomnia for over a year in 74 per cent of individuals (Buysse et al., 2011).

In terms of the process of sleep difficulties, a variety of biological, psychological and behavioural factors are responsible. As such, cognitive behavioural interventions are useful treatment options. Insomnia can be secondary to medical, psychiatric and other sleep disorders. For sleep difficulties to be considered as the primary condition, several factors must be present, for example, hyper-arousal, irregular schedule, excessive time spent in bed and excessive worry, in the absence of other conditions (Morin et al., 2002). The issue of worry is one which can be seen within a variety of mental health problems and, as we are aware, usually has a future focus (Carney et al., 2010). When considering worry in terms of sleep difficulties, however, the worry must be focused on the issue of sleep loss and the perceived impact this can have: in other words unhelpful beliefs and attitudes about sleep (Edinger and Means, 2005).

In terms of worry about the ability to sleep, the client focuses upon the consequences of not getting good or good enough sleep. This in turn increases their state of arousal (hyper-arousal), both physiological and psychological, thereby reducing the probability of an adequate night's sleep (Edinger and Means, 2005). In addition, due to worry and negative thinking styles such as black and white thinking and catastrophizing, any sleep the client does attain is not considered adequate (Carney et al., 2010).

An example of black and white thinking is, 'I must get a full eight hours sleep.' Catastrophic thoughts may include, 'I will never be able to cope if I don't sleep tonight. My work will suffer, I will lose my job.' This style of thinking, in turn, reinforces worry over sleep and creates an attentional bias (looking out for trouble). This attentional bias negatively impacts upon mood, reduces concentration and interferes with the client's cognitive function (Edinger and Means, 2005). One example might be that the person will focus on just how tired they feel the next day, and then start worrying about their sleep that night, reducing their focus even further on what they are doing during the day, which reinforces the belief that they are unable to cope without a full eight hours sleep.

If the person is anxious or depressed, they are likely to have sleep difficulties as part of those illnesses and are also very likely to have negative unhelpful thinking styles. Lying in bed awake for long periods, especially in the early hours of the morning, either ruminating about the past or worrying about the future, is a vulnerable time for clients and is often a time when they experience a dip in mood, as a result. This results in a vicious cycle of worrying/ruminating, not sleeping at night, being tired and feeling less able to cope or do anything much during the day, having day-time naps, worrying about sleeping at night and then not sleeping again. This cycle can feed into the depression or anxiety cycles so it is important to address sleep problems as part of treatment.

Problems with sleep can be a very difficult aspect of anxiety and depression to deal with for clients but cognitive behavioural interventions have been shown to be effective (Morgenthaler et al., 2006), and they produce better long-term outcomes than pharmacotherapy alone (Edinger and Means, 2005). Figure 6.1 (the generic cognitive behavioural model) gives a a representation of the impact sleep difficulties can have.

How much sleep is enough?

Here we examine the issue that creates a considerable amount of confusion among people: how much sleep do we need? Do we all require eight hours a night? Does this remain constant throughout the entire lifespan?

A question which is often asked is how much sleep we actually require. This is not as straightforward to answer as one may think; simply put, we vary a great deal in our need for sleep, not only within the general population but throughout an individual's normal lifespan, and this will also alter depending upon our activity level (Espie, 2010). That said, there is a common myth that we all need around seven to eight hours of sleep a night (Espie, 1999). While this may be the average, some people function quite satisfactorily with four to five hours while others need nine to ten. Winston Churchill and Margaret Thatcher, for example, famously slept for fewer than six hours a night, and both ran the country.

We can therefore state that what is considered enough for one person may be too much for some, but not enough for another. This highlights how unnecessary time spent on worrying about how many hours of sleep an individual should have is. This seven-to-eight-hour rule can be particularly difficult when considering the issue of unhelpful beliefs and attentional bias. If the client is fixed on this seven-to-eight-hour rule as a standard and is unable to sleep for this length of time, this leads to increased anxiety/arousal and, over time, lowered mood due to the worry

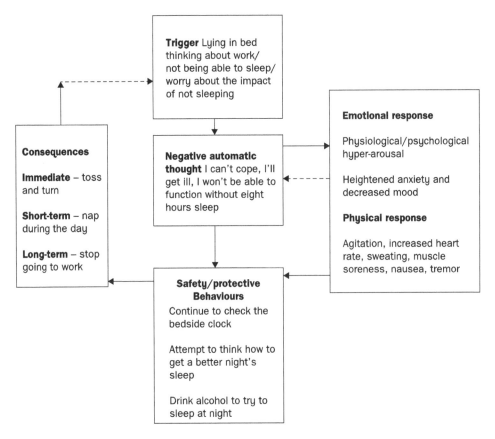

Figure 6.1   Generic cognitive behavioural model of sleep disturbance

and rumination they engage in. Whatever the client's requirements, if the wake-sleep cycle is problematic, it can have a negative impact on psychological, behavioural and physiological processes (Espie, 2010). In addition, if the client is suffering from a medical condition (primary or secondary to insomnia), not experiencing a refreshing night's sleep can heighten the impact of the medical condition (Espie, 2010).

There are different levels of sleep which stretch from a light to a deep sleep; at least four stages of sleep can be identified and broken down into two categories, REM (Rapid Eye Movement) and non-REM sleep (Northumberland, Tyne and Wear NHS Foundation Trust, 2009). As we have said, there is not a set amount of time needed for sleep; however, adults need less than children, and older people generally have less deep sleep. The various stages of sleep are described in Figure 6.2.

REM sleep is a stage which is entered and exited several times during a sleep period and usually occurs for about 25 per cent of the time. It is the phase where most dreaming is thought to take place (Northumberland, Tyne and Wear NHS Foundation Trust, 2009). It is also not unusual to waken on several occasions throughout the

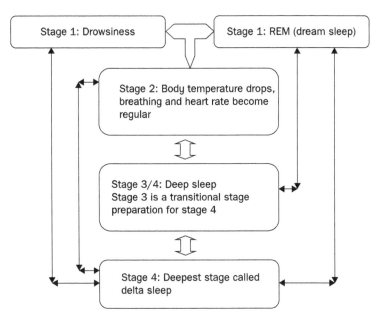

Figure 6.2   Sleep stages

night, although we can often be unaware this has happened. Some clients will experience initial insomnia or difficulty in falling asleep (this is usually linked with anxiety) while others will tend to waken prematurely, also referred to as early morning insomnia, and this is linked to both anxiety and depression (Leahy, 2009).

Why do we sleep and why do sleep problems occur and persist?

This section discusses the reasons why sleep difficulties happen. Issues such as the ageing process, mood difficulties, stress and medical conditions will be discussed.

Sleep is the time for the body to repair and regenerate and is when a lot of growth happens in children, which explains why babies need to sleep a lot. There are a number of reasons why sleep problems develop; the first is the normal process of ageing. When people get older, they tend to sleep less and indeed less deeply (Northumberland, Tyne and Wear NHS Foundation Trust, 2009). This may be misinterpreted as abnormal, but actually less time sleeping is required.

There can also be medical reasons, for example, the need to urinate during the night, chronic pain, obesity (which can result in sleep apnoea) and chest or heart disease. There are of course a variety of other medical conditions that can contribute to sleep difficulties, so it is important to establish any past medical history during client assessment (Northumberland, Tyne and Wear NHS Foundation Trust, 2009). Around 60 per cent of women and 70 per cent of men over the age of 65 get out of bed at least once a night due to pain or the need to urinate (Northumberland, Tyne and Wear NHS Foundation Trust, 2009).

A further reason for sleep disturbance that should be considered is medication, some of which can interfere with sleep. As such, it is necessary to take a comprehensive medication history and refer to the client's GP to ensure medication is not causing a problem. One example might be if the person is taking diuretics (water tablets) which increase urination, so the urge to go to the toilet is waking the person at night. If pain is a difficulty, then the client should be advised to discuss adequate pain relief with their doctor.

Hypnotic or sedative medication can be prescribed for sleep difficulties and while it has proven to be effective in the short term, there can be difficulties with this class of medication in the longer term. For example, this type of medication often becomes tolerated, which means it no longer works at the same dose and people can easily become addicted to it after a few weeks and it can be abused. In older people, sedatives are associated with an increased risk of confusion and falls and the possible accompanying injuries such as hip fractures (Buysse et al., 2011).

Paradoxically, sleeping medication actually reduces the quality of sleep by reducing the amount of REM (or dream) sleep, often meaning that people who take it wake up feeling unrefreshed. Alcohol is often used by people to help them get to sleep, but this also reduces sleep quality and makes sleep disturbance more likely.

So sleep problems can be the result of a variety of factors such as ageing, medical conditions (e.g. bladder problems), pain, stress, anxiety, depression, certain medicines, environmental factors, (including noise and light) and drug or alcohol use. An individual's environment can play a significant part in a disturbed night's sleep as can a changing routine such as that experienced by shift workers. It is therefore important to try to address any possible underlying causes of sleep difficulties. First, though, we will review how sleep is controlled in the body.

There are two main processes which control sleep: the sleep homeostat and the circadian (day and night) rhythm (Espie, 2010). The homeostat controls the client's drive for sleep, while the circadian rhythm controls the 'when' for sleep (Espie, 2010). When thinking of the 'drive' for sleep, the concept of 'sleep debt' must be considered. This posits that for every hour of wakefulness we accrue an hour of sleep debt (Espie, 2010). As such, a person who has no difficulties with sleep has a balance between sleep and sleep debt. This is a particularly good reason to avoid napping during the day if the client experiences some form of insomnia, as this can reduce the body's drive for sleep during the night (Espie, 2010).

This is because the sleep debt has been offset by the client's napping, further feeding the client's sleep disturbance (Espie, 2010). In terms of the circadian rhythm, this is based on the 24-hour day, and stablizes as we grow from infancy to adulthood. For example, a young baby will sleep and wake several times throughout a 24-hour period. Over time, as the baby grows into a child, their routine becomes more stable and sleep settles to the hours of darkness. This is largely dictated by the body's production of the hormone melatonin. During the hours of darkness melatonin production increases (physiologically encouraging sleep) and during daylight it decreases (reducing the physiological desire for sleep) (Espie, 2010). Hence the circadian rhythm is established and works in conjunction with the sleep homeostat; the drive for sleep becomes strong at night, which coincides with increased melatonin production (Espie, 2010).

Those who do not experience sleep difficulties can usually get off to sleep fairly quickly, usually within 30 minutes, and will only wake once or twice during a sleep cycle. This is indicative of the sleep homeostat and circadian rhythm working effectively (Espie, 2010). It is, of course, normal to have the occasional night of poor sleep; this can be, but is not necessarily, due to a stressful event. What is important is that this is a perfectly normal part of everyday living (Espie, 1999).

In terms of mood disorders clients with depression and anxiety can have many types of sleep difficulty. Generally these involve getting less sleep than usual due to hyper-arousal and can include:

- difficulty getting off to sleep – often because of lying in bed with thoughts going around and around in their head. These thoughts can be focused upon the issue of sleep itself, the mood disorder or a combination (worry/rumination, unhelpful beliefs).
- early morning wakening and not being able to get back to sleep, as well as waking frequently during the night;
- heightened physiology/arousal.

(Harvey and Tang, 2003)

Even if clients do get a reasonable number of hours sleep, they often wake in the morning feeling 'unrefreshed' and feel tired throughout the day. Again this creates an attentional bias, as discussed previously, and further reinforces any unhelpful beliefs about sleep and their ability to cope/function.

Assessing sleep

To help assess sleep, the use of a sleep diary should be considered. This can be used in conjunction with the behavioural activation activity monitoring diary, as previously mentioned in Chapter 4 on depression. The sleep diary is used both to gather information and record changes in sleep. Questions which can be asked are as follows:

Sleep diary questions

- What is your sleep routine?
- How do you prepare yourself for sleep? (Describe in detail.)
- How many hours/minutes on average do you think you sleep for?
- What time do you go to bed?
- How quickly do you get off to sleep?
- Before you go to sleep, what goes through your mind?
- Is your sleep a deep sleep?
- Is your sleep disturbed? Do you toss and turn?

- Do you waken easily?
- What time do you waken?
- At what time on average do you get out of bed?
- If you remain in bed, can you get back to sleep?
- If not, what goes through your mind?
- When you waken do you feel refreshed, as if you had a good night's sleep?

(Espie, 2010)

The level of activity during the day and sleeping throughout the daytime can have an impact on the sleep at night. The behavioural activation activity monitoring diary should identify information such as:

- Does the client lie on in bed in the morning? If so, is there an effect on mood?
- Is the client catnapping throughout the day?
- If so, when does this occur and how often?
- During the day are they engaged in any activities?
- If that is the case, what exactly does this level of activity look like?
- Are they drinking lots of tea/coffee? (especially in the evening)

An example of a sleep diary is shown in Figure 6.3. Please see the summary points at the end of the chapter to help with this. The client should be asked to complete this diary every day for a minimum of two weeks, to pick a time each day to complete it and as far as possible to complete it at the same time every day. It is important to be as accurate as possible.

It should be noted that this data collection may reveal the fact that the client is achieving a reasonable amount of sleep, even if they report feeling as if they are not. As such, because they think they require more sleep, the worry this causes can leave them feeling fatigued. It is therefore important to gather a collateral history from family members, loved ones or support workers in order to get a broad overview of the amount of sleep over time the client has been getting.

In this instance, the issue of worry/rumination should be discussed and education provided. If necessary the use of problem solving or sleep stimulus control or sleep restriction can be considered (these are covered later in this chapter). In addition, the use of the behavioural activation activity monitoring diary and sleep diary can be of inestimable value in helping the person see how the vicious cycle of inactivity and daytime sleeping reduces night-time sleep when this data is used to complete a generic maintenance model (see Figure 6.1).

Once you have gathered and analysed the data, the next stage should be to move to sleep psycho-education, unless of course it is identified that more specialist sleep help is required. In which case, in consultation with your supervisor, your client should be stepped up to the appropriate service. One example might be if the client has sleep disturbance due to experiencing nightmares and/or flashbacks in

Name: _____ Date commenced: _____

Date/Day	Day 1	Day 2	Day 3	Day 4	Day 5	Day 6	Day 7
Time you go to bed? What did you do before bed?							
Caffeine/alcohol/ nicotine intake during the day and before going to bed? (number of cups/ glasses/cigarettes)							
What did you do in bed? (read/watch TV/use mobile device/sex)							
How long did it take to fall asleep?							
How many times did you waken?							
How long were you awake throughout the night in total? (hours)							
How many hours sleep do you think you had?							
What time did you finally waken?							
What time did you get out of bed?							
What medications do you take? (consider medications taken for sleep)							
How many naps were taken during the day? How long for? (hours)							
On a scale of 0–8 how would you rate the quality of your sleep with 8 being the worst? 0 1 2 3 4 5 6 7 8							

What did you do when you wakened throughout the night?

What went through your mind?

What was the worst thing that you believed could happen?

Figure 6.3 Daily sleep diary

relation to a previous traumatic event. In this case, a specialist assessment and high-intensity treatment would be required.

With reference to emotional difficulties such as anxiety and stress, clients can report difficulties getting off to sleep, and when they do, the sleep is often restless and clients awaken unrefreshed. With depression or low mood, early morning wakening is often a problem as well as getting off to sleep. In terms of low mood clients often have less activity during the day, due to a lack of motivation and reduced energy levels. As a result they can find themselves napping throughout the day, which will in turn make it more difficult for them to sleep at night.

The same mechanism can be at work with those suffering from anxiety. In this instance the client's coping strategies (avoidance and overcompensation) can reduce the level of activity they would normally engage in so they are less likely to sleep at night. Clients should be encouraged to establish regular sleeping behaviours. This is accomplished through the use of the sleep diary and the behavioural activation activity monitoring diary to identify unhelpful behaviours and then establish new helpful behaviours to promote sleep.

Cognitive behavioural interventions

The following section will outline the most common approaches employed in treating sleep disturbance. There are various strategies which should be considered when treating insomnia.

Strategies for treating insomnia

- **Sleep hygiene** This entails assessing whether there is a sleep problem and providing education about sleep-promoting behaviours including the use of exercise during the day, avoidance of naps and stimulants (e.g. caffeine, alcohol, tobacco, prescription and non-prescription medications, etc.) and the appropriate environment as well as information about the nature of sleep. This approach can be used in conjunction with others but is the mainstay of low-intensity interventions.
- **Relaxation strategies** These focus upon the reduction of physiological hyper-arousal and use rebreathing training and progressive muscular relaxation. They can be used as a primary approach but also in conjunction with others.
- **Sleep stimulus control** This focuses on the issue of the sleep homeostat and the sleep environment. The aim is to change the association the client has with sleep and the sleep environment from an unsuccessful to a successful one. This involves only keeping the bedroom for sleep and sex and having a consistent sleep and wake time. This approach makes use of the 15-minute rule, i.e. only staying in bed for 15 minutes at a time, if not sleeping (Espie, 2010).

- **Sleep restriction** The client's sleep time is restricted each night in such a way as to match the client's time in bed to the amount of presumed sleep they require. This is done by calculating the average total sleep time (ATST). First the client keeps a sleep diary for two weeks, allowing an average sleep time to be calculated. This is subtracted from their rising time, and this is when the client is to plan to go to sleep (Morin et al., 2002; Harvey and Tang, 2003).

We shall now look at these in turn, in more detail.

Sleep hygiene

There are four areas which need to be addressed when we are looking at the promotion of good quality sleep. These are:

1   Investigate the client's current sleep cycle, asking the question: 'Is there a problem?' Use the sleep assessment guide and the sleep diary (Figure 6.3) to help answer this question.
2   With step one in mind, educate the client about what is meant by the wake-sleep cycle and what constitutes good sleep. Emphasize the two main processes which control sleep – the sleep homeostat and the circadian rhythm – as well as the number of hours required and the changing nature of the number of required hours as we age.
3   Again taking into consideration steps one and two, provide information on creating the best possible environment for a good night's sleep. Clients should be advised to do the following:

- **Avoid sleeping throughout the day** However, if the client does engage in napping, it is important to record the specifics of this using the behavioural activation activity monitoring chart. This should be incorporated into treatment – the practitioner and client should work collaboratively to reduce the number of sleep episodes and length of time spent napping throughout the day. The goal is to try to eliminate all daytime napping activity.
- **Exercise during the day** Any exercise is useful, however, outdoors would be preferable. Ensure, however, in the hour or so before bed that the client doesn't engage in any physiological or psychologically stimulating activities.
- **Limit or stop the use of caffeine and nicotine products prior to going to bed, as well as any stimulant or alcohol** In addition, avoid going to bed too hungry or full. We are looking for the Goldilocks 'just right' zone. Ensure that pain relief is adequate and taken before bed, if pain wakes them, and that medication that may interfere with sleep, for example, diuretics (water tablets) are taken as early in the day as possible to reduce night-time urges for the toilet.

- **Ensure the environment is conducive to sleep** The room should be dark and at the right temperature for the client and the mattress should be comfortable. Remove electrical items, for example, TVs and clocks, from the room and attempt to reduce the level of ambient noise.
- **Engage in relaxing activities before going to bed and establish a consistent bedtime routine** For example, set the scene for sleep and prepare the mind and body for sleep. The routine could involve a warm bath, then getting dressed for sleep followed by a warm cup of milk (Harvey and Tang, 2003).
- **The bedroom should be used only for sleep and sex**

Continue to review all three steps in relation to problem solving. The bedroom should be a worry-free zone, so if the client finds they engage in worry/rumination, they should be directed by the practitioner to get up and go to another room (following the 15-minute rule highlighted in the sleep stimulus control exercise). Once there, they should utilize a problem-solving exercise, for example, list all their worries and all possible solutions and then return to the bedroom. If worry continues, again follow the sleep stimulus control exercise until sleep is established (Espie, 2010).

For the low-intensity practitioner, sleep hygiene should be your primary approach but it is useful to be aware of other techniques available, namely relaxation (rebreathing and progressive muscular relaxation), sleep stimulus control and sleep restriction. Brief outlines of these now follow.

Relaxation

While there are a variety of relaxation techniques and scripts that are easy to access, we focus here on rebreathing and progressive muscular relaxation. In terms of sleep, the primary purpose here is to reduce physiological arousal and the secondary is a reduction of psychological arousal (Harvey and Tang, 2003). Consideration should be given to underlying medical conditions for rebreathing and progressive muscle relaxation. Contraindications include respiratory illness such as severe asthma or emphysema, pregnancy, cardiovascular disease, vasovagal syncope (also known as drop attack) or untreated panic disorder. As discussed in Chapter 5 on anxiety, safety behaviours are a very potent maintaining factor, so it is important that you do not introduce them to someone with untreated panic disorder. If there is any doubt about a client's suitability, it is advisable to discuss with your supervisor or the client's doctor.

Rebreathing
The client is instructed to breathe in for four seconds (the use of a second hand on a watch can be useful here), hold their breath for two to three seconds, and breathe out for four seconds. If this is uncomfortable for the client, then the timings should be adjusted. This should be repeated until arousal has been reduced to a comfortable level (Harvey and Tang, 2003).

Progressive muscular relaxation

There are a variety of scripts available; all, however, focus upon the tension and release of the major muscle groups within the body. As with all exercises, first the practitioner must model the behaviour. Tension of individual muscles is maintained for approximately five seconds, followed by release. Each muscle group is only tensed once, and when first instructing the client, the body should be divided into two zones; zone one (hands, arms, neck, shoulder and face) and zone two (back, stomach, buttocks, legs and feet).

The client should be instructed to tense each muscle group for five seconds, feeling the tension, then releasing it before progressing to the next muscle. For example, 'Clench the right fist, hold for five seconds, feel the tension, then release, repeat for the left fist. Then tense the right arm, hold and release, repeat with the left arm. Scrunch up your face, hold for five seconds, then release, and so on.' Once the upper body has been tensed, including the back, shoulders and stomach, move on to zone two. Zone two is everything below the waist – toes, feet, legs and buttocks (Hawton et al., 1989). There are a variety of scripts available and the one outlined by Hawton et al. (1989) is quite effective. When you are satisfied that the client is able to demonstrate they know how to do these exercises, they can then practise them at home and do them before bed.

Sleep stimulus control

The client is instructed to use their bed only for sleep and sexual activity; no other activity is to be engaged in, such as arguments, worry, watching television, etc. The following pre-sleep routine is to be established: one that signals to the body that it is time to go to bed.

- When going to bed, turn out the lights, with the intention of sleeping.
- If you do not fall asleep within 15 minutes, get up, do not stay in bed and worry/ruminate (Espie, 2010).
- Go to another room to engage in a quiet activity, e.g. taking a warm milky drink, until you become sleepy and return to bed (Espie, 2010). It is important that the client does not engage in a stimulating activity, for example smoking or playing a computer game, as these will further disturb the sleep pattern.
- Continue with the above steps as often as is required until a regular and restful sleep pattern is established.

All of the above steps can be used in conjunction with sleep hygiene, relaxation, and sleep restriction.

Sleep restriction

To help a client using sleep restriction, the following steps are used:

- First, the client is instructed to keep a sleep diary which records the number of hours each night they actually sleep. An example of a sleep diary is shown in Figure 6.3.
- This diary should be kept for a minimum of two weeks. Not only will this be useful for calculating the average number of hours per night the client sleeps, but also as an educational and assessment tool (Espie, 2010).
- The diary is used to calculate the individual's total sleep time and then the average sleep time over two weeks. Average sleep (hours) = total sleep in two weeks (hours)/number of nights. For example, if a client works out their average sleep time is five hours and that they get up at 6 am, then a Time In Bed (TIB) prescription can be calculated. They must subtract their average sleep time from their getting up time – five hours from 6 am, which results in an answer of 1 am as the earliest time they should go to bed (Espie, 2010).
- The goal here is to establish a regular pattern: one that is consistent with the number of hours of sleep the client actually gets in bed. A cautionary note here is that the number of hours should be based on no less than five hours. This applies to those clients who identify an average number of hours fewer than five hours (Espie, 2010). If the client wishes to rise later or earlier than the TIB indicates, this can be adjusted. The ultimate goal here is to re-establish the sleep homeostat and the circadian rhythm (Espie, 2010).
- Again relaxation, sleep hygiene and stimulus control can be used to augment this approach.

According to Morgenthaler et al. (2006), sleep hygiene is not recommended as an option for a single therapy as there was not enough available evidence to support its efficacy as a standalone treatment. In Buysse et al.'s (2011) study, a quarter of people with insomnia improved with psycho-education alone. Cognitive behavioural interventions are, however, recommended. This can be broken down into the cognitive component, which is to assist the client to modify their beliefs and adopt more helpful beliefs about sleep, and the behavioural component, which includes stimulus control, sleep restriction and relaxation techniques.

As for all cognitive behavioural interventions, psycho-education plays a key role at the beginning of treatment, in this case sleep hygiene education. In this sense, as part of a combined cognitive behavioural approach there is evidence of combined efficacy (Morgenthaler et al., 2006). Buysse et al. (2011) have established steps based upon sleep restriction and stimulus control principles and these are a useful road map for the low-intensity practitioner. These are:

- reduce time in bed;
- get up at the same time every day;
- only go to bed when you feel sleepy;

- do not stay in bed unless you are sleeping;
- avoid napping.

(Buysse et al., 2011)

Interestingly, Buysse et al. showed that when nurses supported clients in using this approach, rather than providing psycho-education alone, two-thirds of people had an improvement in sleep (as opposed to a quarter). This demonstrates that knowledge about a condition is important for clients (hence the need for psycho-education) but putting this into practice and trying it out for themselves are much more important – experiential learning is very powerful. It is always vital that you encourage clients not just to take your word for it, but to try it out for themselves.

Conclusion

In conclusion, a variety of factors can impact upon a client's sleep pattern, and can have a significant impact on the client's quality of life. It is important to assess the client's sleep pattern, any possible contributory factors to poor sleep including environmental causes, and to identify unhelpful thoughts/beliefs, thinking styles and behaviours. A number of strategies are available which can help identify and treat sleep disturbance. Cognitive behavioural interventions have been proven as particularly effective.

Summary

- Avoid napping during the day.
- Reduce fluid and food intake in the evening. Avoid alcohol, smoking and caffeine.
- The bed should be used for the purposes of sleep and sex only.
- Establish a regular bedtime routine and wake time.
- Avoid physiological and psychological arousal (e.g. arguments, difficult or stimulating tasks, such as computer use) before going to bed.
- Don't try to force yourself to sleep as this results in rumination/thinking errors and body scanning, leading to hyperarousal.
- Do not engage in safety behaviours (e.g. checking the clock repeatedly) (Leahy, 2009).
- Identify thoughts/beliefs about sleep and thinking style errors.

Remember the four steps:

- Reduce time in bed.
- Get up at the same time every day.
- Only go to bed when you feel sleepy.
- Do not stay in bed unless you are sleeping (Buysse et al., 2011).

Recommended reading

Beck, A.T., Rush, A.J., Shaw, B.F. and Emery, G. (1979) *Cognitive Therapy of Depression*. New York: Guilford Press.

Beck, J.S. (1995) *Cognitive Therapy: Basics and Beyond*. New York: Guilford Press.

Espie, C.A. (1999) Cognitive behavior therapy as the treatment of choice for primary insomnia. *Sleep Medicine Reviews*, 3(2): 97–9.

Espie, C.A. (2010) *Overcoming Insomnia and Sleep Problems*. London: Constable and Robinson Ltd.

Espie, C.A. (2011) *An Introduction to Coping with Insomnia and Sleep Problems*. London: Robinson.

Espie, C.A., Inglis, S.J., Tessier, S. and Harvey, L. (2001) The clinical effectiveness of cognitive behavior therapy for chronic insomnia: implementation and evaluation of a sleep clinic in general medical practice. *Behaviour Research and Therapy*, 39: 45–60.

Harvey, A.G., Sharpley, A.L., Ree, M.J., Stinson, K. and Clark, D.M. (2007) An open trail of cognitive therapy for chronic insomnia. *Behaviour Research and Therapy*, 45: 2491–501.

Hawton, K., Salkovskis, P.M., Kirk, J. and Clark D.M. (1989) *Cognitive Behaviour Therapy for Psychiatric Problems: A Practical Guide*. Oxford: Oxford University Press.

Richards, D. and Whyte, M. (2008) *Improving Access to Psychological Therapies*. Rethink Mental Illness. Available at: http://www.iapt.nhs.uk/publications/ (accessed 2 June 2014).

Taylor, S. (2000) *Understanding and Treating Panic Disorder: Cognitive Behavioural Approaches*. New York: Wiley.

7 Recovery and maintaining wellness

Introduction

The purpose of this chapter is to highlight the importance of the client's continued journey towards wellness. Maintaining wellness is a lifelong process, one which the client must be able to continue without the ongoing support of the practitioner. We shall look at the issues of the client as practitioner (or 'self-therapist'), medication use and general advice for staying well.

The client becomes the therapist

So far this book has examined the use of cognitive behavioural interventions in terms of interpersonal communication, assessment, problem identification and goal setting, session structure and the treatment of common mental disorders, namely depression and panic disorder. Throughout, the collaborative nature of the process has been espoused. We would now like to highlight an essential aspect of this collaboration: the client as practitioner. The aim throughout the treatment process is to assist the client to identify problems within their lives and the strategies (useful or not) they employ to overcome them. Of course, it is the aim of the practitioner to assist the client to see that these strategies may not have been effective in the long term. In addition to the primary problem, the strategies being employed themselves may have become a problem-maintaining factor.

The client is therefore guided and encouraged to adopt and test alternative strategies, cognitive or behavioural (or a combination of both), and assess the outcome (Hawton et al., 2003). While this process begins during the treatment session, the burden of this work occurs outside of it as a homework or self-therapy task. It is this move from client to practitioner which is important; the use of cognitive behavioural techniques at home equips the client to work on their own difficulties, not only during treatment but also in the future, long after treatment has ceased. In addition, these new skills can be applied to all areas of the client's life.

The subject of continued wellness should be one that is discussed before the client completes treatment; it should be made a central part of the treatment process, albeit towards the end of the course of treatment. Throughout treatment, however, the client should be socialized to the 'client as practitioner' philosophy, emphasizing that change is accomplished, not by the practitioner, but mainly by the client themselves.

It is in this way that the client continues their journey of recovery throughout the course of their lives. It should be noted that this is often referred to as relapse prevention or creating a 'blueprint' for recovery (Hawton et al., 2003). We

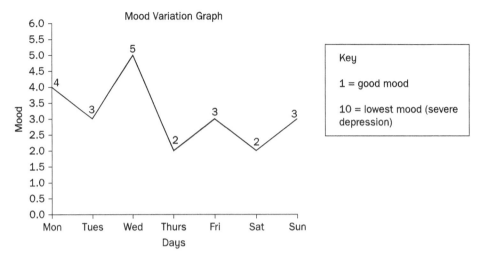

Figure 7.1 Normal mood variations

acknowledge, however, that life is unpredictable for everyone and mood can fluc-tuate throughout a person's lifespan and that this will not necessarily be indicative of a 'relapse'. It is much more helpful to reinforce that a temporary fluctuation in mood is normal and to ask the client to continue to focus on wellness and continued recovery rather than getting caught up in constantly looking for potential 'relapse'. Figure 7.1 can be used with the client to highlight what is considered 'normal mood fluctuation'. This philosophy has been borrowed from evidence-based treatment and recovery of those suffering from even severe mental health problems (Garety et al., 2008).

How do we maintain wellness?

This section will look at how the practitioner can prepare the client to stay well after treatment, including the development of a maintaining wellness plan. The importance of identifying the client's triggers for the initial episode and their main-taining factors will be outlined. Last, there is a section on medication and general advice.

It is important to note that once a person has had an emotional difficulty significant enough to require assistance, even at a low-intensity level, they may be more vulnerable to external (and subsequently internal) stressors. This is espe-cially true in the immediate period following discharge. This is due to the fact that their experience of being unwell is so recent, but also because they now no longer have the practitioner as someone they can rely on to assist them. This point is essential; the client may well form a close 'attachment' to the practitioner and be understandably nervous about coping by themselves. While it is acknowledged that a good therapeutic relationship is necessary for successful treatment, it is also necessary for the practitioner to prepare the client for discharge and ensure that the boundaries of a therapeutic relationship are maintained.

Throughout the assessment and treatment process the practitioner should help the client to identify their own triggers, both external and internal, which led to an unhelpful world view, in terms of negative automatic thinking, unhelpful coping behaviours, upsetting emotions and the accompanying distressing physiology or bodily sensations (Hawton et al., 2003). These triggers and responses are the markers the client should be aware of in terms of maintaining wellness for the future.

As part of the assessment process, data which indicates why the patient began to experience difficulties is gathered. What was happening in their life before they noticed a problem? What did they think about that? How did they interpret it? What impact did this have on beliefs and feelings (both emotional and physiological)? It is important this is included in the assessment and treatment process because these or similar triggers in the future can be indicators of potential difficulty, so self-reflection is important.

Case examples

Depression

When I notice that I feel low, I begin to avoid other people, I gradually stop answering the telephone, keeping to routine becomes difficult, I have problems going to work and with my concentration and memory. Keeping to myself and not interacting with others seem to help me. I feel less of a burden to others and because being with people requires concentration which I find saps my energy, I feel I have more energy for other things.

We can see in this example a strategy of avoidance, designed to improve the client's mood.

'avoid other people, I gradually stop answering the telephone'
'Keeping to myself and not interacting with others . . .'

While in the short term we have already established that this can be quite effective, in the longer term this ultimately causes additional problems.

Panic disorder

Being in crowds at work, on the bus or in the supermarket is very stressful. I notice some rapid breathing, rapid heartbeat and sweating. I also think something bad will happen – I think I will collapse. I have to get home or I need to have someone with me all the time or have access to someone (via telephone, for example). Alternatively I find things much easier if I avoid these situations.

We can identify both avoidance and overcompensatory strategies, avoidance in an obvious sense by wishing to stay away from crowded social situations.

'Being in crowds at work, on the bus or in the supermarket . . . I avoid these situations'

> There is overcompensation in that the client reports the need to have someone with them at all times or easy access to someone for support and reassurance:
> *'I need to have someone with me all the time or have access to someone (via telephone, for example).'*

Examples such as these are typical of the patterns of behaviour clients engage in that cause difficulty in the longer term. It is the job of the practitioner to bring the client's attention to this. With this in mind, as part of preparation for continued wellness, the practitioner should collaboratively identify the unhelpful behaviours and triggers during treatment and then ask the client to reflect on their utility. Useful questions are (Hawton et al., 2003):

- What was life like before you became unwell?
- What changed in your thinking and behaviour?
- How did you deal with relationships with others?
- How did you deal with everyday problems and challenges?

Then:

- What did I change (in my thinking and behaviour) which led to an improvement?
- How can I continue to apply this new learning for the future?
- What are the potential barriers which may interfere with this?
- What can I do to address these barriers (problem solving)?
- Who are the people in my life that are helpful and unhelpful?

(Simmons and Griffiths, 2009)

How can the practitioner help the client develop a maintaining wellness plan?

We will now outline briefly some other useful questions which both the client and practitioner can ask to assist with the process towards the end of treatment. What should they do if they notice they are beginning to have difficulty? Coming up to completion of treatment, the practitioner should ask the client to reflect on their journey of recovery thus far. Completion of a recovery plan, such as those in Appendices 8 and 9), or asking the following types of questions can be useful in this process (Simmons and Griffiths, 2009):

- What is it that I have learned from treatment?
- Is there anything that I found particularly useful?
- Is there anything that I found to be ineffective?
- What sort of things could cause me difficulty in the future? (The client should not only think about the future but what caused them difficulties in the past – this helps establish patterns.)

- Are there any situations, people or any other triggers I need to be aware of that increase my vulnerability?
- What went/goes through my mind (thoughts or pictures)?
- What did/do I notice in my body?
- What feelings did/do I notice?
- What new learning can I apply?
- What are my early warning signs?

Warning signs are specific to each client and should be noted as things for the client to watch out for in the future, before treatment is complete. These early warning signs may include issues such as:

- giving up pleasurable activities;
- self-isolation/avoidance;
- sleep disturbance;
- unhelpful thinking styles becoming more common, e.g. thinking the worst or personalizing;
- thinking too much, e.g. worrying about minor issues or spending a lot of time thinking about the past (rumination).

One way of establishing early warning signs is to ask:

- If you were to go back to when you first started to feel unwell, what was the first sign of trouble that you would notice?

If clients have this information in written form, they will be able to refer to it in the future and revise it, as necessary. The strategies learned during treatment should continue to be practised on treatment completion. It is essential that this becomes a part of everyday life, whether it is the continued use of exposure or behavioural experiments for the treatment of anxiety problems or behavioural activation or a thought record for depression. For example, if a client had been diagnosed as an insulin-dependent diabetic, the client would be advised on the procedure for checking their blood sugar, exercise, eating and of course the importance of taking their medication. It would be expected that this becomes their new lived reality. In short, while the condition does not define the client, it becomes part of their lives, an essential daily pattern. This is the same for ongoing recovery and wellness from anxiety and mood disorders.

What should they do if they notice they are beginning to have difficulty? To identify if any of their triggers or unhelpful responses are involved, the client should ask themselves:

- Is this one of my triggers?
- How did I respond to this trigger? Was it helpful or unhelpful?
- What effect has this had on my mood/my behaviour/my body?

A useful question to remember which the client can be asked or ask of themselves is:

- If you noticed a friend or loved one beginning to have difficulties, what advice would you give to them?

The purpose here is to assist the thinking/problem-solving process. Quite often while we have difficulty arriving at adaptive coping solutions for ourselves, we still retain the capacity to provide very worthwhile advice to others, so this can be a very potent strategy (Simmons and Griffiths, 2009).

It may well be that the client will decide that they have coped well with the trigger and there is nothing to be concerned about. If, however, they decide that this trigger and associated response have the potential to negatively impact upon their thoughts, feelings and behaviours, the client should revise the strategies which worked when undergoing treatment and immediately begin this as self-therapy (Simmons and Griffiths, 2009). They may also ask themselves:

- If I do need to take action, should I contact anyone?
- If so, who would that be (family member, friend, and/or medical practitioner)?

If they, or other people whom they come into contact or are involved with, notice they are beginning to have difficulties or the return of unhelpful coping behaviours, they need to revise their alternative coping strategies or behaviours. To this end it is important to collaboratively create a plan which they can use if they identify that there are potential difficulties.

The client may consider contacting their GP for review if they need to, as the sooner they receive help, the less likely they are to require the same level of assistance they received previously. It can often be helpful to schedule a 'booster session' for the client a number of weeks after treatment ends, so that the practitioner and client can review how they have managed and revise any problem areas, before ultimate discharge.

Treatment continuation

It is important that the client continues to maintain the gains they have made once they are discharged; this means continuing with their newly learnt more adaptive coping strategies. This of course assists with maintaining wellness. Self-therapy or 'blueprinting' (Hawton et al., 2003) should be discussed by the practitioner and client in the last few sessions before treatment completion. Templates outlined in Appendices 8 and 9 can be utilized to assist with this.

It must be remembered that the focus of treatment has at its heart the client as practitioner; in other words, the client (with guidance) essentially treats themselves. Therefore, in order to maintain gains the client should essentially continue with this treatment. As with the formal treatment process, self-therapy tasks (or homework), should be set and adhered to. This ensures the best possible scenario for maintaining wellness and continuing to achieve valued goals. The client should be prepared for this pre-discharge and on discharge.

According to Beck (1995), the client should be encouraged to set aside specific time to engage in self-therapy once a week, moving to one to two times a month, then four sessions per year, with booster sessions annually thereafter. The benefit of following this format is that gains made by the client in treatment continue to be embedded and new behaviours and more balanced thinking styles become established. In other words, with practice, these new behavioural and cognitive styles now become part of the client's everyday life.

Medication

In terms of medication, this is something which the client should discuss with their GP or other medical professional and they should be encouraged to follow the advice given. It would be generally recommended, however, that even if the client is feeling well, they should continue to take their antidepressant medication, as prescribed, for at least six to twelve months, following which they should then consult with their medical professional before considering discontinuation (Paykel, 2001; Royal College of Psychiatrists, 2012). This is because there is a reduced risk of relapse following longer treatment, beyond resolution of symptoms. Some people who have had more than two episodes of depression may be advised to continue antidepressants for longer.

General advice

Clients should be wary of alcohol or illicit drug use and avoid using these as a coping strategy, as in the long term this will only add to their difficulties, including mimicking depressive and anxiety symptoms. The importance of their diet should be reinforced; this should be regular, balanced and healthy. It must be remembered that the body and brain can be considered a machine and, as such, they need fuel in order to function at an optimal level.

It is also important to remember that we all need to factor time into the daily routine to simply relax and have fun. Not isolating yourself and spending time with others is important. To that end, the client should be asked to identify people in their lives who can help with this, such as family and friends (see Chapter 4 on depression which includes behavioural activation). As with diet, exercise and regular physical activity are helpful for the promotion of good mental health. The client should be advised to exercise on a regular basis, as not only can this promote a healthy mind and body, it can also help bring them into contact with others (socialization and behavioural activation). The importance of sleep has been emphasized earlier in the book, however, to summarize, the client should be reminded to get into a good sleep pattern with a regular routine. For advice and strategies, review Chapter 6 on sleep. Lastly, it is important that the practitioner conveys to the client the importance of being generous to themselves. Often clients treat themselves harshly and should be reminded to compare how they treat themselves to how they treat others.

In conclusion, maintaining wellness begins as soon as assessment starts and should increasingly become the focus as the client moves towards the end of treatment. Two useful worksheets are included in Appendices 8 and 9 and can be completed with the client in the later stages of treatment. Both allow the client to reflect upon their course of treatment but importantly ask them to identify potential triggers and warning signs, so that they can construct a potential action plan should action become necessary. Lastly, the client as practitioner theme should always be emphasized as the cognitive behavioural intervention process is one which focuses upon the client effectively treating themselves, dealing with their own thoughts, feelings and behaviours and integrating this into a new way of life.

Summary

- Development of an individually tailored maintaining wellness plan starts at assessment and continues, throughout treatment, until discharge.
- It is vital that clients are aware of potential triggers, early warning signs and maintaining factors to remain well.
- Clients need to be prepared for normal mood variations.
- Continued 'client as practitioner' treatment in the long term needs to be built into the maintaining wellness plan.

Recommended reading

Fava, G.A., Rafanelli, C., Grandi, S., Conti, S. and Belluardo, P. (1998) Prevention of recurrent depression with cognitive behavioral therapy. *Archives of General Psychiatry*, 55: 816–20.

Hollon, S.D., Stewart, M.O. and Strunk, D. (2006) Enduring effects for cognitive behavior in the treatment of depression and anxiety. *Annual Review of Psychology*, 57: 285–315.

Richards, D. and Whyte, M. (2008) *Reach Out: National Programme Student Materials to Support the Delivery of Training for Psychological Wellbeing Practitioners Delivering Low Intensity Interventions*, 3rd edn. Rethink Mental Illness. http://cedar.exeter.ac.uk/iapt/iaptworkbooksandresources/ (accessed 23 May 2014).

8 Supervision

Introduction

In health care, supervision is often cited as important but these sentiments rarely amount to much unless the practitioner and supervisor share an agreed understanding of what it is and what it should include. We have all had different experiences of supervision; these differences impact upon our perception of the practice of supervision and indeed can raise the question, what is supervision?

This chapter addresses what supervision is, or certainly what it can be if you learn how to use it effectively, that is for your personal and professional development as well as for day–to-day caseload management. Guidelines and the evidence base for supervision are outlined. There is a particular emphasis on improved access to psychological therapies (IAPT) low-intensity cognitive behavioural interventions supervision in the United Kingdom, however, the format cited would be a useful template in any clinical supervision context. Examples are given of typical situations for which practitioners may find discussion in supervision supportive, and ethical, cultural and diversity issues are outlined using a case example. Pointers are given to potential pitfalls in supervision and how to avoid them.

What is supervision?

Supervision does not have a universally agreed definition. However, Milne (2007a: 440) has developed a working definition, following a systematic review of 24 empirical studies of clinical supervision, mainly from the learning disability field: 'The formal provision, by approved supervisors, of a relationship-based education and training that is work-focused and which manages, supports, develops and evaluates the work of supervisees.'

What are the functions of supervision?

Milne (2007a) defines the functions of supervision as quality control, maintaining and facilitating supervisees' competence and capability, and helping supervisees work effectively. Supervision covers a range of formative (knowledge and skill development), normative (monitoring and evaluation of practice) and restorative elements (support) (Proctor, 1986), which vary depending on whether the context is educational or clinical.

It is assumed that supervision supports and maintains supervisees' skills, ensures competent treatment for clients and reduces liability for organizations, although this has not been definitively proven (Cape and Barkham, 2002; Trinidad, 2007; Wheeler and Richards, 2007; White and Winstanley, 2010). There is, however, an expectation within a clinical governance framework that supervision of health care professionals, both during training and post-qualification, is necessary. To this end, there are best practice guidelines, which should be followed.

Guidelines on supervision

While supervision is not specifically legislated for, it occurs within a framework of legal, ethical and professional standards, policies and codes of practice, some of which are dependent on the core profession and employer of the practitioner (see Appendix 10). IAPT (2011) have recently produced guidelines for trainees who are not professionally affiliated prior to completion of training, as it is considered so important that ethical principles are adhered to within practice. IAPT have released supervision guidance (Turpin and Wheeler, 2011: 2) and have recognized the role of supervision as: 'a key activity, which will determine the success of the IAPT program'.

IAPT stipulate the regularity of case management supervision (at least one hour per week), that supervision includes clinical outcome evaluation, for example, PHQ–9 (Kroenke et al., 2001) and/or GAD–7 (Spitzer et al., 2006), and that it should be performed by experienced trained supervisors. In addition to case management supervision, low-intensity psychological wellbeing practitioners are recommended to have one hour per fortnight of group/individual supervision aimed at skills development and case discussion (Turpin and Wheeler, 2011).

What is the evidence for supervision?

The literature on specific CBT supervision is sparse and that of cognitive behavioural interventions even more so, as low-intensity intervention programmes are still in their infancy. Much of the CBT supervision literature is drawn from extrapolations of supervision from other mental health fields, particularly psychology and learning disability, and consensus statements about good practice (Ellis and Ladany, 1997; Falender et al., 2004; Roth and Pilling, 2008; Milne et al., 2010). The holy grail of CBT supervision research is proving supervision's assumed impact on client outcomes. This has been difficult due to the inevitable complexities of the supervisor–supervisee–client triad (Ellis and Ladany, 1997; Milne and James, 2000; Lee, 2005; Scaife, 2009).

A definitive model of CBT supervision is not prescribed or universally accepted, however, there is growing evidence that supervision is beneficial in enhancing skills and improving competency within the field of cognitive therapy and allied professions, as well as providing support for staff.

Within the field of mental health nursing a large, randomized controlled trial sought to demonstrate a causal relationship between trained supervisor support for mental health nurses and client outcomes, but no such link could be demonstrated (White and Winstanley, 2010). Supervisees, however, rated trained supervisors significantly better for trust/rapport and importance/value domains on the Manchester Clinical Supervision Scale (Winstanley, 2000). This is a validated supervisee-rated supervision evaluation tool used in nursing, based on Proctor's (1986) normative, restorative and formative elements. Higher-rated supervision was also associated with lower burn-out, which is an important factor in stretched services.

In brief CBT skills or communication skills training it has been found that supervision has a valuable role in maintaining skills and confidence. Mannix et al. (2006) found that both CBT skills and confidence reduced following brief CBT technique training for palliative care staff when they received no ongoing supervision. Those with access to supervision demonstrated improved competence and maintained confidence. Heaven et al. (2006) demonstrated similar effects of supervision on nurse communication skills maintenance. Maunder et al. (2008) also demonstrated a statistically significant improvement in GPs' knowledge and use of CBT skills following a brief CBT training programme by experienced supervisors/trainers, however, there was no follow-up, so it is not known if this was maintained.

Follow-up is important if the trainee is to avoid the 'tendency to return to baseline' following training (Miller and Mount, 2001). This is a common phenomenon and a major function of supervision after training is to consolidate skills taught, ensure those newly achieved skills and competencies are maintained and offer an opportunity to further refine them.

Intuitively, supervisors and therapists are aware of the utility of supervision, so it is the most highly rated method of developing competence for supervisors and supervisees (Lucock et al., 2006). There is also evidence to suggest that following training, without ongoing supervision and support, there is skill and confidence loss (Miller and Mount, 2001; Mannix et al., 2006; Heaven et al., 2006). In other psychotherapy fields, it has been discovered that following training, first development stops, and then practice reverts to previously established models of practice (MacKay et al., 2000). This suggests ongoing training and supervision are necessary for knowledge and skill maintenance and development. Butterworth et al. (2008) conclude that there is an onus on organizations to sustain and develop supervision.

Clinical case management supervision (Richards and Whyte, 2009)

Within the IAPT program, for psychological wellbeing practitioners working with clients using low-intensity cognitive behavioural interventions, supervision is normally conducted by experienced CBT practitioners, working in high-intensity programmes, on a weekly basis. Practitioners have large caseload numbers, so there is a need to prepare in advance of supervision in order to get the most out of the structured sessions. Information technology systems can assist in the preparation for and the execution of supervision.

IAPT (Richards and Whyte, 2009) have stipulated that supervision should cover the following:

Supervision content

- full caseload numbers and management;
- new clients;
- existing clients (at least every four weeks);
- clients with increased risk;
- clients with outcome measures above 15 for PHQ-9 or GAD-7;
- clients for whom the practitioner requests support;
- clients who have not attended/have overdue appointments.

Basic client information required for supervision

- gender;
- age;
- main problem statement;
- level of risk;
- onset and duration of current problem;
- previous episodes/past treatment;
- current scores on clinical measures (at least PHQ-9, GAD-7);
- co-morbidity issues;
- cultural, language or disability considerations;
- employment status;
- treatment from GP or other health care professionals;
- low-intensity treatment plan;
- low-intensity treatment already initiated.

This enables the supervisor and practitioner to decide if this is an appropriate case and management plan.

The following additional information is necessary for existing clients having a four-weekly review, for those clients with higher risk indicated by their outcome measurement scores or for those clients for whom the practitioner is requesting support:

Additional client information

- intervention summary to date;
- number, duration and type of contacts;
- client engagement with low-intensity treatment;
- client response to low-intensity treatment;
- scores on sessional clinical outcome measures;
- low-intensity treatment plan;
- alternative treatment plan including stepping up to high-intensity treatment.

This additional information is to help ascertain whether there needs to be a change to the management plan, including 'stepping up' to high-intensity treatment.

Appropriate cases to select for supervision include:

- the client who has high outcome measure scores (above 15 on PHQ-9 or GAD-7);
- the client who is expressing suicidal ideas or where there are concerns about other risk, including child neglect;
- the client you think is experiencing difficulties beyond your level of competency, for example, co-morbidity, and who may require high-intensity CBT or other treatment.

It should be noted that if you have serious concerns about a client, then you should contact your supervisor or other senior colleague or GP urgently rather than waiting until a scheduled supervision session.

For those clients who have not attended for treatment, dropped out of treatment or where appointments are overdue, the following information, in addition to the basic client information, is required:

- summary of progress before contact loss;
- number of attempts made to contact the client;
- number and methods of contact attempted, e.g. letter/phone call;
- date/time of any telephone calls.

Supervision contracts

We shall now review the importance and use of supervision contracts. In addition, an example template will also be outlined.

It is important to have a supervision contract with your supervisor. This may sound very formal, but if all parties explicitly know the ground rules and expectations it may prevent problems later. How many divorcees later state they wished they had had a pre-nuptial agreement? Contracts should cover the following areas (Townend, 2004; Milne, 2009; Scaife, 2009):

Contract content

- core professional/ethical guidelines followed including confidentiality (and its limits);
- time period and review arrangements;
- practical considerations including: frequency (time/day), place, punctuality, courtesy/respect – including dedicated time and avoidance of interruptions, e.g. mobile phone/email use during supervision and the need for full participation of both parties;
- organizational expectations;

- goals/objectives;
- methods – discussion/role plays/audio/video recording; review/live observation;
- constructive feedback;
- cancellation arrangements;
- action in the event of supervision relationship breakdown;
- indemnity;
- supervision recording arrangements.

An excellent example of a British Association of Behavioural and Cognitive Psychotherapy (BABCP) supervision contract by Townend (2004), which includes most of these elements, is available online (IAPT, 2011).

What do you want from supervision?

Often in a busy role it is easy to get swept along and suddenly realize that another year has gone by. The American philanthropist Elbert Hubbard is quoted as saying: 'Many people fail in life, not for lack of ability or brains or even courage, but simply because they have never organized their energies around a goal.'

Deciding what your goals are for supervision, in other words what you want to get out of it both in the short term (next session) and longer term, is important. Otherwise your supervision will more than likely only include day-to-day case management and limit your ability to get the most from it in terms of your personal and skill development. To be able to do this, it is important to understand where you are coming from by doing a 'needs assessment' (Milne, 2007b):

Needs assessment questions

- What is your background/core profession?
- What skills do you have to bring?
- What areas do you struggle with?
- What do you want to learn more about?
- What is your preferred learning style?

Learning style is another important component of skill acquisition. It is important as it can influence your learning opportunities. Honey and Mumford (2000) built upon Kolb's (1984) integrative theory of experiential learning and proposed that people in a learning situation, such as supervision, move between four stages of learning: learners have an experience (activist), reflect on it (reflector), draw conclusions (theorist) and then put theory into practice (pragmatist). It would be a useful exercise to complete Honey and Mumford's (2000) Learning Style Questionnaire to establish your preferred learning style. One example would be if you have a preference for a theorist style, you may enjoy reading about practice but shy away from role plays and miss the opportunity for experiential learning (activist style). If you have an activist learning style, you may 'jump ahead' and do behavioural experiments with clients before they have been properly planned (theorist style). Knowing your learning style will enable you to establish if you have a bias for particular modes of learning and possibly miss opportunities to expand your learning repertoire.

Supervision can be an uncomfortable experience. It can be associated with feeling deskilled. Training or practising to deliver cognitive behavioural interventions can often involve the trainee practitioner changing from a very directive to a more collaborative approach or from a non-directive stance to a more structured approach. This can prove difficult for the practitioner during training. As an experienced practitioner in a previous health care role, exposing your possible lack of knowledge or skill in a new role to a valued colleague can be potentially frightening.

To understand why learning new things is so difficult we need to review learning theory. Much of adult learning theory is based on Piaget's theories of childhood knowledge growth: that through a process of equilibration, a person resolves incompatibilities between what they know currently and the perception and meaning made of a new experience, which does not fit with current knowledge.

If there is an adequate fit between current knowledge or 'action scheme' and new learning, then the new knowledge will be assimilated (current knowledge is effectively built upon). If, however, there is not an adequate fit between what is known to the practitioner and what is newly learned, then the person experiences cognitive conflict or dissonance, which feels uncomfortable. This can lead to disengagement or resistance to new learning. If, however, the person persists, it may result in a new action scheme for the new knowledge (accommodation) (Atherton, 2009; Scaife, 2009). This is like having a filing system for new knowledge. If there is not an existing file, then you will have to make one up, which is going to require more effort than using an existing pre-labelled file.

Another consideration to take into account when engaged in supervision is the learning atmosphere. It is considered that a certain element of arousal is necessary for optimal learning, above which is panic and below which boredom sets in, both resulting in sub-optimal learning (Csikszentmihalyi, 1975). This means that for effective learning to take place in supervision, it should present a challenge. Milne et al. (2009) have described safety behaviours in supervision, where both parties avoid moving to experiential learning, for example, therapy videos, which means supervision may be a comfortable experience, but it is not going to help improve skill, so is unlikely to improve the quality of treatment clients receive.

We do not come to supervision as blank slates – we come with previous knowledge, skills, experience (good and bad) and beliefs about supervision. This can also influence our learning within supervision.

'To study the phenomena of disease without books is to sail an uncharted sea, while to study books without patients is not to go to sea at all' (Feather, 2008). This statement supports the idea that both declarative (learning about facts and theory) and procedural (putting theory into action i.e. actual clinical practice) knowledge are required to practise clinical skills and that they must go hand in hand. This concept is formulated in Bennett-Levy's (2007) Declarative-Procedural-Reflective model, which adds the element of reflection on practice as an essential feature. Supervision is your opportunity to reflect on your practice, as you prepare and participate. It allows you to consider your knowledge and skills and any deficits which need to be addressed, before putting theory into practice.

Self-practice and self-reflection are thought to result in a more complete understanding of the implementation of cognitive behavioural techniques, making practitioners more enthusiastic and competent about explaining techniques to clients as well as becoming more self-aware (Bennett-Levy, 2007). It is recommended that you should try to use the cognitive behavioural techniques for yourself before ever suggesting them to a client as this will give you a much better idea of the challenges and obstacles that need to be overcome. If you have difficulty completing an activity monitoring record, how difficult will it be for a depressed client? If you are reluctant to complete a thought record and rate just how angry you felt after a row with your partner, what will it be like for your client? After completion of the technique, ask yourself:

- What have I learnt about this technique that will help me to use this with clients?
- What do I need to make sure I explain?

This reflection will help you to understand more fully the practice of CB techniques and develop an understanding of how to implement techniques and develop procedural rules for practice, for example, if . . . then I need to . . .

Supervisee goals

What motivates you? Is your end goal to become a CBT therapist working in a high-intensity programme? Do you want to manage a service? Do you want to be skilled in treating panic disorder? An excellent source of ideas for goals to further your cognitive behavioural intervention practice is Roth and Pilling's (2007) CBT competences framework, which is presented as a map online, with each competence on the map linked to a breakdown of the core knowledge and skills necessary to meet that competence. It is available at: http://www.ucl.ac.uk/clinical-psychology/CORE/CBT_Framework.htm#Map.

It covers five broad areas:

Roth and Pilling's CBT competences framework

- Generic Therapeutic Competence
- Basic CBT Competences
- Specific Behavioural and Cognitive Therapy Competences
- Problem Specific Competences
- Metacompetences

If you wanted to set the goal of being able to adhere to an agenda, what steps would you need to take to get there? To consider this you need to break your goal down into SMART goals (see Table 8.1).

Ultimately, you can make best use of supervision by preparing adequately and presenting a succinct, honest and open account of your work, on the understanding

Table 8.1 SMART goal table

Specific	What precisely do I want to achieve? Who can help me? (e.g. supervisor or colleagues) How? When? Where?	
Measured	How will I measure the achievement of the goal? What stages do I need to measure to ensure I am on track?	
Agreed	Does my supervisor agree that this is a suitable goal?	
Realistic	Given my current knowledge and skills and other commitments, is this a realistic, achievable goal?	
Time limited	Set a date for the overall goal and work back to establish the time limits for the other stages in achievement of the goal. Then ask again, is this realistic?	

that you will receive constructive feedback. It is necessary to take on board feedback and your own practice reflections and apply these to your future practice. If you or your supervisor identify knowledge deficits, then it is important that you take the initiative to remedy this, by looking up a textbook or relevant article and then applying this to your practice (Roth and Pilling, 2007). This is declarative-procedural-reflective learning in practice!

Supportive supervision

As well as being an excellent way to reflect on and hone your knowledge and skills, supervision should also be seen as your back-up and support. It is therefore important that you are able to trust and confide in your supervisor (Bordin, 1983; Scaife, 2009). If you find certain work difficult for personal reasons or if certain cases have a personal impact on you, for example, vicarious trauma, it is important that you are able to discuss this with your supervisor as this may well affect your health and your practice. As mentioned earlier, it can be distressing if a client expresses suicidal thoughts and we reiterate here our recommendation that you should consult a senior colleague/supervisor for advice and support.

In addition, when you start using cognitive behavioural techniques, it can be quite daunting to deal with the level of emotion that clients may experience initially, for example, during behavioural experiments or exposure. In our experience, most trainees instinctively want to reassure and quell the client's anxiety, especially if the practitioner had a previous supportive counselling or other vocational caring role. What effect do you think this will have on the outcome of the behavioural experiment? If you are finding coping with client emotion difficult, this is an excellent topic to bring up in supervision. Remember, your supervisor has more than likely been in the same position and can guide you on how to deal with this.

Occasionally ethical dilemmas occur within treatment, for instance, being asked out by a client and it is important that this is discussed within supervision. A good rule of thumb is that if you behave differently or have a different reaction to clients than is normal, then this is something that should be discussed in supervision (Kent, 2011). This may be an indicator that the practitioner's attitudes or beliefs are interfering with treatment or that additional support is required. If this is not identified and addressed, difficulties within the interpersonal relationship may negatively impact on the treatment process (Prasko et al., 2010).

Case example

Jane is a young (26-year-old) but fairly experienced practitioner who presented a DVD of a case of a 70-year-old lady with a six-month history of depression in supervision. The case had been presented before and the client was not making any progress in terms of her mood and there had been no change in outcome measures after five sessions. The clip of the DVD showed that Jane was still asking the client questions that would usually have been covered previously in assessment. The supervisor was fairly sure they had seen similar questions being asked before at the last supervision session. It seemed that Jane was in a cycle of continuous assessment and had not progressed to using cognitive behavioural interventions. Behavioural activation had not yet been tried.

> Supervisor (S): *I wonder what you think the reason is for the lack of progress in this lady's case?*
>
> Jane (J): *Well, I am worried that I haven't got it right. I don't want to start treating her until I am sure I have it right.*
>
> S: *What would be so bad about that?*
>
> J: *I would hate to get it wrong and then have to change tack half-way through.*
>
> S: *Have you ever had to change treatment before when you get new information about a client?*
>
> J: *Well, yes. But this case is different. She is older so I don't want to ask her to do things, because I know it is more difficult for her, and then get it wrong and have to change treatment. She said she wasn't too sure if this would work for her so I have to get it right.*

In this case, do you think any of Jane's beliefs or attitudes could be interfering with treatment? It is vitally important that we are aware of our own cultural beliefs and attitudes, but it is equally important that we respect the values of others, including clients in our care, who may hold different values to those we have. Diversity is protected by equality and human rights legislation (Human Rights Act, 1998) which has its roots in good ethical principles. This legislation governs the fair treatment of all people regardless of their age, gender, sexual orientation, marital status, religious or spiritual beliefs, disability or sensory impairment and race. Legislation and good ethics underpin the majority of professional standards (see Appendix 10).

In practice this means that all clients should have equal access to care and that steps are taken to try to ensure this is facilitated in a sensitive manner, for example, through the use of a more accessible venue, the use of interpreters and/or involvement of carers (where appropriate). All clients should be actively encouraged to participate in their assessment, treatment and recovery and the practitioner should not make assumptions about what the person may or may not be able to do (Richards and Whyte, 2009). Treatment should be a collaborative process with the practitioner and client working together as a team. In the example above Jane may have held certain assumptions about older people, which were not necessarily consciously discriminatory, but were having an impact on the client's treatment. Do you think Jane may hold any other beliefs about herself as a practitioner that could also be interfering with treatment?

Supervision problems

Most supervisory relationship problems can probably be avoided by having a conversation about ground rules, and making implicit expectations explicit from the beginning (Safran and Muran, 2001; Scaife, 2009). This is further strengthened by a supervision contract, which should set out what to do in the case of a difficulty in the relationship. In the first instance, it is usually advisable to discuss the issue explicitly as professionals, as both parties have a responsibility for maintaining the relationship. The issue may well have been due to a misunderstanding or misinterpretation and can easily be resolved following discussion.

If, however, the issue is more serious, for example, sexually inappropriate behaviour or abuse of power, then it would be advisable to discuss this with a senior colleague for advice and support. Also, if you think that your supervision is not of an appropriate standard or that you are being advised to practise unsafely, this would be a matter to raise with a senior colleague.

One important factor to note is that supervision should not cross over the boundary line to become therapy for the supervisee. If the supervisee considers that they would benefit from therapy, it would be advisable to consult another therapist, with whom there is less likely to be such a power differential within the relationship (Willemyns et al., 2003).

Summary

- Supervision is essential for ensuring competency of practitioners in a supportive way, and therefore client safety.
- Supervision can be effectively used for personal and professional development as well as case management, if the supervisee is adequately prepared and goal-directed.
- Practitioners need to consider their own beliefs and cultural values and how these should not influence the treatment they provide to a diverse population.
- Use of supervision contracts at the outset may prevent later problems.
- Supervision boundaries are important.

Recommended reading

Milne, D. (2009) *Evidence-based Clinical Supervision*. Oxford: BPS/Blackwell.
Scaife, J. (2009) *Supervision in the Mental Health Professions: A Practitioner's Guide*, 2nd edn. Hove: Brunner-Routledge.

Appendix 1: Client history form

Name:	Address:	Tel. no:
GP:	Consultant	Date of birth:
Next of kin:	Date:	Hosp. no.
Contact no.		

Please carefully complete each section below. Try to be as accurate and as honest as you can. If you have any difficulty completing this form please speak to your health care practitioner.

What effect have your current problems had on your social life?

What effect have your current problems had on your ability to work?

Was it you who decided to come for help?

What effect have your current problems had on relationships?

Anything else?

Targets/goals

What do you hope to gain from attending treatment? Specific targets and goals are necessary. For example: after treatment I hope to be able to do the following:

History of current problems

When did you first experience your current difficulties? When did you notice a change?

Are there times when your life has been better than this?

Have you had previous treatment for this problem?

In your view, did it work?

If yes, what helped?

Are you on any medication at present? (If yes, please list.)

Have you been prescribed medication in the past?

If you use alcohol, how much do you drink each week?

How many cigarettes per day do you smoke?

Do you use street or illicit drugs or have you in the past?

How much tea, coffee or other caffeine drinks do you drink per day?

Anything else?

History

Have you ever been treated for this or any other mental health problem in the past?

Have you any medical problems?

Have you ever been in trouble with the police?

Personality

How would you describe yourself before your problems began?

How would you describe yourself now?

Family history/family tree

Family member	Any mental health problems?
FATHER (age, health, type of person)	
MOTHER (age, health, type of person)	
SIBLINGS (age, gender and type of person)	
Are there any problems with how you get on with any members of your family?	
Who was your main care provider as a child?	

Personal history

Where were you born?
What schools and colleges did you attend?
What qualifications did you obtain?

Current social history

Where do you currently live and with whom?
Are you currently employed?
Have you any financial problems?

Work history

Have you ever experienced problems with work?
When did you start work? (types of work)

Have you any hobbies or interests (either now or in the past)?
If currently employed, what is your present job?

Sexual history

When did you reach puberty?
When did you have your first intimate relationship?
Any problems with intimate relationships?

How long have you been in your most recent relationship?
Partner's name, age, state of health?
How might you describe the relationship?
If you have children, list their names, ages and any problems you may have with them.

Mental state

These questions are about how you have been feeling in the last week. Please give details of any change.

How would you describe your mood?
Have you ever thought life not worth living?
What is your normal sleeping pattern and how has it changed?
Has your appetite increased or decreased?
Have you lost or gained weight without actively trying to?
Have you any problems with your memory and concentration?
Have you noticed any change in your energy level?
Have you noticed any change in your level of interest in sex?

Goals for therapy

Please consider the following statements and bring this form to your first appointment.

My current difficulties limit my life in the following ways:

If I did not have my current problems I would be able to:

1.
2.
3.
4.
5.

Name:	Date:	Signed

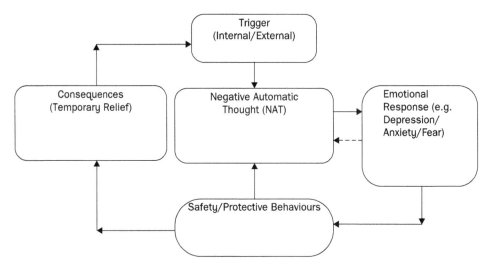

Figure A1 Generic CBT maintenance model

Appendix 2: SMART goal setting form

Specific	Set goals that are as specific as possible. This means setting dates, times, identifying resources needed, etc.	
Measurable	The goal should be capable of being measured to allow you to know when you have met them.	
Achievable	The goals set should be achievable, therefore realistic given the time available, not an exercise in risking setting you up to fail.	
Relevant	Is this important to you, does it concern an activity you value, or will it help you achieve something you value?	
Time limited	Set a time by which you hope the goal will be achieved. If it's longer than a week, then go back to the Achievable section.	

Appendix 3: Client information sheet
What we do and how we feel: behavioural imbalance
(Created in conjunction with Roy Cheetham)

Consider that each of us carries a tank or reservoir of reserves (made up of neuro-chemicals and psychological reserves) that when topped up, and fully functioning, enables us to carry on enthusiastically attending to all we have to do.

When our 'tank' is 'topped up' our energy levels are high and motivation is strong. However, there are, in every life, drains on our reserves; hassles and problems that bounce up constantly and knock us down or cause us grief. These hassles and problems are a constant drain in all our lives. In Figure A2 we see a tank with an outlet pipe that leads to our 'turbine' (this represents drive, motivation and energy).

Because all of us face daily hassles our reserves are constantly being depleted, therefore there is a need to constantly top up our 'tank' or 'reservoir' of reserves. If our level of reserves drop, so too do our energy levels and motivation can be difficult to maintain.

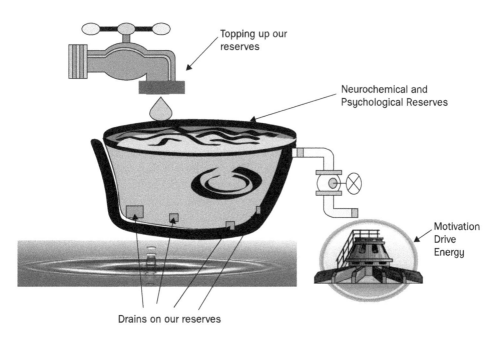

Figure A2

How do antidepressant tablets work?

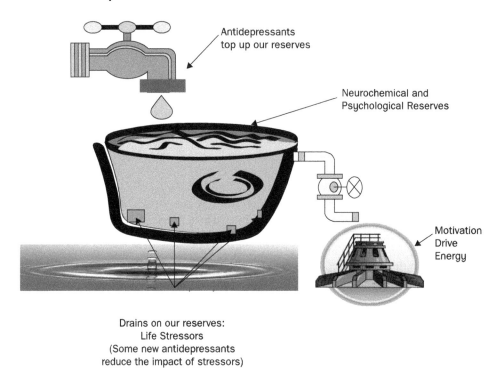

Drains on our reserves:
Life Stressors
(Some new antidepressants
reduce the impact of stressors)

Figure A3

One way of looking at antidepressant medication is that when someone is depressed, those antidepressant medications allow more resources to be made available to the person suffering low mood. They effectively 'turn on the tap' and 'top up' our reserves artificially in an attempt to restore motivation, drive, energy and engagement with life. Antidepressants also improve our ability to manage stress by reducing the stress response. The problem is that when we stop using antidepressants then our reservoir of reserves can become depleted again and slow down our 'turbine', which once again reduces motivation and energy.

What then is nature's or life's antidepressant? When we don't take antidepressants what turns on our 'tap' and replenishes our reserves? The answer is to be found in actively engaging in life. More specifically two forms of activity:

- activities which bring pleasure and are inherently rewarding
- activities which bring a sense of achievement

Both these types of activity are rewarding and it seems it is positive rewarding activities which act as nature's antidepressant. Rewarding activities seem to act as gains which can balance out the losses we endure due to the unavoidable daily hassles of everyday life.

How does activity act as an antidepressant?

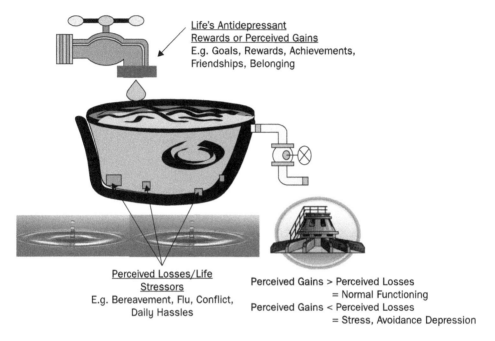

Figure A4

Activities that give us a sense of reward could be considered as perceived gains, while the day-to-day hassles all of us face could be considered perceived losses. A balanced life is therefore one where perceived rewarding gains outstrip (on average) perceived stressors or losses. We know that when people become depressed, for whatever reason, they reduce positive rewarding activity and seem to dwell longer and more intensely on life's stressors.

This contributes to increased stress, often further withdrawal or avoidance, a further depletion of our reserves and a deepening of depression. The difficulty is we don't possess batteries therefore we can't just do one (even spectacular) rewarding activity and hope that keeps depression at bay. We need to engage in rewarding activities (either pleasure or achievement) constantly to keep our reserves topped up.

What kind of activity helps keep us motivated and energized?

The answer to this is to be found by asking what is valuable to us or worth doing in terms of our own personal lives. One way is to tap into those activities you did before you became depressed. How does your activity level and the type of activity you do now compare with your activity level and the type of activity you once would have engaged in? What we could suggest is that you record in a diary what your activity level is now and then. Once completed, think about how it has changed compared to what you used to do before you became depressed.

An example of someone who is fighting the behavioural imbalance

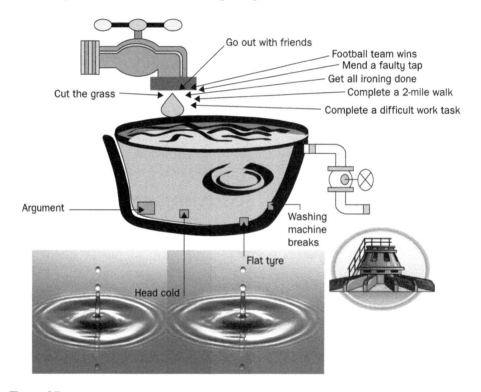

Figure A5

In the above diagram we can see someone who has their fair share of hassles but for whom this is balanced out by a fairly active schedule that offers rewards in terms of pleasure (football team wins, contact with friends) and a sense of achievement (cutting grass, finishing work task, mending tap, etc.). This individual's reserves are being depleted but their active lifestyle ensures their reserves remain topped up.

Now measure: compare your gains to your losses today!

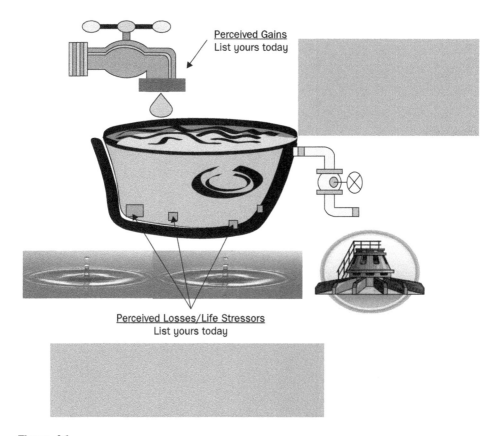

Figure A6

Appendix 4: Client information sheet on bodily changes during stress

In any given stressful situation (real or imagined), humans adopt one of the three techniques to deal with that stress: the fight, flight or freeze response. When this response is activated to deal with real danger we can accept and understand it and it causes us no bother. However, when this response is provoked by an imagined threat or a false alarm (such as believing anxiety symptoms are a sign that you are going mad or going to drop down dead), then the effects of the fight, flight, freeze response can actually add to the person's stress because these harmless self-protective responses can themselves be misinterpreted as further evidence the person is at risk of madness or imminent death.

The aim of this information sheet is to help you understand what these responses mean, as well as understand how they can be activated. Think of the last time you were in a stressful or dangerous situation. What did you do and what did you notice was happening to your body?

The answer is that your body most likely implemented one of the three responses that automatically come into action when any person is faced with a situation that induces stress or is perceived as dangerous: the fight, flight, freeze response. This response is activated in response to both real danger and imagined danger. It is activated both by real threatening situations and worry about potential threatening situations. Worry of being mugged and robbed on the way home is treated the same as actually being attacked and mugged on the way home. In other words it is activated by real danger and the worry about real danger. The response, once activated, means a person's body will adopt any of these three responses (fight, flight, freeze) to deal with and attempt to protect the individual from an actual dangerous situation or the worry that an actual dangerous situation may exist.

These responses are very useful for real life-threatening sources of stress and threats such as being mugged, being chased by a dangerous dog or escaping from a burning building. However, in modern life, sources of stress have escalated to include hectic work deadlines, fear of job loss, fear of being humiliated, fear of making social mistakes, fear of being viewed as a failure and fear of being not as good as others. These relatively new sources of stress still provoke the same ancient fight, flight, freeze responses available to our ancestors 80,000 years ago.

How the body reacts to the fight, flight, freeze response

- The breathing rate increases in order to feed muscle and other vital organs with oxygen in order to help fight or run.
- The heart rate quickens in order to get that oxygen from the lungs to muscle via the bloodstream.

- Muscles tense up in preparation for instant action.
- Pupils dilate or open wider to allow us to take in more information.
- Blood is rapidly transferred from non-vital organs such as the digestive system to our muscles and limbs, providing them with extra energy for fighting or running.

This response makes us overly alert (hypervigilant), feelings of pain are dampened, our responses quicken and overall our body is prepared for an assault. Once the brain perceives the danger has passed, these bodily sensations are turned off and our body returns to its normal state.

Problems with the fight, flight, freeze response

The above response seems like an excellent coping mechanism and has been responsible for our continued survival as a species. However, it was essentially designed to be activated quickly, protect us from danger rapidly and then return to normal quickly. Unfortunately when the threat is not real but is generated in our head in the form of threat thoughts or beliefs, there is no escape from them and therefore this leads to the response being switched on for much longer than it was designed for. The effect of this prolonged use of the fight, flight, freeze system can produce side effects that, while harmless, can feed the fear that something catastrophic is happening to our body.

- The breathing rate initially increases in order to feed muscle and other vital organs with oxygen to help us fight or run. However, if this continues for a long period it can lead to over-breathing (hyperventilation), a sensation of not getting enough air, a sensation of dizziness and a dry mouth and dry throat.
- The heart rate initially quickens in order to get that oxygen from the lungs to muscle via the bloodstream. However, if this mechanism is switched on too long the individual can experience increased heart rate, heart pounding and palpitations.
- Muscles initially tense up in preparation for instant action. Yet if muscles stay tense too long, they can start to shake and become sore and painful. Muscle groups in the legs, arms, chest, neck, back and shoulders can become tight, hot and painful.
- The pupils initially dilate or open wider to allow us to take in more information. But focused attention for a prolonged time can make us jumpy and on edge as well as sensitive to light.
- Blood is initially rapidly transferred from non-vital organs such as the digestive system to our muscles and limbs, providing them with extra energy for fighting or running. However, if this is not corrected quickly the stomach (which needs a good blood supply) can start to churn or the person can begin to feel nauseous.

This response can keep us overly alert (hypervigilant) for much too long (vision and hearing can then become overly sensitive and distorted), feelings of pain begin to be experienced as muscles remain too tense too long and our fight, flight, freeze responses begin to feel dangerous and create a new source of threat. This in turn keeps the fight, flight, freeze response firmly on and so a vicious cycle occurs.

We may try to avoid those bodily sensations and stop doing normal everyday activities because they bring on bodily changes. Before too long we are constantly looking out for any change in our body and this can limit what we do.

Appendix 5: Fear hierarchy

Grade in order of difficulty	Situation avoided	Level of distress 0–8
5		
4		
3		
2		
1		

Appendix 6: Exposure diary

NAME:................................. WEEK COMMENCING:.........................

GOALS FOR 1 ....
THE WEEK 2 ....
3 ....

0	1	2	3	4	5	6	7	8
none		slight		moderate		marked		panic

Rate your distress levels using the above scale

	SESSION		GOAL NO	TASK PERFORMED	ANXIETY			COMMENTS E.g. Avoidance
DATE	BEGIN	END			BEFORE	DURING	AFTER	

Appendix 7: Behavioural experiment worksheet

What negative prediction is to be tested and how much do I believe this thought? (0% = not at all 100% = totally) e.g. 80%

```
```

What is the alternative explanation for what is happening and how much do I believe this? (0% = not at all 100% = totally) e.g. 20%

```
```

How might I test this? What experiment could I devise to check out which belief is more accurate?

```
```

What current safety behaviour/behaviours am I going to have to drop in order to truly test this belief?

```



```

What problems am I going to have to deal with and how may I overcome them?

```



```

Set a time and date for the experiment.

Reflect on what actually happened after the experiment. What did doing this experiment tell me about both explanations? What does it tell me about my thinking?

```



```

Rerate negative prediction (%)

Rerate alternative prediction (%)

Appendix 8: Maintaining wellness form

Name:	Address:	Tel no:
GP:	Consultant	Date of birth:
Next of kin: Contact no.	Date:	Client no.

Please carefully complete each section below. Try to be as accurate and as honest as you can. If you have any difficulty completing this form, please speak to your practitioner.

The following are a series of questions to establish what have you learned that has been helpful.

Cognitive therapy interventions should have been a learning experience. Unlike other forms of talking therapy the emphasis is NOT on tackling every day-to-day crisis or on simply 'talking things out'. The aim is to identify and correct problematic ways of thinking and behaving and most importantly taking action to change unhealthy or counter-productive behaviours and reactions.

Question 1

Try, in your own words, to clearly identify the problems you originally presented with. Please split your answer into the following sections and give a real example to demonstrate each problem.

Problems with thinking or the way you viewed the world (world view):

| |
| |
| |
| |
| |

Behavioural reactions/responses to problems: What behaviour may have helped maintain the problems?

| |
| |
| |
| |
| |
| |
| |
| |
| |

Question 2

Consider your answer to Question 1, then clearly identify and list the specific problems associated with the way you once behaved and reacted.

Question 3

What has changed? (Be definite and specific – point to real behaviour changes such as things that you now can do which were impossible or difficult once.) How did you do it?

_____
| |
_____

Question 4

Give specific examples of how these changes have helped you and those close to you.

_____
| |
_____

| |
| |
| |
| |
| |

Question 5

Please give specific actions you can use alone and independently to resolve any further crisis. Try to think about what you have learned in treatment and how you may employ those techniques if the problems return. (This question is designed to measure if treatment has taught you to be your own practitioner and to enable you to be better prepared should problems return.)

| |
| |
| |
| |
| |
| |
| |
| |
| |

| |
| |
| |
| |
| |

Question 6

If you feel you have not yet got the skills to tackle your problems with thinking or behaving, what part of treatment will you need to concentrate on before formal treatment has finished?

| |
| |
| |
| |
| |
| |
| |
| |
| |

Action plan: finally, can you clearly and specifically list what precise action you will take if the problems we have been dealing with return?

Appendix 9: Summary: staying well

What new learning has taken place?
What was most helpful/what was not?
What new learning should I continue to practise?
What situations are likely to cause me difficulty in the future (be mindful of thoughts, behaviours and feelings both physical and emotional, also extremes)?
What should I do if I begin to have difficulties? (Plan)
Whom should I contact? What are my supports?

Appendix 10: Professional and Ethical Practice Code

British Association of Behavioural and Cognitive Psychotherapists. 2009.
Standards of Conduct, Performance and Ethics in the Practice of Behavioural and Cognitive Psychotherapies. Available at: http://www.babcp.com/silo/files/conduct-and-ethics.pdf
General Medical Council. 2002. Making and Using Visual and Audio Recordings of Patients-Guidance for Doctors. Available at: http://www.gmc-uk.org/guidance/ethical_guidance/making_audiovisual.asp
General Medical Council. 2004. Continuing Professional Development. London: GMC.
General Medical Council. 2006. Good Medical Practice. London: GMC.
General Medical Council. 2009. Confidentiality. London: GMC.
Nursing Midwifery Council. 2008. The Code: Standards of Conduct, Performance and Ethics for Nurses and Midwifes. London:NMC.
British Association of Social Workers (BASW). (2002). British Association of Social Workers. The Code of Ethics for Social Work. Birmingham: BASW. Available at: http://cdn.basw.co.uk/membership/coe.pdf
Royal College of Psychiatrists in partnership with Royal College of General Practitioners. 2008. Psychological Therapies in Psychiatry and Primary Care. *College Report 151*. London: RCPsych.

For practitioners who do not have a professional affiliation before training:

Improved Access To Psychological Therapies. (2011). Ethical codes for non-professionally affiliated staff. United Kingdom: IAPT. Available at: http://www.iapt.nhs.uk/search/?keywords=ethical+code

N.B. The code of practice which is adhered to will be dependent on the profession of the supervision parties, however all professional guidelines are underpinned by human rights, anti-discriminatory legislation and ethical principles. Legislation and policy relevant to your practice will be dependent on your location and is subject to change.

References

Ackerman, S.J. and Hilsenroth, M.J. (2003) 'A review of therapist characteristics and techniques positively impacting the therapeutic alliance', *Clinical Psychology Review*, 23(1), 1–33.

American Psychiatric Association (APA) (2013) *Diagnostic and Statistical Manual of Mental Disorders*, 5th edn. Washington, DC: APA.

Anderson, I.M. et al. (2008) 'Evidence-based guidelines for treating depressive disorders with antidepressants: a revision of the 2000 British Association for Psychopharmacology guidelines', *Journal of Psychopharmacology*, 22(4), 343–96.

Appleby, L., Cooper, J., Amos, T. and Faragher, B. (1999a) 'Psychological autopsy of suicides by people aged under 35', *British Journal of Psychiatry*, 175, 168–74.

Appleby, L., Shaw, J., Amos, T., McDonnell, R., Harris, C., McCann, K., Kiernan, K., Davis, S., Bickley, H. and Parsons, R. (1999) 'Suicide within 12 months of contact with mental health services: national clinical survey', *British Medical Journal*, 318, 1235–9.

Atherton, J.S. (2009) *Learning and Teaching: Piaget's Developmental Theory*. www.learningandteaching.info/learning/piaget.htm (accessed 27 May 2014).

Baker, T.B., Piper, M.E., Majeskie, M.R. and Fiore, M.C. (2004) 'Addiction motivation reformulated: an affective processing model of negative reinforcement', *Psychological Review*, 111 (1), 33–51.

Baldwin, D.S., Anderson, I.M., Nutt, D.J., Allgulander, C., Bandelow, B., den Boer, J.A., Christmas, D.M., Davis, S., Fineberg, N., Lidbetter, N., Malizia, A., McCrone, P., Nabarro, D., O'Neill, C., Scott, J., van der Wee, N. and Wittchen, H-U. (2014) 'Evidence-based pharmacological treatment of anxiety disorders, post-traumatic stress disorder and obsessive-compulsive disorder: a revision of the 2005 guidelines from the British Association for Psychopharmacology', *Journal of Psychopharmacology*. London: British Association of Psychopharmacology.

Barkham, M., Margison, F., Leach, C., Lucock, M., Mellor-Clark, J., Evans, C., Benson, L., Connell, J., Audin, K. and McGrath, G. (2001) 'Service profiling and outcomes benchmarking using the CORE-OM: toward practice-based evidence in the psychological therapies. Clinical Outcomes in Routine Evaluation-Outcome Measures', *Journal of Consulting and Clinical Psychology*, 69(2), 184–96.

Barlow, D.H. (2004) *Anxiety and Its Disorders: The Nature and Treatment of Anxiety and Panic*. New York: Guilford Press.

Baum, W.M. (2004) *Understanding Behaviorism: Behavior, Culture, and Evolution*. Oxford: Blackwell Publishing.

Beck, A.T. (1967) *Depression: Clinical, Experimental and Theoretical Aspects*. New York: Harper & Row.

Beck, A.T. (1972) *Depression*. Philadelphia: University of Pennsylvania Press.

Beck, A.T. (1975) *Cognitive Therapy and the Emotional Disorders*. Madison, CT: International Universities Press, Inc.

Beck, AT., Rush, A.J., Shaw, B.F and Emery, G. (1979) *Cognitive Therapy of Depression*. New York: Guilford Press.

Beck, A.T., Steer, R.A., Kovacs, M. and Garrison, B. (1985) 'Hopelessness and eventual suicide: a 10-year prospective study of patients hospitalized with suicide ideation', *American Journal of Psychiatry*, 142(5), 559–63.

Beck, J.S. (1995) *Cognitive Therapy Basics and Beyond*. New York: Guilford Press.

Bell, A.C. and D'Zurilla, T.J. (2009) 'Problem-solving therapy for depression: a meta-analysis', *Clinical Psychology Review*, 29, 348–53.

Bennett-Levy, J. and Thwaites, R. (2007) 'Self and self-reflection in the therapeutic relationship: a conceptual map and practical strategies for the training, super-vision and self-supervision of interpersonal skills', in P. Gilbert and R.L. Leahy (eds) *The Therapeutic Relationship in the Vognitive-behavioural Psychotherapies*, pp 255–81, London: Routledge.

Bennett-Levy, J., Richards, D.A., Farrand, P., Christensen, H., Griffiths, K.M., Kavanagh, D.J., Klein, B., Lau, M.A., Proudfoot, J., Ritterband, L., White, J. and Williams, C. (2010) *Oxford Guide to Low Intensity CBT Interventions*. Oxford: Oxford University Press.

Bordin, E.S. (1979) 'The generalisability of the psychoanalytic concept of the working alliance', *Psychotherapy: Theory, Research and Practice*, 16, 252–60.

Bordin, E.S. (1983) 'A working alliance model of supervision', *Counselling Psychologist*, 11, 35–42.

Bower, P. et al. (2013) 'Influence of initial severity of depression on effectiveness of low intensity interventions: meta-analysis of individual patient data', *British Medical Journal*, 346, 540.

Butler, A.C., Chapman, J.E., Forman, E.M. and Beck, A.T. (2006) 'The empirical status of cognitive-behavioural therapy: a review of meta analyses', *Clinical Psychological Review*, 26(1), 17–31 epub.

Butterworth, T., Bell, L., Jackson, C. and Pajnkihar, M. (2008) 'Wicked spell or magic bullet? A review of the clinical supervision literature 2001–2007', *Nurse Education Today*, 28(3), 264–70.

Buysse, D.J., Germain, A., Moul, D.E., Franzen, P.L., Brar, L.K., Fletcher, M.E., Begley, A., Houck, P.R., Mazumdar, S., Reynolds, C.F. 3rd and Monk, T.H. (2011) 'Efficacy of brief behavioural treatment for chronic insomnia in older adults', *Archives of Internal Medicine*, 171(10), 887–95.

Cape, J. and Barkham, M. (2002) 'Practice improvement methods: conceptual base, evidence-based research, and practice-based recommendations', *British Journal of Clinical Psychology*, 41, 285–307.

Carney, C.E., Harris, A.L., Moss, T.G. and Edinger, J.D. (2010) 'Distinguishing rumination from worry in clinical insomnia', *Behaviour Research and Therapy*, 48(6), 540–6.

Clark, D.A. and Beck, A.D. (2010) *Cognitive Therapy of Anxiety Disorders: Science and Practice*. New York: Guilford Press.

Clark, D.M. (1986) 'A cognitive approach to panic', *Behaviour Research and Therapy*, 24, 461–7.

Clark, D.M. (1989) 'A cognitive model of panic', in K. Hawton et al. (eds) *Cognitive Behaviour Therapy for Psychiatric Problems: A Practical Guide*. Oxford: Oxford University Press.

Clark, D.M. (1991) 'Anxiety Disorders: why they persist and how to treat them', Behaviour Research and Therapy, 37, s5–s27.

Clark, D.M. et al. (2008) LSE Centre for Economic Performance, 'Working Paper No. 1648: Improving access to psychological therapy: Initial evaluation of two UK demonstration sites', London: IAPT.

Clark, D.M. et al. (1997) *Journal of Consulting and Clinical Psychology*, 65(2), 203–13.

Clark, D.M., Layard, R., Smithies, R., Richards, D.A., Suckling, R. and Wright, B. (2009) 'Improving access to psychological therapy: initial evaluation of two UK demonstration sites', *Behaviour Research and Therapy*, 47(11), 910–20.

Cone, J.D. and Hawkins, R.P. (1977) *Behavioral Assessment: New Directions in Clinical Psychology*. New York: Brunner/Mazel.

Craske, M.G. (2003) *Origins of Phobias and Anxiety Disorders: Why More Women Than Men?* Amsterdam: Elsevier.

Csikszentmihalyi, M. (1975) *Beyond Boredom and Anxiety: Experiencing Flow in Work and Play*. San Francisco, CA: Jossey-Bass.

Department of Health (2008) *IAPT Outcomes Toolkit 2008/9*. www.iapt.nhs.uk. (accessed 30 May 2014).

Dougall, N., Lambert, P., Maxwell, M., Dawson, A., Sinnott, R., McCafferty, S., Moris, C., Clark, D. and Springbett, A. (2014) 'Deaths by suicide and their relationship with general and psychiatric hospital discharge: 30-year record linkage study', *British Journal of Psychiatry*, published online ahead of print 30 January, 2014.

Edinger, J.D. and Means, M.K. (2005) 'Cognitive behavioural therapy for primary insomnia', *Clinical Psychology Review*, 25, 539–58.

Egan, G. (2010) *The Skilled Helper: A Problem-Management and Opportunity Development Approach to Helping*, 9th edn. Belmont, CA: Brooks/Cole CENGAGE Learning.

Ekers, D., Lovell, K. and Playle, J.F. (2006) 'The use of CBT based, brief, facilitated self-help interventions in Primary Care Mental Health Service Provision: evaluation of a 10-day training programme', *Clinical Effectiveness in Nursing*, 9, e88–e96.

Ekers, D., Richards, D. and Gilbody, S. (2007) 'A meta-analysis of randomized trials of behavioural treatment of depression', *Psychological Medicine*, 8, 164–75.

Ekers, D., Richards, D., McMilan, D., Bland, J.M. and Gilbody, S. (2011) 'Behavioural activation delivered by the non-specialist: phase II randomised controlled trial', *British Journal of Psychiatry*, 198, 66–72.

Ellis, M.V. and Ladany, N. (1997) 'Inferences concerning supervisees and clients in clinical supervision: an integrative review', in C.E. Watkins (ed.) *Handbook of Psychotherapy Supervision*. New York: John Wiley and Sons.

Espie, C.A. (1999) 'Cognitive behavior therapy as the treatment of choice for primary insomnia', *Sleep Medicine Reviews*, 3(2), 97–9.

Espie, C.A. (2010) *Overcoming Insomnia and Sleep Problems*. London: Constable and Robinson Ltd.

Falender, C.A. et al. (2004) 'Defining competencies in psychology supervision: a consensus statement', *Journal of Clinical Psychology*, 60, 771–85.

Feather, A. (2008) *Teaching Clinical Skills*. www.faculty.londondeanery.ac.uk/e-learning/teaching-clinical-skills/ (accessed 27 May 2014).

Feeley, M., DeRubeis, R.J. and Gelfand, L.A. (1999) 'The temporal relation of adherence and alliance to symptom change in cognitive therapy for depression', *Journal of Consulting and Clinical Psychology*, 67(4), 578–82.

Garety, P.A., Fowler, D.G., Freeman, D., Bebbington, P., Dunn, G. and Kuipers, E. (2008) 'Cognitive-behavioural therapy and family intervention for relapse prevention and symptom reduction in psychosis: randomised controlled trial', *British Journal of Psychiatry*, 192, 412–23.

Gask, L., Lever-Green, G. and Hays, R. (2008) *Dissemination and Implementation of Suicide Training in One Scottish Region. BMC Health Services* Research 8:246. doi:10.1186/1472–6963–8–246. http://www.biomedcentral.com/1472–6963/8/246 (accessed 27 May 2013).

Gask, L., Rogers, A., Oliver, D., May, C. and Roland, M. (2003) 'Qualitative study of patients' perceptions of the quality of care for depression in general practice', *British Journal of General Practice*, 53(489), 278–83.

Gelder, M. (1997) 'The scientific foundations of cognitive behaviour therapy', in M.D. Clark and C.G. Fairburn (eds) *Science and Practice of Cognitive Behaviour Therapy*. Oxford: Oxford University Press.

Gellatly, J., Bower, P., Hennessy, S., Richards, D., Gilbody, S. and Lovell, K. (2007) 'What makes self-help interventions effective in the management of depressive symptoms? Meta-analysis and meta-regression', *Psychological Medicine*, 37(9), 1217–28.

Ginzburg, D.M. et al. (2012) 'Treatment specific competence predicts outcome in cognitive therapy for social anxiety disorder', *Behaviour Research and Therapy*, 50, 12, 747–52.

Goddard, L., Dritschel, B. and Burton, A. (1996) 'Role of autobiographical memory in social problem solving and depression', *Journal of Abnormal Psychology*, 105(4), 609–16.

Grimshaw J.M. and Russell, I.T. (1993) 'Effect of clinical guidelines on medical practice: a systematic review of rigorous evaluations', *The Lancet*, 342, 1317–22.

Grimshaw, J.M., Eccles, M.P., Walker, A.E. and Thomas, R.E. (2002) 'Changing physicians' behaviour: what works and thoughts on getting more things to work', *Journal of Continuing Education in the Health Professions*, 22(4), 237–43.

Harvey, A.G. and Tang, N.K.Y. (2003) 'Cognitive behaviour therapy for primary insomnia: can we rest yet?' *Sleep Medicine Reviews*, 7(3), 237–63.

Hawton, K., Salkovskis, P.M., Kirk, J. and Clak, D.M. (eds) (1989) *Cognitive Behaviour Therapy for Psychiatric Problems: A Practical Guide*. Oxford: Oxford University Press.

Heaven, C., Clegg, J. and Maguire, P. (2006) 'Transfer of communication skills training from workshop to workplace: the impact of clinical supervision', *Patient Education and Counselling*, 60, 313–25.

Hollon, S.D., DeRubeis, R.J., Shelton, R.C., Amsterdam, J.D., Salomon, R.M., O'Reardon, J.P., Lovett, M.L., Young, P.R., Haman, K.L., Freeman, B.B. and Gallop, R. (2005) 'Prevention of relapse following cognitive therapy vs medications in moderate to severe depression', *Archives of General Psychiatry*, 62(4), 417–22.

Hollon, S. and Kendall, P. (1980) 'Cognitive self-statements in depression', *Cognitive Therapy and Research*, 4, 383–95.

Honey, P. and Mumford, A. (2000) *The Learning Styles Helper's Guide*. Maidenhead: Peter Honey Publications Ltd.

Improved Access To Psychological Therapies (2011) *Ethical Codes for Non-professionally Affiliated Staff*. London: IAPT. http://www.iapt.nhs.uk/search/?keywords=ethical+code (accessed 27 May 2014).

Jacobson, N.S., Dobson, K.S., Truax, P.A., Addis, M.E., Koerner, K., Gollan, J.K., Gortner, E. and Prince, S.E. (1996) 'A component analysis of cognitive-behavioral treatment for depression', *Journal of Consulting and Clinical Psychology*, 64(2), 295–304.

Kahn, R.L. and Connell, C.F. (1967) *The Dynamics of Interviewing*. New York: Wiley and Sons.

Keijsers, G.P., Schaap, C.P. and Hoogduin, C.A. (2000) 'The impact of interpersonal patient and therapist behavior on outcome in cognitive-behavior therapy: a review of empirical studies', *Behaviour Modification*, 24(2), 264–97.

Kendall, P., Howard, B. and Hays, R. (1989) 'Self-referent speech and psychopathology: the balance of positive and negative thinking', *Cognitive Therapy and Research*, 13, 583–98.

Kent, C. (2011) *The 2nd Annual Clinical Supervision Master Class: Making Group Supervision Work: Evaluating Outcomes*. Belfast: School of Nursing and Midwifery, Queen's University, Belfast.

Kolb, D.A. (1984) *Experiential Learning*. Englewood Cliffs, NJ: Prentice Hall.

Kroenke, K. and Spitzer, R.L. (2002) 'The PHQ–9: a new depression diagnostic and severity measure', *Psychiatric Annals*, 32(9), 1–7.

Kroenke, K., Spitzer, R.L. and Williams, J.B. (2001) 'The PHQ–9: validity of a brief depression severity measure', *Journal of General Internal Medicine*, 16(9), 606–13.

Lambert, M.J. and Hawkins, E.J. (2004) 'Measuring outcome in professional practice: considerations in selecting and using brief outcome instruments', *Professional Psychology: Research and Practice*, 35(5), 492–9.

Layard, R. (2005) 'Mental Health: the choice of therapy for all', *Centrepiece*, 10(3), 19–21.

Layard, R., Clark, D., Bell, S., Knapp, M., Meacher, B., Priebe, S., Turnberg, L., Thornicroft, G. and Wright, B. (2006) 'The depression report: a new deal for depression and anxiety disorders', *The Centre for Economic Performance's Mental Health Policy Group*. London: London School of Economics.

Lee, D. (2005) 'An evaluation of prescribed learning outcomes in clinical psychology supervisor training.' Unpublished doctorate thesis. http://www.leeds.ac.uk/lihs/psychiatry/courses/dclin/completed_research/sorps_online06/sorp_david_lee.pdf (accessed 27 May 2014).

Leahy, R.L. (2008) 'The therapeutic relationship in Cognitive Behavioural Therapy', *Behavioural and Cognitive Psychotherapy*, 36(6), 769–77.

Leahy, R.L. (2009) *Anxiety Free*. London: Hayhouse.

Lejuez, C.W., Hopko, D.R., LePage, J.P., Hopko, S.D. and McNeil, D.W. (2001) 'A brief behavioral activation treatment for depression', *Cognitive and Behavioral Practice*, 8, 164–75.

Lejuez, C.W., Hopko, D.R. and Hopko, S.D. (2001) 'A brief behavioral activation treatment for depression. Treatment manual', *Behavior Modification*, 25(2), 255–86.

Lovell, K., Cox, D., Garvey, R., Raines, D., Richards, D., Conroy, P. and Repper, D. (2003) 'Agoraphobia: nurse therapist-facilitated self-help manual', *Journal of Advanced Nursing*, 43(6), 623–30.

Lovell, K., Bower, P., Richards, D., Barkham, M., Sibbald, B., Roberts, C., Davies, L., Rogers, A., Gellatly, J. and Hennessy, S. (2008) 'Developing guided self-help for depression using the Medical Research Council complex interventions framework: a description of the modelling phase and results of an exploratory randomised controlled trial', *BMC Psychiatry*, 8, 91–100.

Lucock, M.P., Hall, P. and Noble, R. (2006) 'A survey of influences on the practice of psychotherapists and clinical psychologists in training in the UK', *Clinical Psychology and Psychotherapy*, 13, 123–30.

MacKay, H., West, W., Moorey, J., Guthrie, E. and Margison, F. (2000). *Training in Sychodynamic-interpersonal Therapy: Primary Care Counsellors' Experiences of Changing their Practice*. British Association for Counselling and Psychotherapy Research Conference, Manchester, May.

Mannix, K.A., Blackburn, I.M., Garland, A., Gracie, J., Moorey, S., Reid, B., Standart, S. and Scott, J. (2006) 'Effectiveness of brief training in cognitive behaviour therapy techniques for palliative care practitioners', *Palliative Medicine*, 20(6), 579–84.

Mansell, W. (2007) 'Reading about self-help books on cognitive-behavioural therapy for anxiety disorders', *Psychiatric Bulletin*, 31, 238–40.

Martell, C.R., Addis, M.E. and Jacobson, N.S. (2001) *Depression in Context: Strategies for Guided Action*. New York: Norton.

Martin, D. and Hamilton, S. (2006) 'How to use non-verbal signs in assessments of suicide risk', *Nursing Times*, 102(2), 36–8.

McManus, S., Meltzer, H., Brugha, T., Bebbington, P. and Jenkins, R. (2009) *Adult Psychiatric Morbidity in England, 2007: Results of a household survey*. Leeds: The Health and Social Care Information Centre.

McNally, R.J. and Foa E.B. (1987) 'Cognition and agoraphobia: bias in the interpretation of threat', *Cognitive Therapy and Research*, 11(5), 567–81.

Maunder, L. and Cameron, L. (2013) *Panic: A Self Help Guide*. Northumberland, Tyne and Wear NHS Trust. http://www.ntw.nhs.uk/pic/leaflets/Panic%20A4%202013.pdf (accessed 23 May 2014).

Maunder, L., Milne, D. and Cameron, L. (2008) 'Pilot evaluation of Brief Training in CBT for Primary Care Practitioners', *Behavioural and Cognitive Psychotherapy*, 36(3), 341–8.

Mead, N. and Bower, P. (2000) 'Patient-centredness: a conceptual framework and review of the empirical literature', *Social Science & Medicine*, 52, 1087–110.

Miller, W.R. and Mount, K.A. (2001) 'A small study of training in motivational interviewing: does one workshop change clinician and client behaviour?' *Behavioural and Cognitive Psychotherapy* 29(4), 457–71.

Milne, D. (2007a) 'An empirical definition of clinical supervision', *British Journal of Psychology*, 46, 437–47.

Milne, D. (2007b) CPD Workshop for New Clinical Supervisors: A Tutor's Guide. Unpublished document available from: www.wiley.com/go/milne (accessed 27 May 2014).

Milne, D. (2009) *Evidence-based Clinical Supervision*. Oxford: BPS/Blackwell.

Milne, D. and James, I. (2000) 'A systematic review of effective cognitive-behavioural supervision', *The British Journal of Clinical Psychology*, 39, 111–27.

Milne, D., Leck, C. and Choudhri, N.Z. (2009) 'Collusion in clinical supervision: literature review and case study in self-reflection', *The Cognitive Behaviour Therapist*, 2, 106–14.

Milne, D., Reiser, R., Aylott, H., Dunkerley, C., Fitzpatrick, H. and Wharton, S. (2010) 'The systematic review as an empirical approach to improving CBT supervision', *International Journal of Cognitive Therapy*, 3, 278–94.

Morgenthaler, T., Kramer, M., Alessi, C., Friedman, L., Boehlecke, B., Brown, T., Coleman, J., Kapur, V., Lee-Chiong, T., Owens, J., Prancer, J. and Swick, T. (2006) 'Practice parameters for the psychological and behavioral treatment of insomnia: an update. An American Academy of sleep medicine report', *Sleep*, 29(11), 1415–19.

Morin, C.M., Blais, F. and Savard, J. (2002) 'Are changes in beliefs and attitudes about sleep related to sleep improvements in the treatment of insomnia', *Behaviour Research and Therapy*, 40, 741–52.

Motl, R.W., Bimbaum, A.S., Kubik, M.Y. and Dishman, R.K. (2004) 'Naturally occurring changes in physical activity are inversely related to depressive symptoms during early adolescence', *Psychosomatic Medicine*, 66(3), 336–42.

Murray, C. and Lopez, A. (1996) *The Global Burden of Disease*. Cambridge, MA: Harvard University Press.

NICE (2003) *Depression*, NICE Guideline, Second Consultation. London: NHS.

NICE (2005) *CG28: Depression in Children and Young People: Identification and Management in Primary, Community and Secondary Care*. London: NICE.

NICE (2006) *TA97: Computerised Cognitive Behaviour Therapy for Depression and Anxiety: Review of Technology Appraisal 51*. London: NICE.

NICE (2007) *CG45: Antenatal and Postnatal Mental Health: NICE Guideline*. London: NICE.

NICE (2009a) *CG90: Depression in Adults: The Treatment and Management of Depression in Adults*. London: NICE.

NICE (2009b) *CG91: Depression with a Chronic Physical Health Problem: A NICE Guideline*. London: NICE.

NICE (2011) CG123: *Common Mental Health Disorders: Identification and Pathways to Care*. London: NICE.

Northumberland, Tyne and Wear NHS Foundation Trust (2009) *Sleeping Problems: A Self-Help Guide*. www.ntw.nhs.uk/pic/selfhelp (accessed 2009).

Overbeek, T., Vermetten, E., and Griez, E.J.L. (2001) 'Epidemiology of anxiety disorders', in E.J.C. Griez et al. (eds) *Anxiety Disorders: An Introduction to Clinical Management and Research*. London: Wiley & Sons.

Overholser, J.C. (2003) 'Cognitive-behavioral treatment of depression: a three-stage model to guide treatment planning', *Cognitive and Behavioural Practice*, 10, 231–9.

Patterson, C.H. (1984) 'Empathy, warmth and genuineness in psychotherapy: a review of reviews', *Psychotherapy*, 21, 431–8.

Paykel, E.S. (2001) 'Continuation and maintenance therapy in depression', *British Medical Bulletin*, 57(1), 145–59.

Philippot, P. and Rime, B. (1997) 'The perception of body sensations during emotion: a cross-cultural perspective', *Polish Psychological Bulletin*, 28, 175–88.

Prasko, J., Diveky, T., Grambal, A., Kamaradova, D., Mozny, P., Sigmundova, Z., Slepecky, M. and Vyskocilova, J. (2010) 'Transference and countertransference in cognitive behavioral therapy', *Biomedical Papers*, 154(3), 189–97.

Proctor, B. (1986) 'Supervision: a cooperative exercise in accountability', in M. Marken and M. Payne (eds) *Enabling and Ensuring: Supervision in Practice*. Leicester: National Youth Bureau and Council for Education and Training in Youth and Community Work.

Rachman, S. (2003) *Treatment of Obsessions*. New York: Oxford University Press.

Rethorst, C.D. and Trivedi, M.H. (2013) 'Evidence-based recommendations for the prescription of exercise for major depressive disorder', *Journal of Psychiatric Practice*, 19(3), 204–12.

Rhodes, L., Genders, R., Owen, R., O'Hanlon, K. and Brown, J.S. (2010) 'Investigating barriers to implementation of the NICE Guidelines for Depression: a staff survey with Community Mental Health Teams', *Journal of Psychiatric and Mental Health Nursing*, 17(2), 147–51.

Richards, D. and Whyte, M. (2009) *Reach Out Educator Manual*, 2nd edn. London: IAPT. http://www.iapt.nhs.uk/silo/files/reach-out-educator-manual.pdf (accessed 27 May 2014).

Richards, D.A. and Suckling, R. (2008) 'Improving access to psychological therapy: the Doncaster demonstration site organisational model', *Clinical Psychology Forum*, 181, 9–16. http://www.iapt.nhs.uk/silo/files/reach-out-educator-manual.pdf (accessed 27 May 2014).

Robertson, I. (2011) *The Winner Effect: How Power Affects Your Brain*. London: Bloomsbury.

Rogers, C.R. (1951) *Client-centered Therapy*. Boston, MA: Houghton Mifflin.

Rosqvist, J. (2005) *Exposure Treatments for Anxiety Disorders: A Practitioner's Guide to Concepts. Methods and Evidence-Based Practice*. New York: Routledge.

Roth, A. and Pilling, S. (2007) *The Competencies Required to Deliver Effective Cognitive and Behavioural Therapy for People with Depression and with Anxiety Disorders*. London: Department of Health. http://www.ucl.ac.uk/clinicalpsychology/CORE/CBT_Competences/CBT_Competence_List.pdf (accessed 27 May 2014).

Roth, A.D. and Pilling, S. (2008) *A Competence Framework for the Supervision of Psychological Therapies*. London: University College London, Research Department of Clinical, Educational and Health Psychology. http://www.ucl.ac.uk/clinical-psychology/CORE/supervision_framework.htm (accessed 27 May 2014).

Royal College of Psychiatrists (2012) *Antidepressants*. http://www.rcpsych.ac.uk/healthadvice/treatmentswellbeing/antidepressants.aspx (accessed 27 May 2014).

Safran, J.D. and Muran, C.J. (2001) 'A relational approach to training and supervision in cognitive psychotherapy', *International Journal of Cognitive Psychotherapy*, 15(1), 3–15.

Safran, J.D., Muran, J.C. and Rothman, M. (2006). 'The therapeutic alliance: cultivating and negotiating the therapeutic relationship', in W. O'Donohue, N.A. Cummings and

J.L. Cummings (eds) *Strategies for Becoming a Master Psychotherapist*. New York: Elsevier.

Salkovskis, P.M. (1988) 'Phenomenology, assessment and the cognitive model of panic', in S.J. Rachman and J. Maser (eds) *Panic: Psychological Perspectives*. New Jersey: Lawrence Erlbaum.

Salkovskis, P.M. (1991) 'The importance of behaviour in the maintenance of anxiety and panic: a cognitive account', *Behavioural Psychotherapy*, 19, 6–19.

Salkovskis, P.M., Clark, D.M. and Gelder, M.G. (1996) 'Cognitive-behaviour links in the persistence of panic', *Behaviour Research and Therapy*, 34, 453–8.

Salkovskis, P.M., Clark, D.M., Hackmann, A., Wells, A. and Gelder, M. (1999) 'An experimental investigation of the role of safety-seeking behaviours in the maintenance of panic disorder with agoraphobia', *Behaviour Research and Therapy*, 37(6), 559–74.

Scaife, J. (2009) *Supervision in the Mental Health Professions: A Practitioner's Guide*, 2nd edn. Hove: Brunner-Routledge.

Shepherd, M. and Rosairo, M. (2008) 'Low-intensity workers: lessons learned from supervising primary care mental health workers and dilemmas associated with such roles', *Mental Health Family Medicine*, 5(4), 237–45.

Simmons, J. and Griffiths, R. (2009) *CBT for Beginners*. London: Sage.

Simon, R.I. (2009) 'Suicide risk assessment forms: forms over substance?' *Journal of the American Academy of Psychiatry and the Law*, 37, 290–3.

Singleton, N., Bumpstead, R., O'Brien, M., Lee, A. and Meltzer, H. (2001) *Psychiatric Morbidity Among Adults Living in Private Households, 2000*. London: The Stationery Office.

Skinner, B.F. (1938) *The Behavior of Organisms: An Experimental Analysis*. Oxford: Appleton-Century.

Spek, V., Nyklicek, I., Smits, N., Cuijpers, P., Riper, H., Keyzer, J. and Pop, V. (2007) 'Internet-based cognitive behavioural therapy for subthreshold depression in people over 50 years old: a randomized controlled clinical trial', *Psychological Medicine*, 37(12), 1797–806.

Spitzer, R.L., Kroenke, K., Williams, J.B. and Lowe, B. (2006) 'A brief measure for assessing generalized anxiety disorder: the GAD-7', *Archives of Internal Medicine*, 166(10), 1092–7.

Strain, J., Hutnik, N., Gregory, J. and Bowers, G. (2006) 'Graduate Primary Care Mental Health Workers: the process of introducing the role into primary care trusts'. www.healthacademy.ac.uk/projects/miniprojects/completeproj/strain.pdf (accessed 27 May 2014).

Sudak, D.M., Beck, J.S. and Wright, J. (2003) 'Cognitive behavioral therapy: a blueprint for attaining and assessing psychiatry resident competency', *Academic Psychiatry*, 27(3), 154.

Taylor, S. (2000) *Understanding and Treating Panic Disorder: Cognitive Behavioural Approaches*. New York: Wiley.

Teasdale, J.D. and Fogarty, S.J. (1979) 'Differential effects of induced mood on retrieval of pleasant and unpleasant events from episodic memory', *Journal of Abnormal Psychology*, 88(3), 248–57.

Townend, M. (2004) *Supervision Contracts in CBT*. Accrington: BABCP.

Trepka, C., Rees, A., Shapiro, D.A., Hardy, G.E. and Barkham, M. (2004) 'Therapist competence and outcome of cognitive therapy for depression', *Cognitive Therapy and Research*, 28(2), 143–57.

Trinidad, A.C. (2007) 'How not to learn Cognitive-Behavioral Therapy (CBT)', *American Journal of Psychotherapy*, 61(4), 395–403.

Turpin, G. and Wheeler, S. (2011) *IAPT Supervision Guidance*. University of Sheffield and University of Leicester: IAPT. http://www.iapt.nhs.uk/silo/files/iapt-supervision-guidance-revised-march–2011.pdf (accessed 27 May 2014).

Veale, D. (2008) 'Behavioural activation for depression', *Advances in Psychiatric Treatment*, 14, 29–36.

Veale, D. and Willson, R. (2007) *Manage Your Mood: Using Behavioural Activation Techniques to Overcome Depression*. London: Robinson Press.

Waller, G. (2009) 'Evidence-based treatment and therapist drift', *Behaviour Research and Therapy*, 47, 119–27.

Webb, C.A., Derubeis, R.J. and Barber, J.P. (2010) 'Therapist adherence/competence and treatment outcome: a meta-analytic review', *Journal of Consulting & Clinical Psychology*, 78, 200–11.

Westbrook, D., Kennerley, H. and Kirk, J. (2007) *An Introduction to Cognitive Behaviour Therapy: Skills and Applications*. London: Sage.

Wheeler, S. and Richards, K. (2007) 'The impact of clinical supervision on counsellors and therapists, their practice and their clients: a systematic review of the literature', *Counselling and Psychotherapy Research*, 7, 54–65.

White, E. and Winstanley, J. (2010) 'A randomised controlled trial of clinical supervision: selected findings from a novel Australian attempt to establish the evidence base for causal relationships with quality of care and patient outcomes, as an informed contribution to mental health nursing practice development', *Journal of Research in Nursing*, 15(2), 151–67.

Whitfield, G. and Williams, C. (2003) 'The evidence base for cognitive–behavioural therapy in depression: delivery in busy clinical settings', *Advances in Psychiatric Treatment*, 9, 21–30.

Willemyns, M., Gallois, C. and Callan, V.J. (2003) 'Trust me, I'm your boss: trust and power in supervisor–supervisee communication', *International Journal of Human Resource Management*, 14(1), 117–27.

Williams, C.J. (2012a) *Overcoming Depression and Low Mood: A Five Areas Approach*. London: Hodder Arnold.

Williams, C.J. (2012b) *Overcoming Anxiety Stress and Panic: A Five Areas Approach*. London: Hodder Arnold.

Williams, C., Wilson, P., Morrison, J., McMahon, A., Walker, A., Allan, L., McConnachie, A., McNeill, Y. and Tansey, L. (2013) 'Guided self-help cognitive behavioural therapy for depression in primary care: a randomised controlled trial', *PLoS ONE*, 8(1): e52735. Doi: 10.1371/journal.pone.0052735.

Wilson, K.G., Sandler, L.S., Asmundson, G.J.G., Larsen, D.K. and Ediger, J.M. (1991) 'Effects of instructional set on self-reports of panic attacks', *Journal of Anxiety Disorders*, 5(1), 43–63.

Wilson, K.G., Sandoz, E.K., Kitchens, J. and Roberts, M. (2010) 'The Valued Living

Questionnaire: Defining and Measuring Valued Action Within A Behavioral Framework', *The Psychological Record*, 60, 249–72.

Winstanley, J. (2000) 'Manchester clinical supervision scale', *Nursing Standard*, 19, 31–2.

Wolpe, J. (1982) *The Practice of Behavior Therapy*. New York: Pergamon Press.

World Health Organisation (2001) *The World Health Report – Mental Health: New Understanding, New Hope*. Geneva: World Health Organisation.

Yerkes, R.M. and Dodson, J.D. (1908) 'The relation of strength of stimulus to rapidity of habit-formation', *Journal of Comparative Neurology and Psychology*, 18, 459–82.

Young, C., Hunte, A., Newell, J. and Valian, P. (2011) *Coping with Panic*. http://www.cpft.nhs.uk/Downloads/Martin/Coping%20with%20Panic.pdf (accessed 27 May 2014).

Index

CBT FUNDAMENTALS
Theory and Cases

Vanessa Skinner and Nick Wrycraft

9780335247738 (Paperback)
2014

eBook also available

CBT Fundamentals: Theory and Cases is an indispensable, introductory guide for all mental health practitioners embarking on CBT training. Designed to be read with no prior knowledge of CBT, the book takes the reader through the essential principles and theory of contemporary CBT in a readable and accessible manner. It then outlines the most commonly used models and applies them to a range of mental health problems a novice CBT practitioner will encounter, from depression to anxiety disorders and PTSD.

Wrycraft and Skinner make an excellent use of the case study format and link theory and practice in an instructive and engaging way, promoting your learning. The cases convey a realistic sense of using CBT and working to both engage and promote therapeutic progress in peoples' lives. While placing an emphasis upon promoting engagement and implementing therapeutic interventions with clients and patients, CBT Fundamentals also addresses the difficulties, limitations and dilemmas encountered in practice in a pragmatic and constructive manner.

www.openup.co.uk